Other Books by Douglas E. Busby
- We Can Help God Heal Us (2020)
- Spirits Can Help God Heal Us (2018)

- Space Clinical Medicine: A Prospective Look at Medical Problems from Hazards of Space Operations (1968)
- Space Biomagnetics (1968)

MY EXPERIENCES
in
MEDICINE, THEOLOGY, AND ALONG THE WAY

Douglas E. Busby
M.D., M.Sc., M.Div., D.Min., Ph.D.

Copyright © 2022 Douglas E. Busby
All rights reserved.

ISBN-13: 9798822103900
ASIN: B0B11VSB7F

Imprint: Independently published

*Dedicated to my wife, Christina,
and our children and grandchildren,
with my gratitude
for suggesting and supporting this project.*

CONTENTS

A. INTRODUCTION	1
B. MY PATH TO A CAREER DECISION	3
1. My Family Background	3
2. My Public and High School Education	10
3. My Career Options and Decision	20
Unforgettable Memories: Playing the Trumpet	21
C. MY EDUCATION IN MEDICINE	29
1. In Pre-Medicine	29
Unforgettable Memories: Summers at Carling Brewery	32
2. In Medical School	36
Unforgettable Memories: Royal Canadian Air Force University Reserve Training Program	45
3. In My Rotating Internship	55
4. As a Graduate Student in Pulmonary Physiology	58
5. As a Senior Intern in Surgery and a Graduate Student in Biophysics	64
D. MY CAREER IN MEDICINE	73
1. As a Senior Staff Scientist at the Lovelace Foundation (Albuquerque, NM)	73
2. As a Senior Research Specialist at Garrett AiResearch (Los Angeles, CA)	86
3. As Director of Medical Services at Continental Airlines (Los Angeles, CA)	88
Unforgettable Memories: Visit to Continental Air Services in Viet Nam and Laos	93
4. As Co-Director of the Emergency Department of Torrance Memorial Hospital and as a Consultant in Aerospace Medicine (Los Angeles, CA)	113
5. As Head of the Civil Aviation Medicine Unit in Canada's Defense and Civil Institute of Environmental Medicine (Toronto, ON)	117
6. As a Consultant in Aviation Medicine in Canada (Toronto, ON)	123
Unforgettable Memories: Crash of Our Piper PA-32-300 Airplane	126
7. As Chief of the Aeromedical Research Branch in the FAA Civil Aeromedical Institute (Oklahoma City, OK)	134
8. As Deputy Federal Air Surgeon at FAA Headquarters (Washington, DC)	144
9. As Chair of the Department of Environmental Health at the Cleveland Clinic (Cleveland, OH)	154
Unforgettable Memories: Serving as an Expert Witness in Friends for All Children v. Lockheed Aircraft	158

10. In the Practice of Occupational and Aerospace Medicine (Cleveland, OH)	165
11. As the Medical Director of the LTV Steel Company (East Chicago, IN)	174
12. As the Medical Director for Medicare in Illinois (Chicago, IL)	177
13. As an Information Analyst for Medtronic and other Medical Technology Companies (Home Office, IN)	186
E. MY EDUCATION IN THEOLOGY	189
1. Background	189
2. In Seminary	196
Unforgettable Memories: From My Field Education	202
3. In Interim Ministry	204
4. In Graduate Theological Programs	206
F. MY CAREER IN THEOLOGY	211
1. Introduction	211
2. As Interim Minister of the First Congregational Church, United Church of Christ (Benton Harbor, MI)	212
3. As Interim Minister of the First Congregational Church, United Church of Christ (Elkhart, IN)	215
Unforgettable Memories: Mention of the Invasion of Iraq in a Sermon	218
4. As Interim Minister of the First Congregational United Church of Christ (Bremen IN)	220
5. As Transitional Senior Minister of the Glenview Community Church, United Church of Christ (Glenview, IL)	223
Unforgettable Memories: Loss of the Functioning of Muscles that Control Vision in My Right Eye	227
6. My Spiritual Healing Ministry	231
Unforgettable Memories: A Spirit Visits My Class on Theology and Medicine	236
Unforgettable Memories: A Woman's Terminal, Metastatic Breast Cancer Disappears after a Spiritual Healing Service	240
7. My Observations of Spirit Involvement in Spiritual Healing	241
Unforgettable Memories: I Receive Invisible Spiritual Surgery	247
Unforgettable Memories: Invisible Spiritual Surgery Destroys a Man's Cancer of the Liver	248
Unforgettable Memories: A Few Other Examples of Spiritual Healing Through Spirits Incorporated by Medium João	253
8. A Brief Description of Spiritism	257

A. INTRODUCTION

Pierre Teilhard de Chardin, the renowned, 20th century French Jesuit priest, scientist, paleontologist, theologian, philosopher, and teacher, described who we are and why we are here. He said, "We are not human beings having a spiritual experience. We are spiritual beings having a human experience." I agree with Teilhard, but would add that our human experience as a spiritual being is divinely intended to be a learning experience on our spiritual path to God.

Teilhard's profound statement on the purpose of our lives on Earth became a reality for me when I passed 85 years of age, and my wife, Christina, and our children convinced me to record for posterity the remarkable experiences that I had in my careers in medicine, theology, and along the way. We decided that I should describe the experiences in a book, rather than on audiotape or disc so that the lessons that might be learned from them would not be clouded by emotional responses to hearing me speak about them. I must say that this project was made productive and enjoyable by Christina's daughter and author, Allison, who suggested that Christina critique what I had written each week as I read it to her on Friday evening over our gin martinis!

In this book, I recall momentous experiences that I had during my careers in medicine, theology, and along the way. In separate chapters, I describe my path to a career decision, my education and career in medicine, and my education and career in theology. And throughout the book, I highlight the "Unforgettable Memories" of experiences that shaped my careers or otherwise made my life quite interesting.

As I finished writing this book, I hesitated to describe my observations of spirit involvement in spiritual healing that I made during many trips to Brazil. I realize that for some, my writing about spirits being involved in healing is "too far out of the box" for a

DOUGLAS E. BUSBY

physician and minister. However, these observations were a significant part of my reality for several years, and so I decided to share some of the experiences that I had while making them.

My Dad used to say to me, "Doug, if you make life much better for one other person, you have served your purpose on Earth." This book shows the successes and failures that I had in my professional careers and related activities. They have certainly been learning experiences for me and, I hope, can be helpful to others.

Enjoy!

B. MY PATH TO A CAREER DECISION

1. My Family Background

I was born on July 24. 1935, at Weston Cottage Hospital in Weston, Ontario, Canada, a western suburb of the city of Toronto. One of my earliest recollections from childhood is when Dad and I stood a few times behind a chain-link fence at Malton Airport just west of Toronto, to watch new, bright-yellow Avro Anson training airplanes start their engines and fly away to Great Britain and World War II.

Avro Anson Trainer

On one occasion, a man on the other side of the fence handed us a small piece of fabric that had covered the wing of an Anson that had just crashed on take-off. Dad held the fabric to my nose so that I could smell the "dope," a plasticized lacquer that had tightened and sealed the fabric. I was often reminded of that day when I used dope in making model airplanes. Many years later, I returned to the Malton Airport, later renamed Toronto International Airport, on two highly-memorable occasions. As a student in the Royal Canadian Air Force (RCAF) during the summer of 1959, I sat in the cockpit of the last of the five Avro CF-105 Arrow interceptor airplanes that were built and destroyed the airport. And on a summer evening in August of 1973, I crashed my six-seat Piper PA-32-300 airplane with family aboard, while attempting to land it at the airport.

My father, Alfred Busby, was born in Oxford, England on February 3, 1910, to John and Harriett Busby. Nothing is known about Grandpa

DOUGLAS E. BUSBY

Busby's life before he met and married Harriett Douglass, who was from a very well-to-do British family that did not approve of their marriage and estranged them. In 1916, Grandpa Busby joined the British army to fight in World War I, sending Grandma Busby, Dad's older brother, and Dad to Canada to be away from the war if it extended into England. While in "live" battle training, Grandpa Busby's left lower leg was badly fractured by an exploding mine. He spent several months in an army hospital, and because of continued discomfort in the leg, he received a medical discharge and a small disability pension from the army. He then joined Grandma Busby and their two sons in the small city of Guelph, Ontario. Grandpa Busby initially worked as a butcher, but being on his feet in this job aggravated his war injury so much that he was forced to take lighter, less-paying employment as the verger, or caretaker and minister's assistant, in the church that the family was attending, St. George's Anglican Church in Guelph. The family grew to five boys and a girl. They lived in borderline poverty, moving from house to house just ahead of being evicted for unpaid rent. One son was born with a lazy eye that became blind and another son had an accident that dislocated a hip, but neither condition received treatment because Grandpa and Grandma Busby could not afford it. Dad excelled in academics and sports in high school, sang tenor roles in community musicals, and participated in the life of St. George's church. In his last year of high school, the church's minister arranged for Dad to receive full tuition and board to study for the Anglican ministry. Grandpa Busby would not allow this because he had decided that as soon as his daughter and four sons graduated from high school, they would remain at home and enter the workforce to supplement his small British army disability pension and meager income as a verger. About 1932, the family moved to Weston where, despite the Great Depression in Canada, Grandpa and Grandma Busby thought that more work would be available for their children. Dad and one of his brothers worked long hours in a local hosiery mill, where they received little pay for long hours on their feet, threading the weaving

MY EXPERIENCES

machines that made silk stockings. To supplement his income before and after he married, Dad played semi-professional baseball and competed in various athletic events for cash prizes. Work and sports produced marked varicose veins, with their treatment causing painful ulcers that kept him from serving in the Canadian armed forces during World War II.

My mother, Louise Harris, was born in Waterloo, Ontario on July 20, 1911, to Everard Ernest and Laura Harris. Everard and his brother, Alfred, were sons of Lord Alfred Harris, a rich playboy who left England under sociopolitical pressure, taking with him a fortune in jewels. He joined the wealthy class in the United States and married Mary Ellen Wrigley, of the Wrigley chewing gum family. When their two sons were still quite young, Mary Ellen died and Lord Alfred took them to Hamilton, Ontario to be brought up by an aunt on his side of the family. Soon thereafter, he died, leaving the remainder of his fortune with the aunt, to be used for the care and education of his two sons. However, the aunt ruled over the boys so harshly that both left home at age 16 - Alfred to join the prospect for gold and silver in British Columbia, and Everard to live in the German-speaking town of Waterloo, Ontario, where he worked for many years in a furniture-making company

In 1903, Everard Harris married Laura Berlet from a first-generation family of German immigrant farmers. Grandma and Grandpa Harris had 11 children; one died in childhood and the other ten, six girls and four boys had full lives with nine of them marrying. The Harris family initially lived in the town of Waterloo, and then in Waterloo County, where Grandpa Harris tried unsuccessfully to farm, and then returned to his former furniture-making employer. The family moved back to Waterloo and finally to a large permanent home in the city of Kitchener, which would eventually become Waterloo's "twin city." The home was large, with six bedrooms, a kitchen with an enormous coal-fired, cast-iron stove that had a compartment for heating water, a dining room with a long, rectangular table that could seat at least 16 persons on side benches and end chairs, a parlor with an upright piano, and an overhang across the front porch; strangely, its only toilet was in a small enclosure in the basement. This home became the center of their family life for many years, being ideal for large gatherings of my aunts, uncles, and numerous cousins on Sunday afternoons, family celebrations, and even the funerals of my grandparents. Until Mom started kindergarten, she could only speak in German, so the school in the predominantly English-speaking community of Kitchener was quite a challenge for her. She had to stop her education after graduating from grade eight to help care for her younger siblings. At age 16, she began to work as a Bell Telephone switchboard operator at the Bell Telephone Company, leaving this company seven years later when she married. Meanwhile, her older brother taught her how to play the saxophone and she joined Kitchener's all-female, all-saxophone marching band, which performed in white dresses, stockings, and shoes.

A fascinating story later told at Harris family gatherings described what became of Grandpa Harris's brother, Alfred. Sometime in the 1920s, he returned to Ontario and tried unsuccessfully to find Everard using a message in Toronto newspapers that asked for help in finding his brother, with whom he wished to share his "fortune" as a successful silver miner. After many years, Dora, Alfred's wife, somehow made contact with Everard. Alfred and Dora were childless, had homes in British Columbia and California, and were strong financial supporters of the Foursquare Church, which had been founded in Los Angeles, California by the Canadian Pentecostal evangelist and media celebrity, Aimee Semple McPherson. Thereafter communications between Dora and Alfred and the Harris family were predominantly Christmas cards, with the cards from Alfred and Dora containing small amounts of money for the Harris family. Alfred died before Dora, and their reportedly large estate went to their church and the person who cared for Dora for several years before she died. In 1940, Grandpa Harris began to have strokes that incapacitated him mentally to the degree that he had to be hospitalized in Hamilton, Ontario until he died four years later.

MY EXPERIENCES

My parents met in the summer of 1932, at the Crystal Beach Amusement Park near Fort Erie, Ontario. They were married in Kitchener on November 11, 1933, during a record snowstorm. They moved into a two-bedroom bungalow that they had rented on Emmett Avenue in Mount Dennis, next to Weston and known for being the home of Canadian Kodak. They had a 1932 Chevrolet, which enabled us to visit the Harris homestead and stay there overnight every few weeks. I recall that on one trip back home from Kitchener, Mom, Dad, and I chewed sticks of Wrigley Spearmint Gum for Dad to use in plugging a hole in the radiator hose. The gum tasted good, in contrast to the Milk of Magnesia which I had to take every morning for chronic constipation.

When I was four years old, I was admitted to Toronto Sick Children's Hospital for bowel x-rays followed by abdominal surgery, which found that the constipation was due to bowel obstruction from my appendix being wrapped around my large bowel. During the surgery, I experienced an out-of-body experience, during which I left the operating room and was able to travel at great speed through interstellar space and stop at will to observe several beautiful, round planets of various sizes suspended in the darkness of space. I believe that this event, which did not frighten me and has since been embedded in my mind, led to my interest in space travel and eventually to my career in aerospace medicine.

At four years old

I had several other memorable moments in childhood. As soon as winter came, Dad would flood our backyard with a hose, to make an ice rink on which to teach me how to ice skate and play hockey.

DOUGLAS E. BUSBY

Although I never excelled in hockey, one of my friends who joined us on the rink said that he intended to be a great hockey player someday, and indeed he did, with the Toronto Maple Leafs; his name has faded from my memory. Dad also tried to teach me how to play baseball, but I quit this sport for several years after the first ball that I struck with a bat flew back and hit me in the face. Mom saw my potential physical abilities in a different light and placed me in a tap-dancing class. I did quite well in tap dance until I went on stage to perform a solo dance number and immediately forgot what to do. Soon thereafter, Mom said it was time for me to get out of this "girls thing" because I had become old enough to wear "breeks," the Scottish word for britches, which are heavy trousers with legs that go just below the knees. And I had even become old enough to meet Dad's fellow hosiery workers as they met in our garage on a few weekends to form a union that negotiated for better working conditions. I remember that the dirt floor of the garage was covered with cardboard, the garage was filled with tables and chairs, and beer and pop, and snacks and sandwiches, were plentiful.

My parents gave me a lot of loving attention. At an early age, I developed an intense curiosity with many questions which they graciously answered, or at least attempted to. When we had a car, my favorite places to go were Malton airport, the beach and amusement park on Toronto's Lake Ontario waterfront, the annual Canadian National Exhibition, and Eaton's Santa Claus Parade. We would also visit Grandma and Grandpa Busby's home every few weeks, arriving to see Grandpa sitting at the dining room table, ready to play the card game of cribbage with Dad, and Uncle John sitting in the parlor, ready to play my favorite marching band records on his gramophone. Grandma Busby usually served an overdone roast of beef, boiled potatoes, and cabbage, and at the end of the meal, Grandpa always poured hot tea for the adults through a small tea leaf strainer. In these visits to the Busby homestead, I learned to be polite "in the English way," and be careful not to bump Grandpa's war-injured leg. Back at home, I also began to learn the difference between good and bad "the

MY EXPERIENCES

hard way," such as when I showed the cardboard house that Dad had just built for me to some older kids, and one of them promptly destroyed it with a lit match.

The year 1940 began with my sister Dianne being born in our home, with all lights having to be turned off at night and air raid sirens periodically tested out of national concern for Canada being bombed by the Germans. Later that winter, another incident occurred to teach me the difference between good and bad. Mom bundled my baby sister between the sidebars on my sleigh, for a trip to a small corner grocery store a couple of blocks and across the street from our home. As a reward to me for watching over my sister under the covered entrance to the store while she went into the store for a few minutes, Mom gave me a box of animal crackers for me to snack on. Just after she went into the store, some older kids came, grabbed the box of crackers from me, and ran away. When Mom came out of the store and I told her what had happened to the box of crackers, she became quite flustered and we quickly started for home. As we crossed the street, she pulled the sleigh so fast over a pile of snow piled along the curb that it tipped over and my sister instantly turned into a slush-covered, crying mess. Too much for Mom and me, so we all cried!

In the late summer of 1940, our family moved to Kitchener in our recently purchased, second early 1930s Chevrolet. We stayed at the Harris homestead until Dad settled into his new job as the production manager of a small local company that made components of army boots. Soon we moved to share a home with an older, rather reclusive man, on St. George Street in Kitchener, and I began kindergarten nearby at the Courtland Avenue Public School. My memory of our time in that home has faded except for playing in a sandbox that Dad built in its back yard, and listening to opera music coming through our neighbor's open window day and night in the summertime. Then, in the late winter of 1942, my parents rented a small three-bedroom home owned by Ontario's hydroelectric company on Talbot Street in Kitchener, just a city block away from the Harris homestead. The property had a long front lawn, at the end of which was a tall hydroelectric tower so that kites could not be flown anywhere near it or the "high tension" wires that it supported. The street in front of our home ended in an up-sloping path through a farm field, suitable for sledding and tobogganing. In the back and on one side of our home was a large vegetable garden with two apple and two plum trees, and a soon-to-be large strawberry and raspberry patches. The property also shared a long "mutual," or shared, driveway from the street to our garage and the garage of an elderly lady who lived next to us, also in a rented hydroelectric company home. This lady would raise a fuss every time our car or even a visitor's car was parked in the driveway for more than a few minutes, even though she did not have a car! Eventually, she moved away and peace came, with the dads in our homes often playing horseshoes and drinking beer together in the new family's side yard, and simply living with the mutual driveway.

2. My Public and High School Education

Immediately after we moved to Talbot Street, Mom took me to J.F. Carmichael Public School, about six city blocks from our home. While she registered me for grade 1, the school's secretary suggested that I go out the school's side door and join my future classmates. I found them engaged in a roaring snowball fight while waiting to line up to come in for first class. When I joined this no-sides battle, I slipped and fell into a deep, slush-filled puddle. I was so wet and cold that my Mom had to take me back home to change my clothes. I should say that this story has a sequel, the setting of which is a shortcut to school in the winter across a farm field and a stream that kids from my neighborhood would walk over when the ice was thick enough to do so. And yes, one day going to school, I broke through the ice into the water up to my waist. My teacher put my wet breeches and shoes over a hot radiator while I sat at my desk in my wet, long underwear as it dried. Needless to say, Mom was not happy about this!

Each class at J.F. Carmichael had about 30 students, who remained together for an entire school year. Many classes were divided into half one grade and half the grade above, to enable a few

MY EXPERIENCES

selected students in the lower grade to progress at a faster rate academically, and possibly "skip" a grade. Every student had his or her desk with an ink well on top and an opening under the top for learning materials. The curriculum in public school included spelling, grammar and reading, penmanship (both printing and cursive writing), arithmetic, social studies, history, art, and physical education, or "PE." Every school day started with the teachers handing a large cod liver oil capsule to each of us and making sure that we put the capsule in our mouth and swallowed it, rather than in another student's ink well to create an awful odor. Every school week started with a brief, biblically-based religion class that ended with The Lord's Prayer and The Pledge of Allegiance. Mid-morning and mid-afternoon class recesses were staggered to enable uncrowded outdoor sports activities, such as baseball, soccer, hockey, marbles, and other games. All students went home for lunch. Every classroom had its wall library with educational books and magazines, and a card system that controlled the length of time that books could be borrowed from it. In retrospect, J.F. Carmichael provided me with a well-balanced education, focusing on three areas that would greatly benefit me in the future. Good penmanship and spelling were a must, with quality of penmanship constantly being graded and in-class spelling competitions being held beyond grade 3. From grade 5 through high school, classes in grammar often included what was called the précis, which involved each student writing a short, accurate summary of a narrative or report read or written by the teacher.

I have many other pleasant memories of my time at J.F. Carmichael. To support the Canadian military engaged in World War II, everyone, teachers and students alike, worked in this school's large "victory garden" at the top of the hill behind the school. In the spring, we raked and planted already-tilled soil, and in the fall, we harvested, washed, and packed carrots, beans, tomatoes, and potatoes for shipment to a military food-processing center. In the summer, teachers and students living near the school weeded and watered the garden, and did some harvesting from it. Year-round, we collected aluminum and tin foil, and tin cans to be recycled for the war effort, and in the fall, we collected milkweed pods for their silky material to be used in lining air force flight jackets and life vests.

We knew that winter was near when a crew arrived at J.F. Carmichael to assemble the boards surrounding a large, rectangular area on the playing field behind the school. With freezing weather, the janitorial staff flooded the area and placed the goalposts, so the ice rink was ready for hockey. The students were responsible for shoveling snow off the ice before any skating could be done. The rink was the center of wintertime recess and PE activities, with the girls usually just skating around, and the boys either playing team hockey or free-for-all hockey, called "shinny." During the winter months, the skates and hockey sticks were placed along one wall of a classroom, ready for recess or PE, or were left behind when we had to "clear the ice." Fortunately, we had a school nurse to treat bumps and bruises, especially from trying to get at a puck. One day while playing shinny at recess, my right knee struck a board along the rink, producing such severe pain in the knee that I had to rest it at home for several days while, according to the school nurse, a "bruise behind the kneecap" healed. Many years later, the inside of the knee was examined by an orthopedist to determine the cause of lingering pain deep in the knee. He found that the cartilage behind the kneecap had at some time been shattered and because of this, the entire knee had developed arthritis. So the nurse was right! And 66 years after the knee was injured while playing hockey at recess, it had to be replaced with an artificial one.

I recall a day when our grade 5 class had to miss morning recess and I got into trouble. A girl's boot had disappeared that morning, so our teacher, Miss Rosalind Adamson, kept the class at their desks until the boot showed up. As we quietly waited for the boot to appear, Ron Moyer, who was seated in front of me and never stopped squirming, moved an elbow backward in the direction of my ink well, so I pushed his elbow away from it. Miss Adamson, who was well known for instant flare-ups of anger in an otherwise pleasant personality, took Ron and me to visit Mr. Judson Brown, the school's principal. He asked

MY EXPERIENCES

us what we had done wrong as he took "the" dreaded leather strap and black record book out of his desk, and waved the strap at us. Ron was speechless and I said that Ron had "made me nervous ..." Before I could complete my answer, Miss Adamson slapped one side of my face and said, "Only your mother has nerves." Mr. Brown immediately sent Ron and me back to our classroom, and nothing more was said about the incident. I also had Miss Adamson as my grade 7 teacher, and never saw her dark side again. She became one of my favorite teachers.

Dad's job as the production manager of a small local company that made army boots came to an abrupt end in 1942, when he declined a transfer to the company's main facility in Westmount, Québec, a suburb of Montreal, Québec. He was soon employed by Four-Wheel Drive (FWD) Waterloo a division of the FWD Company in Clintonville, Wisconsin. FWD Waterloo did the final assembly of large army trucks built in the United States for the Canadian war effort. Dad initially worked in its parts department, but after World War II, he went to Clintonville for training in truck sales and then became the sales manager for eastern Canada in FWD. Dad visited larger Canadian cities out to Newfoundland to sell them FWD snow plows for use mainly at airports. Dad was away from home a lot, traveling by train and airplane to provinces that we learned about in geography class, including Québec, New Brunswick, Nova Scotia, Prince Edward Island, and Newfoundland. About that time, FWD Waterloo became a test center for the so-called "motorized toboggan," the predecessor of the snowmobile, so when Dad was at home in the wintertime, he would arrange for me to get a ride on a motorized toboggan with the FWD test engineer and family friend, Dan Daniels. Several years later, Dan became a stock car racer and offered to train me to drive stock and other race cars, but Dad quickly nixed that.

In the summer of 1944, World War II had limited fresh food in our grocery stores so much that Mom decided to expand the gardening around our home and sell its surplus to relatives and neighbors. Our strawberry plants and raspberry bushes became quite productive and

DOUGLAS E. BUSBY

we had many rows of carrots, lettuce, green onions, beans, and tomatoes. Consequently, my mornings were spent picking the strawberries, and later the raspberries, as well as weeding and watering the garden. Because Mom paid me for my work in our garden, I always had some money to get into the Municipal Swimming Pool for an afternoon of swimming with my friends, and in late afternoons or when it was raining, build model airplanes or read various books, especially about space travel (then called "science fiction"), from the public library.

From 1943 to 1949, Mom and Dad would rent a cabin for a two-week family vacation in Port Elgin, Ontario, a small beach town on the east shore of Lake Huron. I remember the joys of seeing the deep blue water of the lake appear on the horizon and then rushing to get into it, and later having French fries with salt and vinegar on them, playing miniature golf, and roller skating to music at the town's large roller rink. One year, my parents changed this routine, having decided that we would spend our vacation at a full-service lodge on a lake near the village of Fenelon Falls, in the beautiful Kawartha Lakes district northwest of Toronto. Dad rented a rowboat, and he and I fished from it for many hours without a bite. We watched with great interest the testing of a deep-sea diving suit off of the lodge's dock. Someone heard me practicing my cornet and I was invited to play a solo with organ accompaniment during the Sunday service in a local church. Although shuffleboard at the lodge and swimming in the deep lake in front of the lodge were fun, the next summer we were back at the beach in Port Elgin.

In the summer of 1949, Dad was offered the position of new truck sales manager at Mussen Motors, which had its main sales office in Fredericton and satellite sales offices in St. John and Moncton, New Brunswick. Excited by the prospect of our moving to Fredericton, a university city surrounded by forests and lakes, our family traveled by car to see Fredericton and where we might live there. We stopped frequently along the way to "view the sites" in eastern Ontario, Montréal, and along the St. Lawrence River, in Québec City and along

MY EXPERIENCES

the Gaspé Peninsula, and in northern New Brunswick, all of which constituted French-speaking Canada. For me, the highlights of the trip were the magnificent Roman Catholic churches in the small Quebec towns, beautiful quilts being sold along the highway, and numerous small eateries advertising *patates frites*, which in English-speaking Canada were called "French fries. Our reception in Fredericton was very gracious, with the senior management of Mussen taking us on tours of the area, helping us look for a possible home, holding a barbecue for us to meet potential new friends, and taking Dad and me fishing for bass. My parents were told that if we moved to Fredericton, I would be entering a four-year, high school program and might wish to continue my education locally at the University of New Brunswick. Despite the excellent job offer that Dad received from Mussen, Mom and he decided to remain in Kitchener because Grandma Harris was in very poor health and, as one of the oldest of the Harris siblings, Mom felt obliged to continue to live near her. So, dreaming of New Brunswick and of all of the fish that we would probably never catch there, I started grade 9 at Victoria Public School that fall.

The early summer of 1950 began with Dad beginning a new job, as a new car and truck salesman at Hall Automobiles, the Chevrolet, Oldsmobile, and Cadillac dealer for the Kitchener-Waterloo area. While he was saying goodbye on a Friday evening after his last day at FWD Waterloo, he scraped a lower leg on the corner of a wooden pallet in the truck assembly area. Over the weekend, the injury site became infected, and on Monday morning Dad visited our family physician who prescribed the antibiotic sulfonamide for the infection, because the new, preferred drug, penicillin, was not available locally. By Wednesday, Dad was in a coma from a severe allergic reaction to the "sulfa" pills, and Mom drove to the nearby Kitchener-Waterloo YMCA camp, where I was a counselor, to take me to the Kitchener-Waterloo Hospital to say goodbye to him. Fortunately, his intensive care, especially by a Mennonite nurse who spent many hours of her own time at his bedside, helped Dad come out of the coma. Then Dad suffered terribly from an itchy sulfa rash over his body, and developed an ulcer in the infection site which healed after a skin graft from his other leg was placed on it. Later, I heard that the Ontario Workers' Compensation Board refused to pay for Dad's medical care and lost wages because his injury had occurred when he was no longer employed by FWD. Although I was never told how the costs of Dad's medical care were paid, years later I learned that Hall Automobiles placed him on full-time salary on the Monday after his accident at FWD Waterloo.

For my first year of high school, or grade 9, I had to go to Victoria Public School near downtown Kitchener because the Kitchener-Waterloo Collegiate and Vocational Institute (KCI) needed to accommodate an unexpectedly large number of students from German families that had immigrated to our area after World War II. And during that year, my parents purchased a larger home for our family, on Margaret Street, on the opposite side of Kitchener, conveniently several yards from a city bus stop.

Towards the end of the school year, grade 9 students had to choose one of three "career" areas in which to take courses during and beyond grade 10. These areas were "general," which included the science and engineering professions, "commercial," which included the secretarial and accounting fields, and "technical," which included the mechanical and electrical trades. Some courses were available to students in all three areas, at least through grade 11. Graduation from high school occurred for the commercial and vocational students after grade 12, and for the academic students after grade 13. The general students had to pass national examinations, or "councils," usually in nine academic subjects, to enter a Canadian university. With the wise advice of my parents at a time when I had a myriad of ideas about what my career might be, I began grade 10 on the academic side of KCI, taking courses in English composition and literature, Latin, French composition, and literature (second year), physics, algebra, music (choir), and PE. Eventually, my grade 13 councils, all of which I passed, were English composition and literature, French composition and

MY EXPERIENCES

literature, algebra, geometry, trigonometry and statistics, physics, and chemistry.

My high school years were "interesting," to say the least. The assignment of students to homerooms in their grade and career area levels generated a lot of student camaraderie with their homeroom teachers. I recall having Mr. Harvey Class, who taught French, for two consecutive years as my homeroom teacher. He made a special effort to encourage each of us to go on to university. We soon learned that Mr. Class was a diabetic on insulin, and how to help him when his blood glucose (sugar) level got too low for him to think clearly.

I will never forget a disconcerting event that occurred near the end of my year in grade 12 when I was doing well academically and was becoming interested in medicine as a career from working my first of two summers in Kitchener-Waterloo Hospital, as I will describe below. Unexpectedly, the counselor who had been assigned to monitor my progress in high school called me into his office and informed me that my aptitude tests and academic grades showed that I would "never graduate" from "a university." He suggested that I apply to the Ryerson Technical School in Toronto for photography training. I told him that even though photography had become one of my hobbies, I was thinking of going to medical school, and simply thanked him for his advice. When I told my parents about my visit to the counselor's office, Dad said that he had read that aptitude tests can give misleading information and that I should select the career path that I wished to follow. Then for the first time, he expressed his hope that I would go to university, as he had been denied that opportunity by his father. I subsequently learned that the counselor, who became KCI's principal the following year, was following my progress through university, including medical school, with great interest.

A temporary disruption in my high school life occurred during grade 13 when the Korean War was at its worst. The male population of the school, except the conscientious objectors, was unexpectedly "militarized" for several weeks. This involved our being dressed in

DOUGLAS E. BUSBY

army uniforms and being taught by regular army soldiers how to march in formation on KCI's athletic field. At the beginning of this military operation, every student in student in uniform who could play a band instrument was recruited into a marching band to be under my direction when performing with the rest of the "troops." Interestingly, no real or imitation military weapons showed up. Then, after a few weeks of this seemingly-purposeless training, KCI's principal announced that our school's entire student army would be marching on King Street from the front of the school to a park in Waterloo, where it would be reviewed by the Prime Minister of Canada, The Honorable Louis St. Laurent, and many other dignitaries. Surprisingly, this event went off without a hitch, with the Prime Minister stepping down from the reviewing stand to thank the band for its playing of "God Save the Queen," and then several marches as he reviewed the "troops." Thereafter, our uniforms were collected and the band disbanded (pun intended).

A few weeks later, the athletic field was used for another rather unique, non-athletic event. Our grade 13 English literature class was studying Shakespeare's famous play, Hamlet. This included our reading of the "graveyard scene" in Act 5, in which Prince Hamlet sees one of the two clowns who are digging a grave pick up the skull of Yorick, a long-deceased court jester. Prince Hamlet says that when he was a child, he knew the jester well, and then makes several comments about him. As this scene was initially read in class, my close friend, Doug Hammar, said that an intact skull had recently been given to me and that I had named it "Yorick." Then the class's teacher, Miss Lillian Snider, asked me if I would bring the skull to school the next day, and after I replied that I would, she asked Doug and me if we would dig a "shallow grave" in the athletic field for members of the class to enact the graveyard scene. Needless to say, an English literature class standing around a rectangular hole and a skull in the corner of KCI's athletic field created much attention. A picture of this great Shakespearean scene was placed in the KCI's 1954 yearbook, the

MY EXPERIENCES

Grumbler. This picture also appeared on the memories board and in the historical booklet at KCI's 150th reunion in 2005.

At age 15, I joined many of my grade 9 classmates who were working at the new Loblaw's grocery store in Kitchener on Saturdays. I bagged groceries, guided the parking of cars on the store's narrow parking lot, and wrapped head lettuce in the store's produce section. The next school year, I took a better-paying job on Saturdays behind the meat counter in the A&P grocery store across the street. The meat manager was so nasty to his part-time staff, that several months later I welcomed the opportunity to work at the other end of the block at Richardson's Drug Store on Fridays after school and on Saturdays. I was at Richardson's until I moved to London for second-year pre-medicine. The pharmacist who owned the store, Robert "Bob" Richardson, had me make the store's bank deposits, operate the cash register, take weekly inventory, and help two other two pharmacists mix salves and count pills.

For the summer that I turned age 16, Mom got me a job helping Perrin "Perry" Statia, the pharmacist at the Kitchener-Waterloo Hospital. He gave me considerable responsibility, as he often had to rest while recovering from recent major cancer surgery on his neck. I ran the tablet-making machine, counted tablets and capsules, mixed and packaged salves and ointments, and periodically went down a spiral staircase from the pharmacy to a room below it, to double-check the weights of the various chemicals being used in making intravenous fluids. The following summer, I returned to the hospital as an orderly in its radiology department. Although I spent much of my workday transporting patients to and from the department, I again had considerable responsibility, such as developing x-rays in the department's darkroom, assisting with the setting of fractures, applying and removing plaster casts, and removing ureteral catheters. About that time, Dad arranged for me to meet the hospital's pathologist, Dr. Laverne Fischer, to whom Dad had been selling a new Cadillac automobile every year. Dr. Fischer subsequently invited me to his office several times, to show me diseased body tissues preserved in formaldehyde-filled jars or thin-cut for microscopic viewing. Every time I visited Dr. Fischer, he suggested that I give serious consideration to having a career in medicine, of course pointing me in the direction of his medical school at the University of Western Ontario (UWO) in London, Ontario.

I spent my last summer while still in high school working in the service department of Orr Automobiles (formerly Hall Automobiles), where Dad worked in its new automobile and truck sales department. I was the summer "chauffeur," driving customers to their places of business while their cars and trucks were being serviced. My friend, John Alan "Al" Orr, whose father owned the dealership, was the sorter in the parts department. Al and I were often sent to a dealership in another city to deliver or obtain a new Chevrolet, Oldsmobile, or Cadillac for sale at Orr Automobiles. This allowed us to see how fast new General Motors cars could accelerate while we tried to keep them within Ontario's speed limits. One day, Vince Scherer, Orr Automobiles' general manager, and a former Ontario Provincial Police (OPP) officer, met us as we arrived at the dealership after picking up a new Olds 88. He said to us, with Dad watching on, that we had just buzzed so fast through a village that OPP radar at its only intersection could not clock our speeds. He then took a small ruler out of a shirt pocket and began to measure the diameters of bug splats on the windshield of the Olds, commenting that splat size is just as effective as radar for determining car speed. Needless to say, Al and I took Mr. Scherer's little lesson seriously. Thankfully, our jobs were allowed to continue until the end of the summer.

3. My Career Options and Decision

Early in grade 13, I began to think about what career path I should follow. I told our family physician, Dr. William Harvey, that two summers of work in the hospital and Dr. Fischer's fascinating pathology specimens were pointing me towards medicine as a career, and that Dr. Fischer had suggested that I go to UWO for my medical education. Although Dr. Harvey had graduated in medicine from the

MY EXPERIENCES

University of Toronto, he recommended that I take advantage of an academic affiliation that Waterloo College had with UWO, which enabled students to take the same first-year pre-medicine courses as given at UWO, so that they might benefit from being in classes of smaller size. Then he said that large first-year classes contributed to his daughter failing her first year in pre-medicine at the University of Toronto.

I had also developed an interest in theology as a career stemming in large part from having grown up in St. John's Anglican Church in Kitchener and serving as an acolyte, or server, in it. In the fall of 1953, another acolyte and I made separate appointments with the minister of St John's, Rev. Chester Mixer, to ask for his opinion on our entering theology as a career. The other acolyte met first with Rev. Mixer, who immediately asked him whether he had received "God's call" to become a theologian. The acolyte replied, "No," and added that he did not know that God's call to theology was necessary for him to enter it as a profession. Rev. Mixer then terminated the visit with, "You must first receive God's call." When the acolyte told me about his brief encounter with Rev. Mixer, I decided that since I had not yet heard God's call to theology, I would get the same response from Rev. Mixer. So, I decided to make medicine my career.

Yet I recall that during my second year in pre-medicine at UWO, I had second thoughts about having a career in theology, generated in large part from living with theology students in the dormitory of the Anglican seminary, Huron College, on UWO's campus. About mid-year, I told the story of my not having received God's call to theology to The Rev. Canon (later Bishop) Morse Robinson, who was the minister of St. George's Anglican Church near UWO, in which I was serving as a lay reader. He simply advised me to continue to medical school, confident that the right time and opportunity would always exist for me to enter a seminary, as it eventually did in 1994.

Unforgettable Memories: Playing the Trumpet
This seems like a good place for me to tell the whole story of how playing the trumpet was a wonderful part of my life, beginning when

DOUGLAS E. BUSBY

I was 12, and ending when I was 83. It began when two of Mom's brothers who played saxophones in the Kitchener Municipal Band and dance bands in the area around Kitchener encouraged my parents to have me meet Nat Stroh, the genial music teacher and the conductor of the Waterloo Junior Band at the Waterloo Music Company in the hope of my learning to play a band instrument from him. This well-known company in the Canadian band music world had been formed in the early 1920s by two immigrants from the United States, Charles F. "C.F." Thiele, and his wife. They were world-renowned soloists on the cornet, currently being used instead of the trumpet in American concert bands, such as the Sousa Band. C.F. Thiele became conductor of the Waterloo Concert Band, also located at the Waterloo Music Company. The company printed sheet music for bands and manufactured drums, music stands, and other accessories for bands. The Thieles' support of band music in Canada extended to an annual Waterloo Band Festival that spanned over 30 years except during World War II. They funded the construction of a modern band shell in Waterloo Park. They had a "band room" on the second floor of their company, which had a specially-built stage and guest seating at band rehearsals and attendees of company-sponsored workshops for band conductors and instrumentalists. And for his many musical compositions for the band, "C.F. Thiele" eventually became known as "Professor Thiele."

When Dad and I climbed the long flight of stairs to the band room to meet with Stroh, I hoped to receive a cornet on loan from the Waterloo Music Company. However, Mr. Stroh handed me a beat-up E^b alto horn, with its mouthpiece and slides firmly stuck in the horn's tubing, and its three valves barely workable. An E^b alto horn player, Mr. Stroh showed me how to wash and polish the instrument, get its mouthpiece and main tuning slide unstuck and its valves operating smoothly, and, with strong words of encouragement, to start building an embouchure, or the ability to use my lips, tongue, and other facial muscles to make sounds with the horn. Mr. Stroh then gave me weekly private lessons. Several months later, he entered me in a regional band

MY EXPERIENCES

instrument competition in Owen Sound, Ontario, where I received a special mention award for playing my first solo in public, The Bells of St. Mary's.

For Christmas in 1948, Mom and Dad gave me a like-new silver Boosey B^b cornet. Soon thereafter, they placed me under a cornet teacher in Kitchener, Harold Tillsley, who was a cornetist and the conductor of Kitchener's Salvation Army Band. For the next six years, Mr. Tillsley and the Arban's Manual for the cornet would be the dominating forces in my musical life. Eventually, Mr. Tillsley would teach me to play many cornet solos, most of which were the classics of the early 1900s. Each had a cadenza, followed by a theme and variations based on the theme, with the cadenza and variations reflecting the expertise of the cornetist, such as playing wide intervals between notes, double and triple tonguing on the embedded theme, and running complex scales – all made possible by practicing the innumerable cornet exercises in Arban's Manual. As I studied with Mr. Tillsley, my increasing ability to play the cornet led to my being moved from the Waterloo Junior to the Waterloo Concert Band at age 16, and eventually cornet solos (e.g., Carnival of Venice, Old Home Down on the Farm) accompanied by the Concert Band, during its Sunday summer evening concerts in Waterloo and in performances of the band in surrounding communities and at the annual Canadian National Exhibition in Toronto. At one point, my parents helped me improve my cornet performance considerably with the gift of a new Buescher cornet. Meanwhile, I played in the KCI's pit orchestra, which performed before senior student assemblies, and in a band that played in the stands at the school's sporting events. I soloed (e.g., Willow Echoes, Bugler's Holiday) at junior and senior high school assemblies, annually at the high school's spring musicales, and with fellow cornet students in performing duets and trios (e.g., Trumpeter's Lullaby, La Cucaracha) at the musicales. I recall an unanticipated incident while our trio was playing La Cucaracha using our mutes at the Spring Festival. My mute slipped out of my cornet, bounced off the stage, struck the top of a tympani, and finally hit the floor, where it spun

DOUGLAS E. BUSBY

around several times. This noisy mishap, along with audience laughter, made an undesired addition to the only recording made of the festival, and would be avoided many decades later when our trio was asked to play La Cucaracha again at KCI's 150th reunion.

I will always treasure my music education on the trumpet, with countless thanks to those who encouraged me to practice, especially Mr. Tillsley, who was subtle about it, and my Mom, who was not-so-subtle about it. I can still hear her yelling from our front porch, loud enough to interrupt my friends and me while playing baseball in the field across the street, "Dougie, it's time to practice!"

I continued to play with the Waterloo Concert Band throughout high school and in my pre-medicine year at Waterloo College, during which the band played every year on stage at the Waterloo Music Festival. This stage band accompanied such remarkable soloists as Boston cornetist, Walter Smith, New York saxophonist, Sigmund Rascher, and New York tuba player, William "Bill" Bell. I especially remember Mr. Bell, a large man, delighting the audience by slowly lifting a sousaphone and lowering it over his body, and playing Tubby the Tuba (Down in Cuba) with its incredibly fast, triple-tongued finale. During the last time that I played at the festival in 1953, the Waterloo Concert Band shared the stage with the Guelph Concert Band. Seated beside me was a very accomplished cornetist about my age. When I complimented him on his excellent playing, he said that his goal in life was to be one of the best cornetists in Canada. Later, I learned that he was Fred Mills, who became a long-time member of the renowned Canadian Brass.

During my first year of pre-medicine at Waterloo College, I joined the newly-formed Kitchener-Waterloo Symphony Orchestra, which required me to play the trumpet rather than a cornet. I traded in my cornet for a new Buescher trumpet, and for several months also played it a few times in Uncle Ernie's dance band and the dance band of a local German Club. On a memorable 1954 New Year's Eve, I played the trumpet solo in O Mein Papa so many times that I had very sore lips which I soothed with newly-fallen, deep snow as I walked over a half-mile home.

MY EXPERIENCES

With my new trumpet

Near the end of that year, I was invited to play a trumpet solo at a monthly gathering of the staff and students of Waterloo College. I selected the Flight of the Bumble Bee, and the professor of music offered to accompany me on the piano. Although our rehearsals went well, our performance did not, for the professor lost control of a page of his accompaniment while having to turn it over so quickly, that it sailed off the piano. I'll never know whether the spontaneous applause that immediately followed was for my continuing to play without accompaniment, or for the professor retrieving the page and continuing his accompaniment as though nothing had happened.

When I began my second year of pre-medicine at UWO, I joined a large dance band that played mostly for sorority and fraternity formal dances. Often several of us would continue playing at a sorority or fraternity house, of course in return for free beer and snacks. Throughout my four years in the Medical School at UWO, my studies kept me from "keeping my lip (embouchure) in shape," except in my fourth year, when I played both the Carnival of Venice and Trumpeter's Lullaby in "Tachycardia," the annual three-evening Christmas show put on by the UWO's medical students.

When I was a senior intern and graduate student at UWO's medical school and Victoria Hospital, UWO's main teaching hospital, I joined a small orchestra made up of professors, fellow interns, and residents. Its members played quite a variety of instruments, including saxophone, clarinet, trombone, banjo, trumpet (me), drums, washtub bass, and pogo-like pole of cymbals and cowbells called a boombas.

DOUGLAS E. BUSBY

Somehow, our playing (at least our fun in doing so) led to our being asked to play during the reception for a formal dinner at St. Joseph's Hospital, another UWO teaching hospital. When we arrived early in our hospital scrubs to set up the orchestra, we decided to sample the orange punch, which was "boiling" due to a block of dry ice floating in it. Soon we were told that this "swamp juice" (our name for the brew) had been made with far too much vodka and would soon be diluted. But the damage had already been done. Our music sounded wonderful (at least to us), with the banjo player, who was an ear, nose, and throat specialist, wanting to play I'm Forever Blowing Bubbles for the entire shtick. The drummer, who was an obstetrician and gynecologist, lost one set of drumsticks into the crowd. Everyone in our band had a big headache the next day.

The word that we were subsequently "uninvited" to play at any future events at the St. Joseph Hospital did not get through to the planners of an annual dinner at Hotel London to celebrate the Canadian Army's victory at Vimy Ridge in France during World War I. Dressed in World War I Canadian Army uniforms and surrounded by armaments and paraphernalia from World War 1, we played several popular songs from that period. The reception was to be followed by a dinner with the London (Ontario) Orchestra playing classical music during it. All went well at the reception until a large number of veterans, glasses of beer in hand, asked us to extend it with several popular World War I songs that they could sing, including I'm Forever Blowing Bubbles. This impromptu songfest temporarily drowned out the London Orchestra's playing. Needless to say, we were also not invited back to play at another Vimy Ridge dinner. (As an add-on to this story, one of the many people who participated in the songfest was my Dad, who had been attending an automobile sales meeting in the hotel. He heard our music, surprised me with a big hug, and joined the singing with a glass of beer in hand!)

With my heavy post-doctorate schedule, I was unable to maintain my embouchure, even by practicing my trumpet every few days. I sold the Buescher trumpet just before we moved to New Mexico in 1964,

MY EXPERIENCES

where I decided to take up the trumpet again, purchased a new Olds Mendez trumpet, and took private lessons on it in the hope of becoming a church soloist with it. From 1968 to 1976, we lived in California, Ontario (Canada), and Oklahoma, where regular and part-time work, teaching, writing, and family took up virtually all of my free time, so I again lost my embouchure. Soon after we moved to Potomac, Maryland in 1976, I started to play the trumpet again and joined the Silver Spring Brass Band, which recorded turn-of-the-century band music for its weekly Sunday afternoon radio program, and the Silver Spring Concert Band, which frequently gave semi-classical music concerts in the Washington, District of Columbia (DC) area. I played trumpet solos in our Episcopal church in Potomac and a coworker's Methodist Church in Prince George's County, Maryland. Except for playing my trumpet with the University Heights (Cleveland, Ohio) Concert Band for about a year in the early 1980s, I then played it occasionally for personal enjoyment.

In the summer of 2005, I received a telephone call from a high school classmate, Toby Fredericks, asking if I was the Doug Busby who played La Cucaracha with a cornet trio at KCI in 1954. After I said so, recalling that I still had the music for this piece, he asked me to join the other two trio members in playing it after the dinner at KCI's 150th reunion, to be held that fall. Both of the members, Gerry Knipfel of Elkhart, Indiana, and Jim Carroll of Calgary, Alberta were still having outstanding careers in band and orchestra music, so I had to practice "long and hard" for this event. I also made sure that when playing La Cucaracha this time, I would make every effort to keep my mute from falling out of my trumpet to entertain an audience of now 1,200 persons! Our performance, accompanied by a well-known concert pianist who went from the KCI to the Julliard School of Music, received a standing ovation, as it did the following day after an encore at the Kitchener Auditorium.

With my embouchure restored and after some practice reading trumpet music, I successfully applied to be a substitute (and paid) trumpet player during summer seasons in the St. Joseph (Michigan)

DOUGLAS E. BUSBY

Municipal Band, the Michigan City (Indiana) Municipal Band, and the La Porte (Indiana) City Band. I played with the St. Joseph Band for eight full seasons, eventually replacing my aged Mendez trumpet with a new B&S trumpet. During my last two years with the St. Joseph Band, I was privileged to join three other persons in opening each concert with a herald-trumpet fanfare followed by the U.S. National Anthem with the band. Outside of the summer band season, I played with the Southwestern Michigan College (Dowagiac, Michigan) Brass Band and eventually the South Shore Brass Band (Merrillville, Indiana), using a new B&S cornet, and the Valparaiso University Community Concert Band (Valparaiso, Indiana), using the B&S trumpet. And when I served the Glenview (Glenview, Illinois) Community Church as its senior transitional minister, I played the B&S trumpet in the Glenview Community Concert Band.

I have very fond memories of playing innumerable band concerts for large audiences, wearing several different band uniforms (all rather toasty in the summer) and T-shirts emblazoned with band insignia, marching in parades, playing pieces composed for trumpet and organ in several churches, standing numerous times in bands to play the ending bars of Stars and Stripes, and making many musician friends. But my musical adventure had to come to an end in 2018 when increasing hearing loss forced me to permanently return my cornet and trumpet to their cases. That was 71 years after my Dad and I climbed the stairs to Waterloo Music Company's band room.

C. MY EDUCATION IN MEDICINE

1. In Pre-Medicine

In 1954, I began pre-medicine studies at Waterloo College with the 11 students in my class, with all of us taking courses similar to those of other two-year pre-medicine programs across Canada at that time. My first-year pre-medicine courses were in English literature and composition, calculus, general chemistry and qualitative analysis, physics, botany, zoology, library science, public speaking, and PE. I lived at home that year, commuting to the college on my little James 75 cc British motorcycle or the Kitchener-Waterloo bus system.

In addition to the momentary loss of piano accompaniment while playing a trumpet solo, as I described above, I have three other stand-out memories from my year at Waterloo College. The first involved the sport of fencing. Since mandatory PE involved selection and documentation of significant physical activity for the school year, another recent KCI graduate and I introduced a fencing program to the college just like the new program in which we had participated the year before at KCI. At first, we provided our fencing equipment, but within a few weeks, the college's athletic department decided to purchase new foils, masks, and gloves for our growing group of aspiring fencers. This sport quickly became popular, and its participants competed with each other and with fencers from KCI. My second memory evolved from my motorcycle being such a rarity that it drew a lot of attention, so much so that three students decided to ride on it together down University Avenue in front of the college, creating such a distraction in my zoology class that the professor asked me to park it out of sight in the truck delivery area behind the building. This did not work out well for the motorcycle, for a Canada Post truck backed over it. The driver of the truck insisted on being my

DOUGLAS E. BUSBY

chauffeur while my motorcycle was being repaired at Canada Post's expense, with my having to endure sitting quite uncomfortably on a low wooden box on the passenger side of the truck's cab. The motorcycle was sold to another Waterloo College student after the following summer. The third stand-out memory involves a remarkable member of our class, Paul Earl, who told us that after he graduated from high school, he sought his fortune as a trainer of racing horses, eventually for Pearl Bailey, and as a contract bridge player, eventually with Omar Sharif. His father, a prominent Canadian physician, had talked him into returning to Canada for a career in medicine. Those of us who played bridge with him soon found that he had an uncanny aptitude for "reading" cards before they were played, which we surmised was due either to him reading our minds or memorizing and counting cards. In numerous late-evening sessions in the college lounge, Paul "destroyed" every student with whom he competed, fortunately without any money passing hands. To my knowledge, none of Paul's many friends at Waterloo College ever learned what became of him after his first year in pre-medicine.

I took my second year in pre-medicine on the main campus of UWO, hoping to be accepted the following year into its School of Medicine, which at that time was on South Street at the opposite end of London. That year I lived in the dormitory of the nearby Anglican Seminary, Huron College. The seminary's student body at the time was all-male, as were all of the dorm residents. Meals were served buffet style, except at the end of regular school days, when dinner was served family-style. For dinner, everyone had to wear an academic gown over classroom business attire and stand at their tables until grace was said by a senior seminarian at the head table. During my year in the dormitory, I was a family-style waiter, so all of my meals there were at no cost to me. The pre-medicine curriculum was again intense, and essentially the same for most of the approximately 90 hopeful medical students. My courses were: English literature and composition, statistics, organic chemistry, physical chemistry, physics, philosophy, psychology, comparative vertebral zoology, and

MY EXPERIENCES

introduction to embryology. Organic chemistry quickly became the "talk of the town," heard mainly as loud groans as the elderly professor wrote the structures and interactions of chemicals on chalkboards that he usually moved to overlap each other before we could understand or copy what he had just written. And to add to our distress with him, he repeatedly asked examination questions on subjects we had not covered. We could only hope that the biochemistry course in medical school would be much more palatable to us.

My life beyond the classroom while I was in second-year pre-medicine was quite diverse. As I mentioned above, I played trumpet in a large dance band. It practiced Sunday afternoons in the basement of a downtown store, played for many formal university student dances, and folded near the end of the school year when it failed to get a contract to play for the summer at a very well-known lodge in Muskoka. I was active in the university's Canterbury Club, which met at St. Paul's (Anglican) Cathedral for worship, guest lectures, and dances. At one gathering, the university's president and the club's honorary president, Dr. G. Edward Hall, described the research he did while at the Royal Canadian Air Force (RCAF) Institute of Aviation Medicine (IAM) in Toronto during World War II. Little did I know at the time that the IAM would play a launching role in my medical career.

Throughout my second year in pre-medicine, I served as a lay reader and acolyte for early morning communion services in the chapel of Huron College, as well as a lay reader for Sunday evening services at St. George's Anglican Church near the university's main campus - which brings to mind a rather humorous incident that occurred one morning in the chapel. The evening before it occurred, the dean of Huron College had commented to some students during a gathering for coffee and conversation that seminarians seemed to be bored while reading the same words in the Anglican Book of Common Prayer every morning after morning during worship service in the chapel. Surprise! Every Book of Common Prayer in the chapel's pews disappeared that night, causing a humorous sort of chaos as the seminarians searched for prayer books. As the acolyte that morning, I had a prayer book in hand, so I had to become the sole responsive voice in the congregation.

I found that student pranks were not unique to Huron College. Convocation day at UWO was celebrated annually in the fall as a university holiday, with a sit-down lunch in Convocation Hall being followed by a prominent speaker, who in 1955 was Sir Robert Watson-Watt, the renowned British pioneer of radar technology. The master of ceremonies began the event by announcing that after grace was said by the university's chaplain, we could open the wrapped large boxes on the tables in front of us, each containing gifts for us. The boxes contained thousands of dry dinner rolls, which immediately became a cloud of projectiles. Flying rolls struck everyone, but those at the head table, including Sir Robert, were given large serving trays to protect themselves. Calm was eventually restored and a fine meal was served. However, as soon as Sir Robert began to speak, the university's marching band entered, parading around the head table and through the hall to a rousing march which soon generated a snake line. I recall that after the student body calmed down a second time, Sir Robert gave a great speech.

Another mischievous event involved a blinding white light, appropriately nicknamed "the chastity light," that shone from the top of the tower in front of Brescia Hall, a convent and women's residence, onto the straight narrow road to its main entrance. One day, two students posing as electricians tried to get into the tower to "service" and undoubtedly disable the light, but a perceptive nun turned them away. This led to some sort of a high-powered gun being used at some distance from the hall, to destroy the light and unfortunately a piece of the tower. The perpetrators were never caught, but the light and missing piece of the tower were soon replaced.

Unforgettable Memories: Summers at Carling Brewery
This seems to be an appropriate place in my story to describe my four summers of employment at the Carling Brewery in Waterloo, starting

MY EXPERIENCES

after high school. Each summer, Carling used students from the graduating grade-13 class at KCI, Waterloo College, and returning home from colleges and universities for the summer, to help it meet an upcoming great need for its Black Label Lager and Red Cap Ale. The students received the same hourly pay as Carling regular employees, had to join the brewery workers' union, and while at work had to wear a Carling uniform consisting of a khaki work shirt with a bright red "Carling" stitched across the back of it, khaki trousers, black steel-toed shoes, and the bright red Carling baseball-style cap. When employees over age 21 "punched in" for work, they were given four free tickets, for two bottles of beer at lunch and two bottles of beer after work - a practice which was welcomed in the hot weather, but otherwise appeared to contribute to substantial alcoholism among the regular employees. Most of the students were initially assigned to the evening (3:00 p.m. to 11:00 p.m.) and night (11:00 p.m. to 7:00 a.m.) shifts in the company's bottling department, which had its bottle-receiving, beer-bottling, and bottle-shipping functions in one large building. I started in receiving, and during my first midnight shift ever, had to stand alone on a temporary platform just outside of the building and transfer cases of 24 returned-empty beer bottles from one conveyor belt to another for the entire 8-hour shift and, unexpectedly, 2 hours of overtime. Throughout the summer, I usually went home quite "tired and stinky" from passing innumerable cases of supposedly-empty beer bottles from hot railroad boxcars onto conveyor belts.

My second summer at the Carling Brewery in Waterloo began in the beer-bottling area where three filling machines bottled and capped bottles with lager (white bottles) or ale (green bottles) at a rate of over 500 bottles a minute. The beer-bottling process was preceded by the bottles being washed in one of three machines. At each machine, four of us reached into cases of empty beer bottles passing by on a conveyor belt and placed four bottles at a time into the machine's intake system on the other side of the conveyor. Lower back discomfort that occurred from having to lean and reach in moving bottles from cases to the washer was usually relieved by our being rotated, one person at a time, to sit facing a conveyor belt to inspect full bottles of beer rapidly moving by on it in a single line from a pasteurizer to a labeler.

Midway through that summer, the brewing department posted a job for a person with "laboratory experience" to work for the rest of the summer as a quality control technician in the bottling department. In applying for this position, I cited my summer work in the hospital pharmacy and a year in pre-medicine as my experience, which led to my being selected and trained for it, and a few days later again being assigned to work the night shift. This job's major tasks were verifying by the taste that the beer being bottled was lager or ale, routinely inspecting newly-washed bottles for cleanliness, and checking the operating temperatures of the bottled-beer pasteurizers. Concerning taste testing, I was trained to be sure that at any time of the day, especially after "tasty" meals and snacks, I could easily detect the difference in taste between lager and ale. As an example of what could happen if I failed at this, I was told that one of two regular quality control technicians had recently failed to detect an accidental lager-ale changeover error when a new 8,000-gallon tank of beer was put online for bottling, due to his having eaten a hamburger covered by a thick slice of onion just before coming to work. Wrong beer, wrong bottle color, wrong bottle caps, and wrong labels could lead to numerous bottles of beer having to be "dumped" and never consumed. Although wrong bottle caps and labels occurred several times during my four summers at Carling, the fresh onion story remained a strong reminder to watch what I ate before I reported to work as a quality control technician.

At the beginning of my third summer at Carling, I was assigned to work the night shift for a few weeks in the company's brewhouse, as a partner to a long-time employee there. Our jobs were to clean the inside of the copper kettle used in the first stage of making each 8,000-gallon batch of beer and to clean the inside of a circular, open, steel mixing tank after the second stage of beer-making. This two-stage process involved the boiling of water, malted grain and hops in the

MY EXPERIENCES

kettle, followed by churning them in the tank. Finally, a sugary liquid, called "wort," was drained from the tank to be fermented into beer, leaving pulp, grain, and hops, together called "mash," for us to remove from the floor of the tank. To clean the kettle, the "cleaner" used a single key to turn off the power to a large mixing blade at the bottom of the kettle, and while keeping the key, donned a protective suit, rubber boots, and face mask, and descended a ladder into the kettle and washed it with a mixture of sulfuric acid and charcoal. For cleaning the tank, the "cleaner" used a single key to turn off the power to its numerous small mixing blades mounted on rotating crossbars, and while keeping the key, donned a protective suit, rubber boots, and face mask, and descended a ladder into the tank to push the mash through holes in the tank floor and clean the inside of the tank with a less hazardous chemical than the sulfuric acid used to clean the kettle. I have described our work here in some detail to say that even though my partner and I took precautions to avoid a disastrous accident, as had been recently reported in the news, I have often wondered how safe we were in such a hot environment at night, with my partner drinking several "hidden" bottles of beer during our work shift and rushing our work so that he could get a few moments of sleep on a bench in the dressing room.

Just before my assignment to the brewhouse ended and I was to be a quality control technician again, the brewmaster for the Carling Brewery in Waterloo invited me to come to his office late that afternoon. After he introduced me to the brewery's apprentice brewmaster, I was invited to join them in a "blind" tasting to compare the newly-bottled beer at the Carling Brewery in Waterloo, with beer from other breweries, including the Carling and O'Keefe breweries in Toronto, and the Molson Brewery in Montreal. Fortunately, I was able to "identify and approve" the newly-bottled beer from the Carling Brewery in Waterloo. After the tasting, the brewmaster offered me a brewmaster apprenticeship, which would involve my completing a bachelor's degree at the Ontario Agricultural College in Guelph, Ontario, by transferring my pre-medicine course credits from Waterloo

College and UWO to it, and taking several courses in microbiology at it, to fulfill requirements to enter an apprenticeship and become certified as a brewmaster. This offer, including a substantial salary and coverage of the cost of my education and work-related expenses, was quite enticing. However, I received acceptance to enter the Medical School at UWO a few days later, and making beer and tasting a lot of it simply did not substitute for a career in medicine.

I worked the remainder of my third and my entire fourth summer in the quality control laboratory in the bottling department of Carling Brewery in Waterloo. The fourth summer was hot, with much public demand for beer and much company demand for overtime work, which occasionally involved the dumping of bottled beer. I will always remember a rather unique incident that led to a large beer dumping, as well as a clean-up of a lot of broken glass. I had just walked onto the mezzanine floor of the shipping area on my way to my night shift in the laboratory, when I saw a regular Carling employee back a forklift into the main water pipe to the bottling department, splitting the pipe wide open. Immediately, water started to flow across the mezzanine and fall onto hundreds of stacked cases of beer in the shipping area below, soon creating a mess of collapsing cases and breaking bottles. This incident had also shut down the supply of water, but not steam, going to the main pasteurizer. Water to a pasteurizer was heated by the steam and sprayed onto just-filled, cold bottles of beer to gradually increase the temperature of the beer in them to 140-142 degrees Fahrenheit and, after a one-half-hour holding period, gradually lower the temperature of the beer to near room temperature. As I ran to the bottling area to assist with shutting down the steam lines, all I could hear was the noise of beer bottles exploding from the heat of the steam. A lot of overtime work was needed to dump hundreds of bottles of beer. That's sure been quite a story to tell at a party over the years!

2. In Medical School

I enthusiastically started medical school at UWO in early September of 1956. There were 58 of us, 45 of whom had "survived" pre-

MY EXPERIENCES

medicine at UWO. The 13 medical students who had not been in UWO's pre-medicine program had comparable pre-medical academic backgrounds at UWO or another Canadian university, or an American or European university. Some had already been in the workforce, including a pharmaceutical representative, a research pharmacist, a psychologist, an RCAF pilot, a television news broadcaster and drama host, and a professional baseball player. Two had recently immigrated to Canada from countries in Europe.

On my first day in medical school, our class was introduced to the school's teaching staff and its anatomy, physiology and pharmacology, clinical chemistry and bacteriology, histology and pathology laboratories, and its library. In the anatomy laboratory, 10 cadavers, covered with a transparent waxy material, had been placed on high, marble tables, ready for their complete dissection by groups of six of us over the next nine months. We were also instructed on the use of our microscopes, which included the new Japanese Olympus microscope that I introduced and sold to class members for a local medical supply company. That evening, we gathered for a get-acquainted party at the nearby "frat house" owned by the local chapter of the international medical student fraternity, Alpha Kappa Kappa (AKK).

During my first two weeks in medical school, I gradually realized that the environment of the home in which I was living in London was incompatible with my being able to study comfortably and effectively. Mr. and Mrs. Bruce Dinsmore had a very neat and clean home which was a short walking distance from the medical school. Recently retired, Mr. Dinsmore had taught mathematics and had been an assistant football coach at London Central High School, and at the time, especially at the dinner table, was interested only in how well the school's football team was doing. Unknown to me when I moved into their home, Mrs. Dinsmore was a diehard teetotaler. I was placed in a small upstairs bedroom, with Mrs. Dinsmore ordering me to never sit on the edge of the bed, despite there being no chair in the room! To study, I had to share a small room above the garage with a graduate

DOUGLAS E. BUSBY

student at UWO. I had a very small desk, the top of which could not hold both a textbook and a notebook. And to wash my clothes, Ms. Dinsmore said that I could use the water in the washing machine after she washed her family's clothes, or simply send or take my dirty clothes home for my mother to wash them. The event that finally led me to decide to move out of the Dinsmore's home occurred at the dinner table after my third day at medical school when Mrs. Dinsmore asked me if I had any friends in AKK, and before I could answer her, referred to the local chapter of AKK as a "bunch of drunks." I replied by saying that I understood that AKK is a medical student fraternity and has several alumni on the faculty of the medical school supporting its academic activities for all medical students. She vociferously held to her negative perception of AKK, adding that she would not tolerate my coming into her home with alcohol on my breath, as had occurred after the welcoming party at AKK after my first day at medical school. I thought, "What if Mrs. Dinsmore discovers where I had worked during the summer?"

I decided to look for another place to live, and a day later saw that a Mrs. Hazel Hughes had posted an announcement on the medical school's bulletin board, that she had a room available for a medical student in her apartment on Grand Avenue, a very short walking distance from the school. There I would have a large bedroom with a moderate-sized desk and small side table, and use of Mrs. Hughes' refrigerator and her telephone, and the apartment's laundry. I stayed with Mrs. Hughes through my first three years at medical school. I had dinner with Mrs. Hughes for the first year, and due to her busy work and church schedule, thereafter had dinner at the AKK fraternity house, having become a member of AKK in my first medical school year. In her early 80's when I moved into her apartment, Mrs. Hughes was the First Reader in London's Christian Science church, manager of this church's Reading Room, and an avid student of the Holy Bible and the writings of her church's founder, Mary Baker Eddy. Even though Christian Science teaches that sickness is an illusion that can be corrected by prayer alone, Mrs. Hughes never said anything contrary

MY EXPERIENCES

to the field of medicine and it as my choice of career. When I taught about prayer for healing in a seminary many years later, I would reiterate what I had learned about Christian Science healing from her.

All medical students at UWO had the same curriculum throughout medical school. The first-year classes were in anatomy, histology, biochemistry, physiology, preventive medicine, and psychiatry. Except for preventive medicine, which was an introductory course in biostatistics, and psychiatry, which was an overview of psychological disorders, this curriculum, as well as the second-year curriculum, was designed to administer a pretty strong dose of the basic sciences that are foundational to the practice of medicine. One of my most captivating professors that year was Dr. Alan Skinner, an anatomist and classical scholar who wrote a famous book on the origin of medical terms. Dressed in a black academic robe, Dr. Skinner began each anatomy class with a lecture on the area of the human body that we were to dissect, using colored chalk on a blackboard to illustrate the anatomic structures we should be able to identify during our subsequent dissection. Curiously, Dr. Skinner never stepped into the anatomy lab, so an assistant professor of anatomy and two second-year surgery residents assisted us during, and quizzed us after, the dissection on which he had just lectured.

Another of my most interesting professors that year was Dr. Murray Barr, who taught histology, or the study of the microscopic structure of tissues. He began each histology class with a lecture during which he projected slides of the various tissues of the human body and then had us use colored pencils to draw pictures of tissues as viewed through our microscopes. In his first lecture, Dr. Barr showed us how he and an associate had identified a dark spot in the cells of human females, and how he had developed a simple test to determine the sex of a person using the cells being shed from the lining of the mouth. He said that he had observed that this spot, since called the Barr body or sex chromosome, is abnormal in persons with congenital disorders, such as Down's syndrome. Throughout my time in medical school and beyond, Dr. Barr's research on chromosomal abnormalities and their relationship to such disorders helped to open the field of genetic medicine for which he was accorded many honors.

During my first year in medical school, several professors referred to their research in aviation medicine which they and the President of UWO, Dr. Hall, had conducted at the RCAF IAM during World War II. I recall hearing Dr. Hall speak about research at the IAM to the Canterbury Club the year before and with this additional information on aviation medicine from the professors, I became curious about this specialized area of medicine.

The courses during my second year in medical school were neuroanatomy, pathology, biochemistry, physiology, bacteriology and immunology, preventive medicine, psychiatry, medicine, surgery, and obstetrics and gynecology. Neuroanatomy was taught by Dr. Barr, who had written a classic text on the human nervous system that made understanding the anatomy and functions of the brain much easier. As I studied neuroanatomy, I often wondered whether the human soul is located in the brain and because the soul does not appear to be a distinct physical entity in the brain, I also wondered whether it is some sort of energy within the brain. Pathology was taught by Dr. John Fisher, who extended the use of our microscopes from histology to the study of diseased tissues, including non-malignant and malignant cancer. Dr. Fisher's lectures concluded with the room lights being turned off and his using a slide projector to show us what we would be seeing through our microscopes, which led to several in the class falling asleep and Dr. Fisher raising his voice to awaken them.

Courses in medicine and surgery were also given during my second year in medical school. They focused principally on learning how to take a medical history and physically examine patients with the class formed into small groups, each led by a specialist on the clinical staff of the medical school. I will never forget my first history and examination, with the patient being a large-breasted young woman who was hospitalized for treatment of heart failure from mitral heart valve insufficiency while pregnant. After taking the medical history relevant to her heart problem, I exposed her chest and, as we had been instructed, began to observe it for any abnormal

MY EXPERIENCES

movement associated with her leaking heart valve. Our clinical teacher then asked me to describe what I was doing at this point in my examination of the patient, and without thinking about how to reply discretely, I said, "Having a good look." Everyone in the room, except me, responded to what I had just said with momentary loud laughter. So, on my first day ever having contact with a patient, I learned the hard way that what a physician says in front of a patient can be misconstrued.

I will never forget an experience that I had in the fall of my second year in medical school, and in retrospect predicted a major aspect of my medical career. I had joined the Caduceus Society, a small group of students in our class that met monthly at the AKK fraternity house to hear three of its members each "give a paper" on a medical subject of interest, and then be critiqued on its content and presentation by a guest professor from the medical school and the other attendees. I decided to speak on the evolution of aviation medicine into a new specialty, aerospace medicine, to protect and treat humans from medical problems from hazards of space travel. Major sources of information for my presentation were an article on space medicine recently published in the journal, *Ciba Symposia*, and my imagination. The majority of students who voted on my presentation felt that my topic was too futuristic, but the guest professor, Dr. Alan Burton, Chair of the Department of Biophysics at UWO's medical school, disagreed with them, citing his extensive experience in aviation medicine at the RCAF IAM during World War II. And on October 4, 1957, just a few days after the Caduceus Society meeting, the Russians launched Sputnik 1, the first artificial Earth satellite, inaugurating the "Space Age" and stimulating international interest in the possibility of human travel into space.

My last two years in medical school provided my core knowledge in clinical medicine through a variety of direct learning experiences. One of these experiences was of especially great value to me. As I subsequently learned from many years of contact with American and other "international" medical graduates, the Canadian medical education system was unique in stressing the importance of the "detailed medical history" in diagnosing a patient's health problem.

DOUGLAS E. BUSBY

Our Professor of Medicine, Francis "Frank" Brien, would repeatedly remind us of how Canada's renowned physician, teacher, philosopher, and author, Sir William Osler, would astound his students and colleagues by making a diagnosis from a patient's answers in a detailed medical history consisting of a few well-crafted questions directed to the patient and, if necessary, the patient's family and friends. But Dr. Brien would never forget to mention that added to making a diagnosis should be "a thorough physical examination and the judicious use of laboratory, x-ray, and other diagnostic tests." Dr. Brien's teaching was a prophetic warning about the looming high-cost shift in the diagnostic component of a patient's medical management away from a time-consuming medical history and physical examination toward rapidly evolving laboratory and other diagnostic tests, substantially stimulated by misconceived liability for not using them.

My third-year courses in medical school were in preventive medicine, psychiatry, medicine, surgery, obstetrics and gynecology, pediatrics, ophthalmology, otolaryngology, pharmacy, physical medicine, pathological chemistry, radiology, and anesthesia. And my fourth-year classes were in preventive medicine, medicine, surgery, obstetrics and gynecology, pediatrics, ophthalmology, and otolaryngology. In the third and fourth years, we were increasingly involved in the diagnosis and treatment of patients, functioning as "doctors" in the various outpatient specialty clinics, going on "rounds" with physicians of various specialties while they visited their hospitalized patients, and attending "grand rounds" in medicine and surgery where patients usually with complex medical and surgical problems were presented to the students, interns, residents, and medical staff members for a discussion of their problems. We met as a class for lectures and were divided alphabetically into small groups from which students in their fourth year would be assigned to take the medical histories of, and do physical examinations on, patients just admitted to the hospital. Over the two years, our scope of "training and practice" expanded from the 1,200-bed Victoria Hospital adjacent to the medical school to three other large healthcare institutions in London: St. Joseph's Hospital, Westminster Veterans' Hospital, and the Ontario Psychiatric Hospital. With a rapidly-growing

MY EXPERIENCES

population of 276,000 in 1960, its birth rate easily provided ten babies whom each of us had to help deliver during our fourth year of medical school.

During my third and fourth years in medical school, I became a member of two additional medical student organizations, the Alpha Omega Alpha (AOA) Honor Medical Society and the Osler Medical Society, while my activities in the Caduceus Society continued. AOA is an international society of medical students who have been elected to it because of their scholastic ability, contributions to the field of medicine, and moral character. In my last year of medical school, our chapter had 15 members – ten from my class and five from the third-year class. Its monthly meetings, usually held in the home of a medical school professor, consisted of a presentation on a research or clinical topic by a student or professor. The Osler Medical Society is a Canadian organization of medical students founded to perpetuate the memory of Sir. William Osler and the study of medical history. In my last year of medical school, our chapter had 19 members – 11 from my class and eight from the third-year class. For its monthly meetings, various members presented papers on historical characters and events in medicine. The Osler Medical Society also supported the medical school's Osler Corner, which contained medical items of historical interest.

The annual banquets of the AOA and the Osler Society were quite popular among the students and faculty of the medical school, in large part due to their having well-known speakers. I have distinct memories of two of the speakers, albeit for quite different reasons. The speaker at the AOA banquet in my third year of medical school was the renowned neurosurgeon and director of the Montréal Neurological Institute, Wilder Penfield, who had become widely known for his mapping of the human brain. Since I had become interested in the nature of the human soul from studying neuroanatomy during my second year in medical school, I hoped that Dr. Penfield might say something about the soul, or human spirit, in his presentation. Indeed, he did, by simply mentioning during his speech that "in performing hundreds of operations on the human brain, I have yet to identify a soul." The speaker at the Osler Society banquet in my fourth year of medical school was the Chair of the

DOUGLAS E. BUSBY

Department of Anatomy in the medical school at the University of Toronto, Dr. J. C. B. Grant, who wrote a very popular atlas of anatomy. As the president of the Osler Society, I was responsible for meeting and chauffeuring the speaker. After Dr. Grant arrived in the late afternoon at London's train station, I drove him to Hotel London, presumably to rest for an hour before going to the banquet. However, Dr. Skinner and he reminisced about old times over a bottle of Crown Royal in Dr. Grant's room, and when I arrived to take Dr. Grant to the banquet, he had just stepped out of the shower, quite wet and tipsy. Needless to say, I was able to get Dr. Grant dried and dressed in his tuxedo (fortunately with a clip-on bowtie), and then to the reception for the banquet just a bit late and seemingly sober. His fascinating speech was on the origin of the names of various cities around the world, in a way reflecting Dr. Skinner's book on the origin of medical terms.

Late in the summer between my third and fourth years of medical school, I was married to Barbara Timm, and we moved into the apartment building on Grand Avenue, down the hall from the apartment in which I had lived with Mrs. Hughes. We were to live there as I finished medical school and did a rotating internship, sharing the same experiences, including the start of a family, with many of my classmates.

The culmination of medical school was taking examinations of the Medical Council of Canada, to become a licentiate of the council as the first step to being qualified to practice medicine, and the second step to be in a rotating internship. About one month at the end of our final school year was set aside for individual study. The examinations were proctored, written in the medical school's gymnasium on small desks well separated from each other. The time allotted for each examination was three hours, during which we selected five of seven questions to answer in writing. Each of us also had an oral examination in each of including medicine, surgery, obstetrics and gynecology, and pediatrics, given by physician specialists on the faculty of the medical school. We did not receive the results of the Council examinations, which were included in the final grading for the year. My average

MY EXPERIENCES

grades and class standings for my medical school years were: the first year, A, second of 60; the second year, A, second of 55; the third year, A, first of 54; and the fourth year, A, first of 54. On June 4, 1960, 54 of us graduated from UWO with the degree of Doctor of Medicine (M.D.), with three of us, including me, receiving our M.D. *cum laude*.

Over the years I have been asked several times if how I studied for examinations and answered their questions were in part responsible for my getting good grades in medical school, to which I have replied, yes, and if desired, repeat the following advice that I was given and applied throughout and beyond medical school. Early in my first year of medical school, Dr. Charles "Chuck" Gowdey, Professor of Pharmacology, joined several of my classmates and me at lunch in the medical school's cafeteria. It was a frustrating time for me because I had just failed my first (and only) examination in university - in biochemistry. He seemed quite interested in how we were adapting to medical school, so I decided to make an appointment with him to ask him for advice on how to get good grades. He began by informing me that the primary goal of UWO's medical school was to graduate physicians who would be "safe" in their practice of medicine, so medical students should be particularly attentive to "pearls" taught with an emphasis in the classroom and at the bedside. With regards to the taking of examinations, he suggested that all questions be thoroughly read before answering the first one selected, the same time be allotted to answering each question, each answer begin with a brief statement on what the answer will involve, and good penmanship with correct spelling and grammar being used. Later, I added outlines, especially of some of the more complex answers to be given, as suggested to the medical students by Dr. Angus McLachlin, Chair of the Department of Surgery at UWO's medical school.

Unforgettable Memories: Royal Canadian Air Force University Reserve Training Program
Dr. Gowdey was one of my professors in medical school whom I had heard had worked at the RCAF IAM during World II. In a casual conversation with him in early 1958, I mentioned my interest in

aviation medicine. He suggested that if I wished to know about it as a potential medical specialty for me, I should visit IAM, especially to see some of the aeromedical research being conducted in support of the Avro CF-105 Arrow interceptor becoming operational. For this, he placed me in contact with IAM's commander, Group Captain Donald "Don" Nelson. A few weeks later, I met with Dr. Nelson at the IAM's main facility on Avenue Road in Toronto, after which he had several members of his staff show me its research and teaching operations there and at its satellite facility in RCAF Station Downsview, just north of Toronto. At the Avenue Road facility, I saw a human centrifuge, one of the first built in North America to study the effects of "G" forces on pilots. At the Downsview facility, I saw a newly-constructed decompression chamber being used to study the protection of airline pilots and their passengers from sudden exposure to high altitudes. After the tour, Dr. Nelson recommended that if I was interested in a career in aviation medicine, I join the RCAF University Reserve Training Program (URTP) at UWO, and spend the last two summers while in medical school assisting in aeromedical research programs at IAM.

When I subsequently visited the RCAF recruiting officer on UWO's main campus, I learned that if I joined the RCAF URTP, I would be given the entry-level rank of flight cadet, and have to go to the RCAF Officers' School at the Royal Military College (RMC) Saint-Jean in Quebec for five weeks at the beginning of my first summer of duty. Moreover, I would have to attend monthly meetings of all of the military reserve students at UWO and serve for three full summers with the RCAF. (I did not realize at the time that I would be unable to serve the third summer, due to being in a rotating internship immediately after graduation from medical school.) So, after being "sworn in" and fitted with full winter (blue) and summer (khaki) RCAF officer uniforms and a wedge cap with markings indicating that I was a flight cadet, I began to attend the monthly meetings of the military reserve students on the UWO campus. And a day after my final examinations in second-year medicine, I boarded a train for RMC Saint-Jean, knowing that because of an extended medical school year at UWO, I would be several days late for classes there.

RMC Saint-Jean was one of three undergraduate military colleges in Canada, with the other two being the Royal Military College (RMC)

MY EXPERIENCES

of Canada near Kingston in Ontario, and the Royal Roads Military College (RMC) near Victoria in British Columbia. Its parade square bordered the beautiful Chambly Canal, which parallels the Richelieu River as it flows north from Lake Champlain to the St. Lawrence River. When I arrived at RMC Saint-Jean, I was ushered to the last class of the morning, then to lunch, and finally to my dormitory room. There, I met my three French-Canadian roommates from the University of Montréal, who had also just arrived and, as I soon discovered, had so little command of the English language that even bed selection was quite a challenge. After unpacking and donning our uniforms, the four of us were rushed outside to join our "flight" of 30 flight cadets, including several medical students, on the drill field. All walking and marching at the school required us to raise our arms to shoulder level and our thighs to horizontal level.

Most of the URTP students arrived at RMC Saint-Jean with no drill experience, including giving drill commands. Drill was taught on the parade square by cadets who were full-time students at RMC of Canada, who would finish the summer at RMC marching in formation, wearing a historic military uniform and pill-box cap, and shooting guns and cannons for the numerous seasonal tourists who visit the RMC campus. We did not appreciate them loudly berating us for every mistake we made during a drill session. So, one hot afternoon, a flustered cadet in my flight marched us down a ramp between the parade square and the Chambly Canal, with many of us descending up to our knees in water. Our instructor screamed at us to stop and then commanded us to "about face" and "march" up the ramp, which splashed a lot of welcome, cool water on everyone. The cadet who was responsible for this fiasco, created deliberately or not, had to appear "on charge" before the student court later that afternoon and was punished by having to march around the perimeter of the parade square for an hour that evening.

In addition to drill, the education of all flight cadets at RMC Saint-Jean included classes in Canadian military history, current world military affairs, military organization, leadership, use of a military pistol, PE, and the table set-up, dress, and etiquette at an officers' mess dinner. Military history focused mostly on World War II and the integration of Great Britain's Royal Air Force with the RCAF during

DOUGLAS E. BUSBY

World War II. Current world military affairs dealt almost exclusively with the Cold War, covering the responsibilities of the North Atlantic Treaty Organization (NATO) and the North American Air (later Aerospace) Defense Command (NORAD), and how to protect military and civilian populations in a thermonuclear war. Military organization, to which I had no prior exposure, was fascinating for me, for at least I would now know whom above me in rank to salute. Leadership was a broad overview of how leaders can function effectively, with information that I have used my entire life.

We were required to learn how to maintain and use the Browning 9 mm pistol, which had just been chosen by NATO for use by all of its military forces. A session of firing the pistol involved several of us standing in a line behind a narrow, long table, and shooting straight ahead at our own "bullseye" paper target which was mounted about 30 feet away on a bank of dirt sloping upwards to a vertical concrete wall. During one session, the fight cadet next to me placed his hands over his chest and fell to the ground saying, "I've been shot!" In turning to see what had happened, all of us still standing in the line turned towards our fallen comrade, inadvertently pointing our pistols in his direction as the instructors screamed at us to place our pistols on the table. The flight cadet rapidly developed a large, tender bruise in the front of his chest from this one-of-a-kind event, at least according to the instructors. A flattened 9 mm bullet was found where the cadet had been standing at the time of the incident and was subsequently presented to him to serve as a reminder of the "day I shot myself."

PE was also quite an experience for me. We were introduced to a small team of exercise physiologists who had just developed two exercise routines for the RCAF - one consisting of 5 basic exercises for women, called the 5 BX, and the other consisting of 10 basic exercises for men, called the 10 BX. Published together, their popularity around the world helped to launch the modern fitness culture. But when the team visited RMC Saint-Jean, 5 BX and 10BX were still being tested on their feasibility for use "in the field." We "volunteered" to contribute to this testing by doing the exercises during PE, with the exercise physiologists observing our performance of them and recording our heart and breathing rates. I continued to use the 10BX throughout that

MY EXPERIENCES

summer, after which my physical environment while at medical school, especially in the apartment, prevented me from engaging in it.

Finally, we learned about etiquette at a mess dinner, an institution of the Canadian military dating back several centuries in the British Empire for its officers. In our first class on this dinner, we were told that how it is conducted is standard among the military services. Consequently, instruction on table set-up, dress, and etiquette at a mess dinner is conducted for every officer in training so that the officer knows how to dress and behave at the dinner, which in some instances means altering cultural norms. We were taught how to set and use the place setting at the dinner table, such as where seemingly vast arrays of glassware and silverware are placed and used. Then several traditions were to be followed. The "cocktail hour" before a mess dinner does not begin until the commanding officer arrives, during which a designated officer gives a "call to order" and everyone stands in to acknowledge her or his presence. Before dinner begins, the Queen is toasted with water, without a clinking of glasses. Then a decanter of port is provided to each dinner table and passed from right to left without touching the table until each officer's glass is filled.

One mess dinner tradition - no one is to leave the dinner table until the meal has ended - was unexpectedly demonstrated to us at the mess dinner following our graduation from RCAF Officers' School at the RMC. Midway through dinner, a flight cadet stood up and waved at the vice president of the mess seated at the head table, to get his permission to go to the washroom. For several minutes, the vice president of the mess ignored the cadet, who was making his need to empty his bladder more and more evident. With everyone now watching this evolving scene, the vice president of the mess stood up and fired a Browning 9 mm pistol at the cadet, who took a step backward, collapsed, and fell to the floor. Frozen silence. Then, before anyone could react to what had occurred, the vice president of the mess and the flight cadet took their seats and waved to each other.

About a week before we graduated from officers' school, our training on the drill field began to include the commands and maneuvers that we would have to perform at our graduation, including our flights marching in military formation by a reviewing stand on which would be an air vice-marshal from RCAF Headquarters in Ottawa, Ontario, Canada, military dignitaries from the area, and the school's leadership. I thought that I was doing quite well in this training until a drill instructor asked me to step away from my flight, and without telling me why, sent me to the commander of the school. My apprehension for possible bad news shifted to anxiety when the commander told me that I had been selected to be the attaché to the air vice-marshal at the graduation ceremony and post-graduation reception. My responsibilities would be to brief the air vice-marshal on the school's officer training program, and then take him first to the reviewing stand and then onto the drill field to meet several flight cadets. I recall that this unexpected event in my life went quite well, not only in my briefing, but in my taking the right steps and turns on the drill field. At the reception after graduation, I met an RCAF pilot who offered me a ride from the nearby RCAF Station St. Hubert to the RCAF Station Downsview the next morning. So, my first flight ever was in the copilot seat of a twin-engine, multi-passenger Beechcraft C-45 Expeditor. The pilot gave me some instructions on how to fly the airplane, with my flying all over the sky!

Beechcraft C-45 Expeditor

I spent most of my two summers in the RCAF at its IAM facility at the RCAF Station Downsview, which had a large officers' mess for meals and socializing, an officers' dorm, and an indoor pool. This facility was involved principally with research and training in its decompression chamber on the protection of airplane pilots and passengers from hypoxia, or a reduced amount of oxygen in the tissues, due to a fast loss of the atmospheric pressure inside of an airplane, or rapid decompression to actual altitudes of up to 40,000 feet. Moreover, the RCAF was concerned with protecting fighter pilots who might be exposed to actual altitudes of up to 45,000 feet during aerial combat, and the Avro CF-105 Arrow interceptor pilots who might be exposed to actual altitudes of up to 60,000 feet during flight

MY EXPERIENCES

testing of this airplane. This research and training involved the use of a decompression chamber comprised of two essentially-tubular sections – a large section that could comfortably seat about 10 adults along its sides, and a small section. To simulate a rapid decompression, the atmosphere in the large section would be decompressed to the altitude normally used in the cabin of a pressurized aircraft, and the atmosphere in the small section would be decompressed to a much higher altitude. Then, a pressure control valve would be opened between the sections to allow their rapid equalization of pressure, with a predictable "timed ascent" of the large chamber to a predictable "simulated altitude."

I had two main responsibilities in the decompression chamber unit during my two summers at RCAF IAM. First, I served as a safety officer in rapid decompressions for testing the effectiveness of emergency oxygen delivery systems, including those used for airline passengers, and in training RCAF fighter pilots in hypoxia recognition and oxygen management. Second, I revised the RCAF pilot training manuals on altitude physiology, including protection from hypoxia and decompression sickness. On my first day in the decompression chamber unit, I joined a group of military and airline pilots who were being qualified for high-altitude flights with a routine in which I would be participating many times as a safety officer. This routine had the pilots first experiencing hypoxia during exposure to a simulated altitude of 35,000 feet, and then being exposed to a rapid decompression from 8,000 to 40,000 feet and donning an oxygen mask within the time of useful consciousness, or the time to don an oxygen mask to prevent loss of consciousness (about 15 seconds at 40,000 feet).

One day at lunch in the officers' mess, I met an RCAF pilot who offered to "take me up" in a T-33 *jet trainer* while he met his required monthly flight time. I was fitted with a helmet and mask in the decompression chamber unit and shown how to position myself for ejection from the T-33 by a member of its ground crew. Then, with my camera in hand, I was buckled into the combined ejection seat and parachute and told to keep my right hand off of the canopy lever and ejection seat handle unless the pilot ordered me to pull on one of them.

DOUGLAS E. BUSBY

Canadair T-33 trainer   Niagara Falls – upside down!

First, the pilot flew fairly low over Niagara Falls, during which he suggested that I hold my camera pointing straight upwards as he snap-rolled the plane for me to take a picture of the falls looking straight down through the clear canopy of the aircraft. Next, we headed north over Hamilton and then up Highway 400. Over the Barrie area, he put the plane into a steep climb. Then he flew it "over a hump" into a controlled dive, producing several seconds of simulated zero-gravity and a pencil floating in the cockpit atmosphere. During weightlessness, I felt slight nausea, but I did not have to use a readily-available "barf bag." I remember that during my second summer at IAM, I flew in the same plane with this pilot, who showed me some of the acrobatics he planned to use in the airshow at the Canadian National Exhibition. Again, no use of a barf bag, but lingering dizziness made my getting out of the cockpit a very slow process.

Back in the officers' mess after my first flight in the T-33, an RCAF URTP flight cadet who was working in the air traffic control tower at RCAF Station Downsview for the summer requested a ride in the T-33 from another pilot. The flight cadet was known in the officer's mess as having a nervous disposition, so he had to make his request several times before the pilot relented. During his decompression chamber training, the cadet had a "block" in his ears and the decompression chamber had to be raised and lowered in altitude several times to "equalize the pressure" in his ears, the last time using a potent norepinephrine nasal spray to decongest his Eustachian tubes. Despite his ear-clearing problem, the cadet somehow convinced the flight surgeon who commanded the decompression chamber unit, Squadron Leader Wilson "Bill" Leach, to clear him for high-altitude flight. When the T-33 was being flared for landing at the end of his flight, the cadet panicked and accidentally pulled on the opening lever for the airplane's canopy. The open canopy scooped so much air that the

MY EXPERIENCES

airplane was forced nose-up, momentarily terrifying the pilot as he unexpectedly had to correct the landing. That incident was not the end of the flight cadet's rise to popularity. Several days later, he was working alone in the control tower when a T-33 pilot notified him that he was unsure whether the nose gear of his airplane was completely lowered for landing. Instead of inspecting the airplane through binoculars to determine whether its nose gear was down, the flight cadet immediately shot a red emergency flare into the air over the airfield. The pilot landed the T-33 safely. However, the flare ignited the tall dry grass that covered most of the airfield, creating a huge column of smoke and a noisy parade of RCAF and Downsview community firetrucks. I never saw the cadet after that.

My second summer at the IAM facility at the RCAF Station Downsview began just after the Canadian government decided to terminate production of the Avro CF-105 Arrow interceptor and destroy five flight-ready Arrows, because of the high cost to produce this airplane and the lack of an international market for it. Dr. Leach invited me to come with him to Malton Airport to witness the destruction of the last of the Arrows. I will never forget looking upwards at its large electronics cable bundles being divided with blowtorches, and then climbing up a long ladder to sit in its cockpit, holding onto its joystick and looking out over its large delta-shaped wings, letting my imagination fly this "pride of Canada."

Avro CF-105 Arrow interceptor

A few weeks after I witnessed the last CF-105 Arrow interceptor being destroyed, Squadron Leader Leach asked me to visit the pilots of the RCAF's new aerobatic flying team, the Golden Hawks, which was performing in air shows across Canada with the Canadair Sabre (F-86 in the USA). The U.S Air Force (USAF) had reported that members of its acrobatic team were experiencing lower chest discomfort due to

DOUGLAS E. BUSBY

partial lung collapse from breathing pure oxygen during air shows, and Dr. Leach wanted me to ask the pilots in the RCAF's acrobatic team if this was also occurring among them. I met the RCAF team in the officer's mess at the RCAF Station St. Hubert near Montréal, just before the team was to fly to Winnipeg, Manitoba, to be in an air show there the next day. One of its members, Flight Lieutenant Jeb Kerr, graciously helped me get the information I needed: the RCAF team was not breathing pure oxygen and not experiencing chest discomfort while performing in air shows. On August 10, 1959, he was killed when his F-86 Sabre collided with a private aircraft that had illegally entered the landing pattern reserved for the RCAF team while landing at the Calgary, Alberta airport.

Towards the end of the second summer, Dr. Leach arranged for me to spend two weeks at the RCAF Station Trenton, an RCAF flight training base and the hub for RCAF air transport operations in Canada and abroad so that I could participate in the operations of its clinic and hospital, and most especially, observe the work of a flight surgeon in a clinical setting. At the time, I was applying for an RCAF incentive program for medical students who were currently flight cadets in the URTP. In this program, the cadet would receive a regular officer's salary and benefits during his or her fourth year of medical school and a subsequent year of rotating internship, in return for three years of full-time service in the RCAF. When I returned to IAM for the remainder of the summer, I discussed the program with Dr. Nelson, who said that he would sign my application for it. He then recommended that upon completion of my internship, and with his support, I receive training and experience as an RCAF flight surgeon, and thereafter study at the School of Public Health at the University of Toronto and the USAF School of Aerospace Medicine at Brooks Air Force Base in San Antonio, Texas, to become certified as a specialist in aerospace medicine by the American Board of Preventive Medicine. This became an exciting possibility, to which my fiancé, Barbara Timm, agreed, and my application was soon approved for the URTP. However, when I arrived at medical school to begin my fourth year there, the RCAF recruiting officer on UWO's main campus informed me that the program had just been changed so that I would be receiving RCAF officer pay and benefits only in my internship year in return for four years of full-time service in the RCAF. I did not accept these changes and remained in the URTP. The following spring, I was assigned to the IAM for the last of the three summers required in the URTP, but fortunately received a waiver for this due to having to enter a year of rotating internship at the beginning of July. Years later, I learned that these changes in the RCAF incentive program for medical students who were currently URTP flight cadets were generated by an influx of newly-graduated British physicians into Canada to serve their two years of obligatory military service in the RCAF instead of the British military.

Although my status as a flight cadet in the RCAF URTP ended when I graduated from medical school, Dr. Gowdey, who was the deputy commanding officer of the Medical Reserve Unit at the RCAF Station London, located at the Crumlin (later London International) Airport, invited me to become a member of the unit. I was given the rank of Flight Lieutenant and joined several physicians from the staff of the medical school and community, and a few administrative personnel, in monthly "readiness" exercises to support the RCAF should it have to use its remaining medical facilities at the airport in the event of a war or civil disaster. The unit was decommissioned a year later, after a final mess dinner.

3. In My Rotating Internship

On July 1, 1960, I began a one-year rotating internship at the Victoria Hospital. In those days, this type of internship was necessary beyond being a licentiate of the Medical Council of Canada, in order to be granted a license to practice medicine in the Province of Ontario. We spent time in each of the clinical specialty departments, with some exposure to the subspecialties in them, as well as in the emergency department of the hospital. For being on call overnight or simply resting, we had rooms in a dormitory with a telephone next to each of our beds as our only way of being contacted when we were not physically on duty. The internship was an excellent way for "hands-on" learning in all of the medical specialties, helping many of us to determine which medical specialty to select and often where to be trained for it.

DOUGLAS E. BUSBY

During the rotating internship, I became interested in surgery, especially cardiac surgery, and in internal medicine, especially cardiology. I also gave thought to becoming a specialist in aerospace medicine. In a visit to Dr. Nelson at the RCAF IAM, he suggested that I contact the personnel office in the USAF School of Aerospace Medicine to discuss possible options for being trained in aerospace medicine in the USAF, one of which might require my enlisting in the USAF. He also suggested that the potential for my being accepted for training in aerospace medicine in the USAF might improve substantially if I first obtained a graduate degree in aerospace physiology. When I mentioned to him my interest in high altitude physiology stemming from my summers at the IAM, he recommended that I look into the possibility of studying under Dr. Hermann Rahn, an expert in pulmonary and environmental physiology who was Chair of the Department of Physiology at the University of Buffalo.

The USAF School of Aerospace Medicine referred me to the coordinator of specialty training in aerospace medicine in the USAF in Washington, DC. When I visited him in the fall of 1960, he described how I might enter the program, first by immigrating to the United States, then by being assigned a U.S. Selective Service ("Draft Board") classification of 1-A, "Available for military service," and finally by enlisting in the USAF through his office. He agreed with Dr. Nelson that obtaining a graduate degree in aerospace physiology between my rotating internship and enlisting in the USAF could enhance the potential for my being selected for training in the specialty of aerospace medicine in the USAF. Upon my return to Canada, I contacted the Selective Service office in Albany, New York, to affirm the potential for my receiving a 1-A draft classification with the military's representative there, an officer in the U.S. Army. After I described my medical and RCAF training, family status, and desire to become a specialist in aerospace medicine in the USAF, he stated that if I "permanently" immigrated to the United States on a U.S. Immigration "green card," I would have to register with the U.S. Selective Service after 6 months, and would then receive the 1-A draft classification necessary for me to enlist in the USAF. Early in 1961, I visited Dr. Rahn, who invited me to study under him for a Doctor of

MY EXPERIENCES

Philosophy (Ph.D.) degree in an area of pulmonary physiology relevant to aerospace medicine.

My rotating internship was an excellent learning year, despite all of the routine stuff that physicians at "the bottom of the totem pole" have to do. Much of what interns did in the operating room involved holding tissue retractors for hours on end. We were constantly "on call" to insert intravenous fluid needles, nasogastric tubes, and urinary catheters, remove drainage tubes and stitches, and inject intravenous drugs and contrast agents. A particularly difficult and odiferous task was removing the intravaginal radiation pack used to treat cancer of the cervix. We did not do cardiopulmonary resuscitation (CPR) in those days, because it had not been "invented" yet, but we were called to "pronounce death." I greatly enjoyed the challenge of "working up" new patients - taking a medical history, doing a physical examination, ordering diagnostic tests, and then presenting what I had determined about the patient's medical problem to a resident, the name given to a medical or surgical in training. A special event that occurred during the year of my rotating internship was the use of the cardiopulmonary bypass pump and deep hypothermia by Dr. Charles "Charlie" Drake, a neurosurgeon, so that he could successfully close off arterial aneurysms at the base of the brain. He subsequently performed this operation in many centers in Canada and the United States.

On September 5, 1960, the first of my three daughters, Suzanne, was born quite prematurely at Victoria Hospital following detachment of an unanticipated very low placenta (*placenta previa*) that day. Suzanne, who weighed just 3 pounds and 4 ounces, was placed in an "incubator" in the hospital's newborn nursery, and because of her being so premature, was to have her breathing monitored and restored by tapping one of her heels if it slowed or stopped. (In those days, a neonatal intensive care unit with its array of electronic devices for monitoring vital cardiopulmonary functions in a baby, did not exist.) I was on duty at the hospital that night and was awakened in my room at about 3:00 a.m. by the pediatrics resident, Dr. Margaret Churchill, who asked me to come to the nursery immediately. When I arrived in the nursery, Margaret told me that the student nurse who was responsible for monitoring Suzanne while her supervisor was "at dinner" had not seen that Suzanne had stopped breathing while talking with her boyfriend on the telephone. Fortunately, the supervisor had returned to the nursery just in time to successfully resuscitate Suzanne, who had turned "very blue" from anoxia (lack of oxygen). Margaret was very concerned that Suzanne would not survive the night. I stayed with Suzanne the rest of the night, praying that she would stay alive. Suzanne continued to breathe on her own after her resuscitation. However, the long period of anoxia appears to have been the cause of her cerebral palsy.

4. As a Graduate Student in Pulmonary Physiology

Early in July of 1961, my wife, Suzanne, and I moved into a very nice apartment on Allenhurst Road in Buffalo, New York, planning for me to receive a Ph.D. in pulmonary physiology in about two years, and then join the USAF, hopefully at its School of Aerospace Medicine. On my first day in the Department of Physiology at the University of Buffalo, I met Captain William "Bill" Robertson and Captain Dominic "Dom" Maio, aerospace physiologists from the USAF School of Aerospace Medicine who were also there to obtain a Ph.D. in pulmonary physiology. Soon they assured me that my path to becoming a specialist in aerospace medicine was quite reasonable, in light of many research and clinical opportunities available in the USAF and becoming available in the National Aeronautics and Space Administration (NASA).

Bill, Dom and I were supervised by Dr. Leon Farhi, a pulmonary physiologist and an associate of Dr. Rahn. That summer, Dr. Farhi gave us a course on the application of respiratory gas exchange theory to the selection of safe breathing atmospheres for pilots and astronauts. Because we were working on a Ph.D. for which proficiency in two languages besides English had to be demonstrated, Dr. Farhi arranged for us to take an intensive course in scientific German. Also, I brushed up on my high school French by reading weekend editions of the popular Canadian newspaper, La Presse, so that I was able to pass the proficiency tests for German and French that fall.

MY EXPERIENCES

Until my first day in the Department of Physiology at the University of Buffalo, I was unaware that it had a compression chamber unit, headed by Dr. Edward "Ed" Lanphier, an expert in diving medicine and physiology. Dr. Farhi assigned me to work with Dr. Lanphier for the remainder of the summer, on a study to determine whether a Swiss mathematician's recent controversial proposal that carbon dioxide rather than nitrogen is responsible for nitrogen narcosis. Also called "rapture of the deep" and "martini effect," nitrogen narcosis is a problem for deep-sea divers, who experience increasingly-poor judgment, incoordination, euphoria, short-term memory loss, and difficulty with mental concentration when breathing air at underwater depths greater than 100 feet, and can lose consciousness and die at depths greater than 300 feet.

In this study, the compression chamber was occupied by a human subject, a technician, and a device to measure the partial pressure of carbon dioxide in the subject's blood. First, the chamber was rapidly pressurized to a simulated depth of 225 feet (6.8 atmospheres), with the subject breathing air, and the technician breathing a helium-air mixture to prevent nitrogen narcosis. At "depth," the technician immediately removed a small amount of arterial blood through a previously-placed needle in one of the subject's arms and measured the partial pressure of carbon dioxide in the blood. Finally, the chamber was rapidly decompressed using the U.S. Navy (USN) Diving Tables to prevent decompression sickness, or "the bends," from occurring in the subject and technician. Dr. Lanphier was the first subject and I was the technician, with the "run" being successful. I was the second subject and Bill was the technician, with the run being successful except for bleeding from the needle-insertion site producing a tender and painful bruise in the arm.

The third subject was Bill Robertson, and I was the technician. Our compression began on Friday afternoon, just before the very warm and humid Labor Day weekend. As I was withdrawing the arterial blood sample at depth, some bleeding began to occur around the needle in Bill's left arm. Dr. Lanphier told me to apply pressure over the bleeding site as we went through decompression, and I soon recognized that the pressure was trapping dissolved nitrogen in the arm, with nitrogen bubbles beginning to form in it. The atmospheric pressure in the chamber was immediately increased, and after the bubbles were no longer detectable, it was slowly decreased as recommended for the treatment of divers with decompression sickness in the USN Diving Tables. This process took over 50 hours, during which the chamber's air compressor had to be replaced with one from the city's fire department. Moreover, the air conditioning to the building automatically shut off at 6:00 p.m. on Friday for the upcoming weekend, requiring us to cool the chamber continuously with water-soaked blankets draped over it and fans blowing on the blankets. After Bill came out of the chamber, he was observed in the university hospital for two days and was treated for multiple small boils in his skin attributed to his exposure to the high temperature and humidity inside the chamber. After Bill's experience, the study was discontinued, but from limited results obtained in it, carbon dioxide as the cause of nitrogen narcosis seemed highly unlikely. Several years later, Bill and I worked together on spacesuit testing at Garrett AirResearch in Los Angeles, during which we shared the story of this high-risk study many times.

In early January of 1962, I asked Dr. Farhi what research I might be doing for my Ph.D., and he replied that it would be accurately determining the "tissue compartments" of nitrogen washout from the human body. In a physiology lecture in medical school, I had learned that atmospheric nitrogen, dissolved in tissues throughout the body, can form bubbles to produce symptoms of decompression sickness if the atmospheric pressure is lowered too quickly to allow equalization of the partial pressure of nitrogen in the tissues with the partial pressure of nitrogen in the atmosphere. In this process, a higher level of nitrogen dissolved in the tissues is "picked up" by the blood flowing through them and released by the blood into the lungs as gaseous nitrogen. Scientists had recently shown that the rate of this equalization process differs for various tissues depending largely on their blood supply and fat content, and is complicated by the fact that

MY EXPERIENCES

nitrogen is at least five times more soluble in fat than other tissues. They had also shown that this process has at least three simultaneously occurring phases – two rapid phases with half times of a few and several minutes, and a slow phase of about two hours, and most importantly, that this "washout" of nitrogen can be hastened by breathing pure oxygen. Since the Department of Physiology at the University of Buffalo had just received a recently-invented instrument for measuring the amount of nitrogen dissolved in the blood, I concluded from Dr. Farhi's comment on my potential research project, that I would be engaged in defining nitrogen washout phases more precisely with subjects breathing air or oxygen, or even a mixture of helium and oxygen as had recently been suggested, with data from this project being relevant to the prevention of decompression sickness from lowering spacecraft cabin and space suit atmospheric pressures in space. In January and February of 1962, Dr. Farhi had the Japanese student and me work together on validating the effectiveness of the new instrument, as Dr. Farhi and I continued to discuss my research project.

Also in January of 1962, I registered with the U.S. Selective Service, assuming that I would receive a 1-A draft classification. However, in late February I received a letter from the service, stating that it had given me a 5-A draft classification, "Registrant over the age of liability for military service." I immediately attempted to make telephone contact with the military representative in the U.S. Selective Service in Albany, with whom I had previously discussed my receiving a 1-A draft classification. His secretary said that he was "on travel," but after I described my possible misclassification by the U.S. Selective Service to her, said she would ask the military representative to telephone me as soon as possible. Minutes later, she informed me that she had discussed my classification with the representative, who told her to inform me that the Board had decided to give me the 5-A draft classification "because of your age and you have a family." I decided to "stay put" in my Ph.D. program at the University of Buffalo, and when possible, discuss the potential effectiveness of appealing

DOUGLAS E. BUSBY

my 5-A draft classification by telephone or in person with the representative. Then, a few days later, I received a second letter from the U.S. Selective Service, which stated that I now had a 1-A draft classification, and ordered me to report on a March date to the Buffalo U.S. Army recruiting center to be commissioned as a general medical officer in the U.S. Fifth Army. When I told Dr. Rahn that I had been drafted, he said that from his experience with graduate students being drafted, an appeal to rescind or modify an order for military service would be highly unlikely, and declined to support an appeal.

A few days after I received the 1-A draft classification and order to report to the recruiting center, my wife and I decided to return to Canada. In the interim, I contacted Dr. McLachlin, Chair of the Department of Surgery at UWO's medical school, by telephone. I indicated my interest in training to be a general surgeon, and he replied that if I wished, I could be a starting resident ("senior intern") in his general surgery residency program, to begin that July. Then he advised me to contact Dr. George Manning, Chair of the Department of Cardiology at UWO's medical school, saying that Dr. Manning might wish to use my assistance with a research project in cardiology until I entered his surgery program.

We moved back to Canada during the second week of March of 1962, purchasing a small new home on Knight's Hill Road in London. Just before I was due to report for commissioning into the U.S. Army, I talked with the military representative of the U.S. Selective Service in Albany by telephone. He denied ever having discussed my 5-A draft situation with his secretary and advised me to report for commissioning, but in doing so to say that I had surrendered my U.S. Immigration green card and show the commissioning officer my Canadian Passport as proof of my Canadian citizenship. He assured me that he would have the record of my disastrous relationship with the Board "set straight," so that I could re-immigrate to the United States in the future if I so wished. I was not commissioned into the U.S. Army.

As I look back on our decision to return to Canada, another "force" seems to have been at work in leading me to make it. In January of

MY EXPERIENCES

1962, Suzanne, then 16 months of age, could not yet walk without support, and she crawled very slowly and awkwardly. When I mentioned Suzanne's walking and crawling problems to Dr. Farhi, he suggested that she be evaluated by a pediatric orthopedist who was a close friend of his. The orthopedist ordered x-rays of Suzanne's hip joints, and without taking her medical history, quickly examined her hips and had her walk with support. He said that she had congenital dysplasia (abnormal development) of the acetabula (joint sockets) in her hips, and prescribed full-leg "twisters" that would forcibly rotate her legs inwards to correct this problem. A few days after we returned to Canada, we took Suzanne to Dr. Robert "Bob" Nicholson, the pediatrician who had cared for her from birth until we moved to Buffalo. After thoroughly examining Suzanne and having her seen in consultation by Dr. John "Jack" Kennedy, Chair of the Department of Orthopedics at UWO's medical school, Dr. Nicholson informed my wife and me that Suzanne had spastic cerebral palsy involving her lower extremities. Susanne was referred to the Crippled Children's Treatment Centre at Victoria Hospital to begin a program of physical therapy at the center and daily stretching exercises on her legs at home.

When I met with Dr. Manning a few days after I returned to Canada, he invited me to work with him on a unique research project in cardiology, which he had designed and was ready to begin. The purpose of this project was to evaluate the effectiveness of two separate drugs in preventing the death of dogs after acute blockage of a major coronary artery in them. Dr. Manning had developed a surgical procedure for producing the blockage, which would involve my accurately placing an open ligature for later closure around the origin of the left coronary artery in anesthetized dogs. Although I would not like to take dogs' lives in the name of medical progress, so little was known at that time about the prevention of death from sudden coronary artery occlusion in humans that I decided to work with Dr. Manning on the project, the results of which I reported at a scientific meeting in Québec City.

5. As a Senior Intern in Surgery and a Graduate Student in Biophysics

My next post-graduate undertaking, which involved both surgery and biophysics, requires some explanation. In the 1960s, the Royal College of Surgeons of Canada required four years in a general surgery residency program beyond the rotating internship; training, followed by a specialty certification examination; sub-specialty training, such as in cardiovascular surgery or urology, would then follow certification as a specialist in general surgery. At Victoria Hospital, eight surgical residents were spread across the four years of training. The first year was spent as a senior intern in surgery at this hospital, caring for public ward surgical patients and assisting in all sorts of surgical operations. The second year was spent in a basic science in medicine, with the surgery residents either teaching anatomy or conducting research in physiology or biophysics. The last two years were spent mostly in the supervised practice of general surgery - one year as a senior resident at one of the two other teaching hospitals in London, and the last year as one of the two chief residents at Victoria Hospital. During the time that I spent with Dr. Manning in the Department of Cardiology, I had become interested in cardiovascular surgery and learned that Dr. Alan Burton, Chair of the Department of Biophysics at UWO's medical school, was widely known for his research in cardiovascular biophysics. Subsequently, Dr. McLachlin approved my request to spend my basic science year in biophysics under Dr. Burton's tutelage.

Dr. McLachlin, who was known to his residents as "The Chief," was a very thorough and dedicated teacher. Most of my time during my senior intern year at Victoria Hospital was spent in the operating room, assisting Dr. McLachlin and other surgeons on his staff, and beginning to perform "supervised" operations, such as hernia repairs and uncomplicated appendectomies. I was on duty at the hospital during the daytime and on alternate nights on Monday through Friday, and full-time every other weekend.

MY EXPERIENCES

The senior interns and chief residents had to accompany Dr. McLachlin on his weekday and Sunday morning rounds (visits) of his patients in the private surgical ward and of the general surgery patients in the public surgical ward. The senior, basic science and chief residents had to attend grand rounds for medical students and surgical staff in the hospital's auditorium, with the senior residents presenting the patients and Dr. McLachlin lecturing and challenging his senior interns and chief residents with questions on each patient's condition. Every Saturday evening, Dr. McLachlin would dictate to a telephone operator at the hospital's switchboard a question that would be similar to one on the written examination for the specialty of general surgery. All eight of us had to retrieve the question from an operator and write the answer to it in 35 minutes, as would occur in the three-hour, five-question specialty examination. When we met with Dr. McLachlin on Sunday morning, he would read aloud the answers to the question written by the chief residents and the answer of one of the senior residents or senior interns, and then dictate what he considered as being an "ideal" answer. I have to say that my year as a senior intern in surgery was one of the busiest of my graduate training, to the point that when Dr. McLachlin grabbed a snack off a food cart in the operating room lounge or visited a washroom when on rounds, the senior interns and chief residents also had to do so or wait for the next pause in his work.

My year in biophysics under Dr. Burton began in July of 1963, during which I studied the unique distensability of the major brain arteries in the human, including changes in their distensability with age. Also that year, I learned much from Dr. Burton about the effects of environmental stresses such as temperature and altitude on the human body, which began to rekindle my interest in aerospace medicine, but this time in the involvement of this medical specialty in the U.S. Space Program. Dr. Burton's teaching sessions began during a 9:00 a.m. coffee break, usually attended by all four of his graduate students, and lasted all morning - that is, unless we stopped for a round of golf with Dr. Burton leading the way.

DOUGLAS E. BUSBY

One summer day on the golf course, Dr. Burton mentioned to me that he had just read about the interesting work that the Lovelace Clinic in Albuquerque was doing in selecting astronauts for NASA and conducting research on the aging of airline pilots. I subsequently telephoned the Clinic to ask for information on its work in aerospace medicine, and was routed to Dr. Albert "Al" Schwichtenberg, Head of the Department of Aerospace Medicine and Bioastronautics in the Lovelace Foundation for Medical Education and Research, in a building connected to the Lovelace Clinic. In a long conversation with Dr. Schwichtenberg, he asked me about my educational background, to which I added my summers of experience in the RCAF IAM and my current research in biophysics. He described his department's various activities, including astronaut selection, research on airline pilot aging, and performing information analyses for NASA Headquarters in Washington, DC. He also mentioned that the Lovelace Foundation was participating in the aerospace medicine residency program being conducted by the Department of Preventive Medicine at The Ohio State University.

In September of 1963, my wife and I drove to Albuquerque for a two-day visit to the Department of Aerospace Medicine and Bioastronautics in the Lovelace Foundation. While there, we stayed with Dr. Schwichtenberg and his wife in their adobe home and had our first taste of New Mexican cuisine in Old Town, Albuquerque. Dr. Schwichtenberg described the information analyses that his department was performing for NASA Headquarters in much greater detail than in our earlier telephone conversation. The analyses involved gathering and assessing information relevant to safe travel into space from various sources, including a large on-site document library, a university library system, and data from visits to aeromedical research facilities in NASA, the USAF, the United States Navy (USN), and several universities. He said that at the time, this work was being done by two other physicians in the department, and suggested that I might wish to join them in it. When I expressed concern that this type of work would take me away from the practice of medicine, he

MY EXPERIENCES

assured me that if I obtained a license to practice medicine from the New Mexico Medical Board, I could perform Federal Aviation Administration (FAA) airman medical certification examinations in the department and work part-time in the emergency department of the Lovelace Clinic.

After I returned to London, I telephoned Dr. Schwichtenberg to thank him for his hospitality and to say that I had decided to complete my training in general surgery before working in aerospace medicine or even getting the education necessary to become a specialist in it. As he later told me, his response to my decision lived up to his being called a "bull-headed Dutchman," for he responded to my decision by asking me to compare professional fulfillment from being in the NASA Space Program with professional fulfillment from being in a surgery residency program, when he believed that my future would be in aerospace medicine anyway. So, after considerable weighing of surgery versus aerospace medicine, I accepted Dr. Schwichtenberg's offer of a senior staff scientist position in the Foundation's Department of Aerospace Medicine and Bioastronautics, to begin there soon after I defended my thesis for a Master of Science (M.Sc.) in biophysics in September of 1964. Dr. McLachlin graciously accepted my resignation from the surgery program.

I have many other lasting memories from this time in my life beyond playing in the doctors' band, serving in the local RCAF medical reserve, and deciding to make career changes. On November 10, 1962, my daughter, Sharon, was born at Victoria Hospital, a foot and her bottom arriving first. She was delivered by two of the obstetrics residents at the hospital: Dr. Paul Harding, who had played trombone when we were members of the Waterloo Band, and Dr. Kenneth "Ken" Stuart, who was one of my classmates in medical school. A very loud cry from Sharon after she took her first breath indicated that she was healthy and ready to take on the world. On Christmas day in 1963, Suzanne was standing in her maternal grandparents' living room using a coffee table for support, when she unexpectedly let go of the table and for the first time began to walk, looking surprised and repeatedly saying "look, I'm walking." Barbara and I, and her grandparents and grandparents cried with joy.

On January 15, 1964, my daughter, Stephanie, had an induced, premature birth at St. Joseph Hospital due to being in heart failure from her red blood cells being destroyed by a reaction between her and her mother's cells due to their having different Rh blood types. Immediately after Stephanie was born, Dr. Nicholson began to replace Stephanie's blood with donor blood which had to be taken from cold storage without it being rewarmed. The initial injection of the cold donor blood through Stephanie's umbilical vein produced a nine-minute standstill of Stephanie's heart. During his pediatrics training at the Johns Hopkins University in Baltimore, Maryland, Dr. Nicholson had learned from Dr. Archer Gordon, a cardiac surgeon who was developing CPR, how to perform closed-chest compression for CPR of a baby using the index and middle fingers of one hand. So with Dr. Nicholson using Dr. Gordon's new CPR technique on Stephanie and my giving her pure breathing oxygen from an anesthetic machine, her heartbeat returned. Over the following two days, Stephanie had more blood exchanges, which were only partially successful. She was then transferred to UWO's Department of Pediatrics at Victoria Hospital for blood exchange by a "continuous drip" system which was under development at Victoria Hospital and had not yet been used on a human being. This invention was remarkably successful in stopping Stephanie's red blood cell destruction, and she had no lasting side effects from the Rh reaction or cardiac event. Interestingly, Dr. Gordon was engaged in research on external electrical defibrillation of the heart when I subsequently arrived at the Lovelace Foundation, and while I was assisting him in surgery at the Lovelace Clinic, I had the opportunity to tell him about Stephanie's resuscitation, which Dr. Nicholson had learned from Dr. Gordon while at Johns Hopkins.

During my year in biophysics research, I took flying lessons and ground school at London's Crumlin Airport to get my pilot's license, with most of the cost of this training being reimbursed by the Canadian Government. I learned to fly in a two-seat Cessna 150, from the owner of the Crumlin flight center, George Walker, and his chief instructor, Fred Thompson, who would become an Air Canada pilot. I soloed (flew the airplane alone) after 9 hours of flying time, and did my solo cross-country flight from London to Windsor to Chatham to London without any problems. However, a fellow solo cross-country student just behind me made his approach to the main Chatham runway too low. Unknown to the student at the time, his airplane's propeller struck a power line, cutting off electricity to part of Chatham; he landed successfully. In retrospect, my flight training was uneventful except for the day that I taxied the Cessna 150 out to the main runway at Crumlin to do practice landings and decided not to because of gusty winds crossing the runway. George ordered me to "get back up there," presumably to overcome my obvious fear of wind in safely landing an airplane. With renewed determination and thanks to George, I learned that day, particularly how to make safe crosswind landings without being frightened of them.

Cessna 150

My basic science year ended with a lost opportunity to make an important contribution to neurosurgery and, as Dr. Burton said, to conduct a relatively straightforward project for a Ph.D. in biophysics or physiology. By way of background, Dr. Burton asked me to determine if an inert silicone casting material could be injected into the brain arteries of rabbits to assess their reaction to adrenaline (epinephrine) and noradrenaline (norepinephrine). This project was successful, and Dr. Burton asked me to describe it as an add-on to my M.Sc. thesis on the distensibility of the major brain arteries in the human being. As I was searching in the scientific literature for information related to the silicone-casting project, I found the report of a recent study that showed that the serotonin released from platelets as they form a blood clot in the brain causes blood vessels around the clot to constrict, reducing the flow of blood through these vessels. I began to wonder whether the local accumulation of serotonin during repair of a ruptured cerebral aneurysm is the cause of often-fatal post-operative intracranial arterial spasm after a repair is done with the patient in profound hypothermia. This explanation for serotonin being the cause of the spasm seemed even more plausible to me when I found another report of a recent study that showed that the metabolism of serotonin is slowed and preserved by cold. I theorized that if serotonin is the cause of this intracranial arterial spasm after repair of a ruptured arterial aneurysm with a patient in profound hypothermia, then if a serotonin-blocking drug is placed in the operative site during and after surgery, it might prevent the spasm. I had the opportunity to present my theory to Dr. Drake and his associate, Dr. Nicholas "Nick" Gergeley, when they examined me for my M.Sc. degree. They seemed very interested in it at the time, but no follow-up activity on it apparently occurred at UWO after I went to the Lovelace Foundation. I subsequently discovered that my theory was correct, from research conducted in the late 1970s at the Radcliff Infirmary in Oxford, United Kingdom.

Before my story shifts to our move to New Mexico and then to around the United States over the years, I should describe how I became licensed to practice medicine in New Mexico, and subsequently in several other states. In the early 1960s, the medical licensing boards in many states required that a graduate of an American or Canadian medical school pass a written examination prepared by an individual state medical board or the National Board of Medical Examiners. To take this examination, licensing boards required that the medical graduate have a basic science certificate, which could be obtained by passing a state board examination in the basic medical sciences after completing the first two years of medical school. At the time, most states would issue a license to practice medicine on a reciprocal basis, and some states accepted licensing by the Medical Council of Canada; apparently, the U.S. armed forces accepted all medical licenses issued in both countries. Since I had

MY EXPERIENCES

originally planned to move to the United States after I completed my rotating internship, I successfully wrote the examination for a basic science certificate in Michigan at the Wayne State University in Detroit, Michigan during the spring of 1961. Although I did not apply for a medical license by reciprocity in the State of New York while I was at the University of Buffalo, I began to do so for New Mexico in the spring of 1964, after I decided to join the Lovelace Foundation. As required by the regulations of the New Mexico Medical Board, I submitted to the Board an application for a license to practice medicine in New Mexico, along with copies of my basic science certificate and my license to practice medicine from the Medical Council of Canada. The Secretary of the Board, Dr. John Dearborn, immediately replied to my application with a letter saying that I could not be licensed to practice medicine in New Mexico because I had not graduated from a "Class A American medical school." When I showed the letter to Dr. Douglas Bocking, Dean of UWO's medical school, he said that the reason for the denial was invalid and obtained a document from the archives of the medical school to show me why. This document was a letter written in the early 1900's by the Flexner Committee, which had been formed by the American and Canadian Medical Associations to evaluate each medical school in the United States and Canada for the quality of its medical education. The UWO was one of the Canadian medical schools that did not meet professional staffing requirements, but this was quickly resolved and, as the document from the Flexner Committee said, UWO's medical school was designated a "Class A Medical School" by the Committee. Dr. Bocking sent a copy of the document to Dr. Dearborn, along with a letter stating that UWO's medical school has subsequently maintained its Class A status without interruption over the years. Neither Dr. Bocking nor I received a response from Dr. Dearborn.

Soon after I arrived at the Lovelace Foundation, I learned that Dr. Dearborn had been a surgeon at the Lovelace Clinic and left the Clinic under hostile circumstances. He then broke his non-compete agreement with the Clinic in setting up a surgical practice in Albuquerque and, after being legally forced to close the practice, had

DOUGLAS E. BUSBY

moved to Santa Fe. I also learned that other international medical graduates whom the Lovelace Clinic wished to employ had been having considerable difficulty obtaining a license to practice medicine in New Mexico. Because I did not need a license to practice medicine in New Mexico in order to work as an information analyst in the Lovelace Foundation, I decided not to make my having a license an issue between the Lovelace Foundation and Dr. Dearborn at that time. However, when I was in the Aerospace Medicine Residency Program at The Ohio State University in 1966, I learned that Ohio had a reciprocity agreement with New Mexico for a license to practice medicine. I successfully wrote the medical licensing examination in Ohio, and then re-submitted the basic science certificate along with a copy of my Ohio license to practice medicine to the New Mexico Medical Board. Again, Dr. Dearborn responded with a letter of denial, but this time under the presumption that I deliberately went out of New Mexico as my state of residence to take the licensing examination in Ohio rather than in New Mexico. The Lovelace Clinic successfully appealed this for me for the reason that Ohio was my state of residence when I wrote Ohio's medical licensing exam. I subsequently obtained medical licenses by reciprocity with Ohio to practice medicine in California, Oklahoma, Maryland, Indiana, Illinois, and Indiana.

D. MY CAREER IN MEDICINE

1. As a Senior Staff Scientist at the Lovelace Foundation (Albuquerque, NM)

We moved to Albuquerque in September of 1964, into a rented southwest-style home on Washington Street Northeast. There, we had a phenomenal view of the nearby Sandia Mountain Range as it changed in color from brown to red at sunset. The families of those with whom I would be working helped us get settled, and even gave h a welcoming party for us. Everyone wanted us to know about New Mexico's comfortable, sunny weather, fascinating history and sights, and its unique southwestern cuisine. On my first and every day of going to and from my office through the large lobby of the Lovelace Foundation, I was exposed to one of the largest collections of western art in the United States, including many original paintings by Russell, sculptures by Remington, and the unique blackware pottery by Maria Martinez of the San Ildefonso Pueblo - all under the watchful eyes of a friendly guard. The spacious Department of Aerospace Medicine and Bioastronautics had separate offices for Dr. Schwichtenberg as the head of the department, and Dr. Emanuel ("Jocko") Roth, Dr. T. Morris Fraser, and me in its information analysis group, space outside our offices for our secretaries and a room to be equipped for performing Federal FAA airman medical certification examinations in the department. Next to our suite was a large library of unclassified and classified documents in aerospace medicine and bioastronautics, managed by two document librarians. The work of our group required us to have a formal ("secret") security classification, and, since I was still a Canadian citizen, required me to sign a Declaration of Intention to become a U.S. citizen after five years of living continuously as a civilian in the United States.

DOUGLAS E. BUSBY

Dr. Schwichtenberg was a retired USAF Brigadier General who last commanded all USAF medical operations in the Pacific. He had joined the Lovelace Foundation to direct the evaluation of astronaut candidates in Project Mercury, as depicted in the movie, "The Right Stuff." He coordinated the topics for information analyses that were assigned to our information analysis group by NASA Headquarters. He was also a consultant in aerospace medicine at the test pilot facility at the Edwards Air Force Base in California and several aerospace companies. An academic genius, Dr. Roth had studied for his medical degree at the Harvard Medical School while independently taking courses at the Massachusetts Institute of Technology. Thereafter, he conducted research in aerospace physiology for several years at the USAF School of Aerospace Medicine, spending much of his time there with Dr. Hubertus Strughold, the internationally-recognized "Father of Space Medicine." The majority of his information analysis work at the Foundation involved spacecraft cabin atmospheres. Dr. Fraser had graduated from the Medical School of the University of Edinburgh, and served as a physician in the Royal Air Force and then the RCAF, ending his RCAF career in 1962 as a specialist in aerospace medicine and Commanding Officer of the RCAF School of Aerospace Medicine in Toronto. The majority of his information analysis work at the Foundation pertained to the psychology of long-term living in space.

A few days after I began to work at the Lovelace Foundation, Dr. Schwichtenberg invited me to his office to meet Dr. W. Randolph ("Randy") Lovelace II, whom I found was very interested in my academic background in surgery and biophysics, and experience in the RCAF. Later, I learned that his uncle, William Randolph Lovelace, founded the Lovelace Clinic in the early 1900s and that Dr. Randy Lovelace established the Lovelace Foundation in 1947. Dr. Randy Lovelace had graduated from the Harvard Medical School and had been trained in general surgery at the Mayo Clinic. During his residency in surgery, he conducted aeromedical research and participated with two associates in developing the Boothby-Lovelace-Bulbulian (BLB) high-altitude oxygen mask, initially for pilots. Later, he served in the U.S. Army Air Corps Aeromedical Laboratory at the

MY EXPERIENCES

Wright Field in Dayton, Ohio, where he personally performed experiments on emergency escape from airplanes flying at high altitudes. That research culminated in his personally identifying the marked jolt from a parachute opening at high altitude. He "jumped" at 40,200 feet, at which the parachute-opening jolt temporarily rendered him unconscious and tore the glove from his right hand with it sustaining frostbite. In 1958, he was appointed Chair of the NASA Special Advisory Committee on Life Sciences, which played a key role in the selection of the Project Mercury astronauts, and in 1964 he became NASA's Director of Space Medicine. In the late 1940s, he developed a surgery practice at the Clinic, which he continued until his death in December of 1965, when the pilot of a small plane in which he and his wife were flying into Aspen, Colorado, became disoriented in a snowstorm. The plane crashed in a blind canyon and the three of them perished.

I am very grateful for having known Dr. Randy Lovelace, especially in talking with him about the future of aerospace medicine during various social gatherings. On one occasion in his home, I had the opportunity to meet and discuss pilot disorientation during high altitude flight with Charles ("Chuck") Yeager, the record-setting test pilot who was the first in history to break the sound barrier in level flight. And on another occasion, Dr. Lovelace strongly urged me to become qualified to take the specialty examination in aerospace medicine through the Aerospace Medicine Residency Program at The Ohio State University and the Lovelace Foundation. Sadly, I would not see him again after he and his wife attended a going-away party for my family and me just before I left the Foundation for a year of specialty training in aerospace medicine at Ohio State in June of 1965.

Unexpectedly, the request for my first information analysis did not come from NASA Headquarters, but from Serendipity Associates, a well-known corporate "think tank" that was engaged in a study with the rocket propulsion manufacturer, Aerojet General. This study involved the identification of spacecraft and space crew requirements for a long-distance space mission. Through Dr. Schwichtenberg, I was asked to suggest what medical provisions should be placed on a spacecraft to maintain the health and welfare of its crew. At that time, the longest planned space mission was 14 days in Project Gemini that in turn would determine whether NASA could go ahead with making safe Project Apollo flights to the moon. When I began to consider possible provisions for a space crew on a long-distance space mission, I assumed that these provisions would be contingent on the duration of the mission and its distance from the Earth, either with the spacecraft staying in Earth orbit or traveling into deep space, either being for a long period. I discussed the type of mission and consequently anticipated kinds of provisions with the head of the Serendipity-Aerojet study, who told me to consider a deep space mission lasting months to years, and only to list the provisions in my report for the study.

I do not have a copy of the report, but remember some of the key provisions listed in it. I thought that the most important provisions would relate to crew protection from hazards of space operations and the management of possible medical problems from the various hazards. The hazards included a decrease in atmospheric pressure and increase of carbon dioxide in the spacecraft cabin or space suit, weightlessness, suspended particles in the spacecraft cabin, heavy structures in motion, sharp and pointed structures inside and outside of the spacecraft, heat and cold, fire, toxic fumes from burning plastic, electrical current from various sources, solar radiation, and meteorites. Next, I identified provisions that would sustain a crew's health and welfare, including an appetizing and nutritious diet, effective equipment for male and female hygiene, laundry, regular changes of clothing, exercise equipment to maintain cardiovascular health and musculoskeletal fitness, comfortable spaces and colors in work and living areas, an electronic reading and reference library, various forms of entertainment, ample quiet personal space for relaxation and sleep, and, perhaps most importantly, a means for private audiovisual communication with family and friends back on Earth. Finally, I stated that the spacecraft should have state-of-the-art diagnostic and treatment capabilities for managing minor-to-major health problems, and for immediate audiovisual communication and diagnostic data transmission for consultation with medical and

MY EXPERIENCES

surgical specialists, including specialists in aerospace medicine, back on Earth.

I completed the list of provisions for maintaining the health and welfare of the crew of a spacecraft on a long-distance space mission for the Serendipity-Aerojet study in about two weeks. Immediately thereafter, Dr. Schwichtenberg provided me with a NASA Headquarters' request for a detailed information analysis that would keep me occupied for much of the next three years. This project would require me to describe the characteristics and suggest the management of possible medical problems from hazards of space operations, specifically during an interplanetary mission when a medical problem would have to be managed on the spacecraft by medically-trained personnel in a specially-equipped diagnosis and treatment facility. It covered decompression effects (acute hypoxia, the ebullism syndrome, "explosive" decompression injuries, decompression sickness, aerotitis media, and aerosinusitis); heat disorders, including dehydration; cold injury and hypothermia; possible medical problems from weightlessness; acute radiation effects; injuries from meteoroid penetration; burns; injuries from mechanical forces; and carbon dioxide toxicity. Finally, it considered the general aspects of the diagnosis and treatment of medical problems in space. During the project, I sought the advice of many experts in the field of aerospace medicine during visits to NASA Headquarters, the NASA Manned Spacecraft Center in Houston, Texas, and the NASA Ames Research Center in Mountain View, California. One of the potential hazards of weightlessness that I covered was contamination of the spacecraft cabin atmosphere by particles and droplets floating in it, which became the subject of a luncheon speech that I gave as a stand-in for Dr. Randy Lovelace at the Annual Scientific Meeting of the American Association for Contamination Control in Bal Harbour, Florida, in the spring of 1965.

About a month after I arrived at the Lovelace Foundation, Dr. Roth, Dr. Fraser and I attended a conference on space medicine conducted jointly by NASA and the USAF, at the USAF School of

DOUGLAS E. BUSBY

Aerospace Medicine. Invitees to the conference included specialists in aerospace medicine, aerospace physiologists and other life scientists, and spacecraft and spacesuit environmental systems engineers. They came from military and civilian centers in the U.S., Canada, Great Britain, Germany, and other countries that were conducting aerospace medical research and development in support of the U.S. Space Program and the newly-formed European Space Research Organization, a precursor of the European Space Agency (ESA).

The conference was so interesting and informative to me that I remembered the names and topics of many of its presenters. Dr. Charles ("Chuck") Berry, chief physician and "the astronauts' doctor" at NASA's Manned Spacecraft Center, presented essentially-normal physiological data obtained from the Project Mercury astronauts during and after their one-man flights of up to 34 hours and 19 minutes in duration. In the subsequent discussion period, several conference attendees predicted that physiological data from the upcoming two-man Project Gemini flights of up to 14 days would show that a space mission in space of over 14 days could expose astronauts to a significant health risk. Christopher "Chris" Kraft, Jr., developer and director of NASA's Mission Control operation during Project Mercury, spoke on the challenges of communicating with astronauts during space flight. Wernher von Braun, the leading figure in the development of rocket technology in wartime Germany and now director of the NASA Marshall Space Flight Center in Huntsville, Alabama, described the rocket systems that would be used in Project Apollo. Hubertus Strughold, director of military research in aviation medicine in wartime Germany and now Professor of Space Medicine at the USAF School of Aerospace Medicine, outlined challenges in selecting safe spacecraft cabin and space suit atmospheres. Dr. J. Allen Hynek, chair of the Department of Astronomy at Northwestern University in Chicago, Illinois, who became the nation's foremost expert on unidentified flying objects (UFOs), used statistical calculations to show that many of the immense number of solar systems in the universe should contain a planet that supports life, including intelligent life. Finally, I recall that Dr. James Van Allen, head of the Department of Physics and Astronomy at the University of Iowa in Iowa City, Iowa, described his discovery of two zones of

MY EXPERIENCES

magnetically-trapped electrons and protons encircling the Earth, now called the Van Allen Belts, and emphasized the need to protect astronauts from receiving a harmful dose of radiation if they have to pass through them.

I left this conference wondering whether my information analysis topic from NASA Headquarters was realistic in light of our not knowing whether or not space flights longer than just 34 hours and 19 minutes could be a health risk to astronauts. Upon my return to the Foundation after the conference, Dr. Schwichtenberg assured me that NASA Headquarters was so confident in the ability of humans to adapt to the space environment and in developing measures to protect and maintain the health of the astronauts during long-term, long-distance space missions, that it was already in the early planning stage for sending a crewed spaceship to Mars.

In early 1965, I responded to the suggestion by Dr. Randy Lovelace that I become a specialist in aerospace medicine through the aerospace medicine residency program at The Ohio State University and the Lovelace Foundation. I wrote a letter to Dr. Harold Ellingson, Chair of the Department of Preventive Medicine in The Ohio State University College of Medicine in which I asked him how this might be possible. A retired USAF colonel, Dr. Ellingson had recently been Commander of the USAF School of Aerospace Medicine. At Ohio State, his department directed an aerospace medicine residency program that allowed its participants to get up to two years of experience in aerospace medicine at the Lovelace Foundation. He was President-Elect of the American Board of Preventive Medicine (ABPM), which certified physicians for proficiency and specialization in general preventive medicine, public health, occupational medicine, and aerospace medicine.

In his reply, Dr. Ellingson said that my rotating internship and year as a senior intern in surgery would meet the general clinical training requirement of the Board and that my working for at least two years as an information analyst in aerospace medicine would fulfill the board's requirement for the supervised practice of aerospace medicine. However, he pointed out that I would have to spend a year in the department of preventive medicine of a university that gave classes covering general preventive medicine and aerospace medicine, and would require me to write a research-based thesis for a master of public health (M.P.H.) or M.Sc. degree. Later, he informed me that since I had an M.Sc. in biophysics, his department and the ABPM would allow me to forgo the thesis.

In June of 1965, we moved into a rental unit on Woodhill Drive in Grandview Heights, Ohio, near The Ohio State University. With three other residents in aerospace medicine, I immediately began to take the year of classroom education required by the ABPM. Fortunately, I had time during the year to work part-time on my clinical space medicine project for NASA. My classes covered methods in epidemiology, safety engineering research, environmental physiology, environmental health, applied toxicology, industrial hygiene, environmental control, and infectious disease and immunization. Some classes included field trips to course-related facilities, including a refinery, a foundry, several manufacturing companies, a sewage treatment plant, and the food preparation and aircraft maintenance operations at the Wright Patterson Air Force Base. We were also familiarized with the important research that two of the department's professors, Dr. Charles "Charlie" Billings and Dr. Robert ("Bob") Wick, Jr., both specialists in aerospace medicine, were conducting on the effects of various blood alcohol levels (from consumption of alcohol-containing beverages) on pilot performance.

While I was at The Ohio State University, I met Ron Passi, a classmate in medical school who had just completed the surgery residency program under Dr. McLachlin and was taking a year of advanced training in gastrointestinal surgery at this university's hospital. Ron and I decided to study together for the mid-year, state-wide written examination for a license to practice medicine in Ohio, mainly by sharing our thoughts on answers to currently-relevant medical practice questions that might be asked. With just a few hours of study and having been out of medical school for over five years, both of us passed the examination, with Ron being first and me being second in the state. I received a higher grade in surgery than Ron and was later told that Dr. McLachlin enjoyed announcing this to his surgery residents. I left my year at Ohio State with an "A" in 20 and an "S" (for satisfactory) in one of my 21 classes.

MY EXPERIENCES

We were back in Albuquerque in June of 1966, looking forward so much to living there for a long time that we purchased a home, on Bellrose Avenue Northeast. I moved back into my former office in the Lovelace Foundation. I joined the USAF Reserve and was immediately assigned to command a unit of 12 medical reservists that met and trained one weekend a month and two weeks a year for giving emergency backup support to the clinic at the Kirtland Air Force Base in Albuquerque. As I described previously, I was able to obtain a license to practice medicine from the New Mexico Medical Board, which enabled me to perform FAA airman medical certification examinations in the Department of Aerospace Medicine and Bioastronautics and to maintain exposure to emergency medicine by working a 12-hour shift on weekends in the Lovelace Clinic and by assisting in surgical operations in the Clinic.

I remember that my first FAA airman medical certification examination was on a famous female pilot who was visiting the Foundation, Jacqueline ("Jackie") Cochran. A holder of numerous speed, distance, and altitude records and the first woman to break the sound barrier, Ms. Cochran, along with 12 other female pilots, had recently been rejected as potential astronauts during the selection of the original seven male astronauts chosen in NASA's Project Mercury. In my work in the Clinic's emergency department, I had to treat medical problems that I seldom encountered during my medical training and experience in Canada, including pulmonary (lung) edema (fluid accumulation) due to heart failure from high-altitude exposure even when driving through the Sandia-Manzano mountain pass into Albuquerque, acute asthma from inhaling juniper wood smoke from fireplaces, and injuries from skiing in the nearby mountains.

One Saturday morning, I was assisting Dr. Archer Gordon with an emergency appendectomy when he invited me to visit his laboratory to see the progress he was making in developing CPR, which at that time involved treatment of ventricular fibrillation with external electrical shock, and the design and testing of the manikins, Resusci Anne and Resusci Baby, for use in training people how to perform mouth-to-mouth breathing and external cardiac compression for CPR. While I was there, he described a remarkable incident that had occurred earlier in the week. He and two internal medicine residents

DOUGLAS E. BUSBY

at Lovelace Clinic had produced ventricular fibrillation in a dog and were attempting to reverse it with a newly-developed device that sent a brief "shock" of electricity through a pair of metal plates placed on the dog's chest. One of the residents accidentally received a shock from the device, and immediately went into ventricular fibrillation and lost consciousness. Dr. Gordon quickly defibrillated the resident with the device, and the resident completely recovered.

My space clinical medicine project culminated in a 434-page, typewritten report with 1,158 scientific references. The report was critically reviewed by over 25 experts familiar with its contents, and then published as a NASA Report, in the journal Space Life Sciences, and as a book. During the two-month review process, Dr. Schwichtenberg had me conduct an information analysis for NASA Headquarters on the possible adverse effects on astronauts of their being exposed to magnetic fields of low and high intensity. I reviewed the scientific literature on the effects of magnetic fields on biological systems, known as biomagnetics. I also visited scientists doing research in biomagnetics at the Hahnemann Medical School in Philadelphia, Pennsylvania, the Northwestern University Department of Biology in Evanston, Illinois, and the US Naval School of Aviation Medicine in Pensacola, Florida. The findings in this project were published as a NASA Report and in Space Life Sciences.

Aside from completing my clinical space medicine and space biomagnetics reports, the first six months of 1967 were quite eventful for me. Dr. Fraser and I taught a semester-long course on human factors in aviation in the Department of Engineering at the University of Colorado in Boulder, Colorado. Dr. Roth and I spent several days at NASA Headquarters editing proposals being written by aerospace engineers in NASA for the Voyager 1 and 2 interstellar probes of our solar system. The three of us took a course on computer programming using Fortran, the language of the Foundation's computer. On a weekend when I was on duty in the USAF Reserve, Paul Villa, a local person of Native American and Spanish descent, handed me several photographs of unidentified flying objects (UFOs) reportedly taken by him, which he had decided to turn over to the USAF. I gave the pictures to Dr. Schwichtenberg, who said that he would pass them to Project Blue Book, a current USAF study of reported sightings of UFOs

MY EXPERIENCES

in the United States being conducted at the Wright Patterson Air Force Base. Several weeks later, Dr. Schwichtenberg returned them to me, saying that the photographs were fake; I was unable to contact Mr. Villa to give them back to him. But this story was not over, as I will describe later.

In the spring of 1967, Dr. Schwichtenberg, Dr. Roth, Dr. Fraser, and I were invited to attend a classified-as-secret meeting held for NASA and USAF aerospace scientists and several aerospace contractors, at Kirtland Air Force Base. The purpose of this meeting was to inform those in the aerospace community with "a need to know," that the Los Alamos National Laboratory in New Mexico had invented a spacecraft engine that generates ions and propels them with a high-energy magnetic field to produce sustained acceleration and deceleration of a spacecraft. Consequently, this engine could greatly shorten the duration of a long-distance space mission, such as an exploration of Mars. We were also told that testing of the engine in space had been put on indefinite "hold" out of international concern that the radioactive material used to generate the ions could be released into the Earth's atmosphere if a spacecraft exploded on its launch pad or during launch. Now I had an indication of why NASA seemed to be so confident in the future of long-distance space travel that it had asked for the information analyses that I had been conducting. Interestingly, the content of this meeting was reported a few weeks later in the British newspaper, the Manchester Guardian, making it no longer secret.

Just before the Annual Scientific Meeting of the Aerospace Medical Association in Washington, DC, in May of 1967, I received a letter from the Canadian Government saying that I had been selected by "Operation Retrieval," a program designed to entice graduates of Canadian universities who were working abroad to return to Canada to teaching and research positions. This letter invited me to inquire about open positions in the Department of Preventive Medicine at the Dalhousie Medical School in Halifax, Nova Scotia, the Department of Physiology at the McMaster University School of Medicine in Hamilton, Ontario, and the School of Engineering at the University of Waterloo in Waterloo, Ontario. Since I had planned to drive to Washington via Kitchener-Waterloo, I made appointments to visit the

DOUGLAS E. BUSBY

McMaster University and the University of Waterloo which, I recall, were made more out of curiosity than of necessity. A professor of pulmonary physiology in the medical school at McMaster University "picked my brain" on areas for research in environmental physiology, without mentioning an opening for a teaching or research position in the school. However, the dean of the engineering school at the University of Waterloo was looking for someone to develop and direct a teaching and research program in human factors, which at the time seemed to me to be beyond my levels of knowledge and experience in human factors. At the Aerospace Medical Association meeting, Dr. James "Jim" Waggoner, Corporate Medical Director and Director of Life Sciences at Garrett AiResearch in Los Angeles, California, offered me a recently-opened position of senior research specialist in the Life Sciences Division of Garrett AiResearch, adding that I would be an associate of Dr. Bill Robertson, the USAF aerospace physiologist who had been a classmate at the University of Buffalo.

After I returned to the Lovelace Foundation on the Monday after the Aerospace Medical Association meeting, I was telling Dr. Fraser about my visits to the McMaster and Waterloo universities when Dr. Roth stormed into Dr. Schwichtenberg's office and loudly asked Dr. Schwichtenberg why he had not relayed a written message from Dr. Roth to NASA's Office of Space Medicine when he visited it while attending the Association's meeting. After a short and unintelligible conversation between them, Dr. Roth the facility. About an hour later, Dr. Schwichtenberg told Dr. Fraser and me that because Dr. Roth had insulted his integrity, he was transferring the Foundation's information analysis contract with NASA either to The Ohio State University or the Roswell Institute in Buffalo, New York. Later, Dr. Fraser and I surmised that the message from Dr. Roth to NASA's Office of Space Medicine might have stemmed from his reaction to the Apollo 1 command module fire that had occurred that January and killed three astronauts. Before this catastrophic event, Dr. Roth had been conducting a detailed analysis related to the selection of safe spacecraft cabin and space suit atmospheres, including the potential for cabin atmospheres supporting fire. He had reported that the use of a pure oxygen atmosphere of 5 psi (pounds per square inch) in the Apollo command and lunar landing modules during Apollo missions is

MY EXPERIENCES

a fire hazard. Moreover, this hazard would markedly increase if either module would be pressurized with oxygen at 5 psi over a sea-level atmospheric pressure of 14.7 psi already created with pure oxygen while testing the internal systems of the modules on the launch pad. This had occurred in the Apollo 1 command module.

Unfortunately, Dr. Schwichtenberg would not retract his seemingly-hasty decision to terminate the Foundation's information analysis contract with NASA, even though Dr. Fraser and I, and others in the Lovelace Foundation and Clinic, tried desperately to change his mind. A question that was never answered was why Dr. Clayton "Sam" White, who had been with the Lovelace Foundation since Dr. Randy Lovelace founded it in 1947, and had been its director since Dr. Lovelace died in 1965, did not step in and reverse Schwichtenberg's decision, in spite of some sort of unsolvable animosity having existed between him and Dr. Schwichtenberg for some time. In the following six weeks, Dr. Roth returned to his office daily to complete his work, with no personal communication with Dr. Schwichtenberg, and then joined the Department of Physiology at the University of New Mexico School of Medicine in Albuquerque, to conduct research on kidney dialysis; he subsequently took his own life. Dr. Fraser developed a highly-successful human factors program in the School of Engineering at the University of Waterloo.

After I searched unsuccessfully for a position at the Lovelace Foundation, Lovelace Clinic, and the University of New Mexico, I decided to join Garrett AiResearch. I notified the USAF Reserve that I would be leaving my reserve unit at Kirtland Air Force Base and was reassigned to the outpatient clinic in the USAF Space and Missile Systems Center at the Los Angeles International Airport, to serve as a general practice physician for one day a month and two weeks a year. Since my work at Garrett AiResearch would require me to have a license to practice medicine in California, I was able to obtain it through California's reciprocity agreement with Ohio before we left for California. Our departure from Albuquerque due simply to a conflict of personalities was very stressful for us, as I said goodbye to a professionally-rewarding life at the Lovelace Foundation and Clinic, and we to our beautiful home, our many friends in the German Club, and the United Cerebral Palsy Association of New Mexico, and New

DOUGLAS E. BUSBY

Mexico's enchanting history, captivating scenery, and wonderful cuisine.

2. As a Senior Research Specialist at Garrett AiResearch (Los Angeles, CA

We moved to the Los Angeles area in early July of 1967, into a home on Cedarbluff Drive, high on Palos Verdes Peninsula and with the back of it facing the Pacific Ocean. The home was above the heavy smog that filled the Los Angeles basin most of the year, so we always had an excellent view of the ocean, along with passing boats and whales. Unfortunately, I had to drive over 20 miles from home to Garrett AiResearch near the Los Angeles International Airport, either through four beachfront cities or along the crowded Pacific Coast Highway.

The aerospace medical research at Garrett AiResearch focused principally on using simulated "spacewalks" and "moonwalks" to estimate the amount of oxygen that would be used and the carbon dioxide, heat, and metabolic water that would be produced during physical activities of astronauts using the life support system in the backpack of the Apollo spacesuit. Data from this research would be incorporated into the design and operation of the life support system so that it would supply breathing oxygen, remove carbon dioxide, provide cooling, and control the suit's humidity within safe and comfortable limits during spacewalks and moonwalks during Apollo missions. This research was conducted on firemen from local fire stations who had physical characteristics and exercise programs similar to the Apollo astronauts, and had volunteered for it. For a simulated spacewalk, the subject wore a fully-operational Apollo spacesuit underwater in a pool and was made neutrally buoyant to simulate weightlessness. In this condition, he would conduct a series of physical tasks, such as turning nuts and bolts with specially-constructed tools and moving heavy objects, while using various foot and hand supports to control movement generated by Newton's third law of motion (for every action, there is an equal and opposite reaction). For a simulated moonwalk, the subject's fully-operational Apollo spacesuit was connected to a gimballed apparatus that limited any movement in a downwards direction to the moon's force of

MY EXPERIENCES

gravity, which is one-sixth of the Earth's gravity. Then the volunteer walked on a mixture of stones and sand being continuously dropped onto a large, moving conveyor belt several feet in front of him. From before to after each simulated spacewalk or moonwalk, Bill Robertson monitored the volunteer's oxygen consumption and carbon dioxide output, and the temperature and humidity in the spacesuit, and I monitored the volunteer's, electrocardiogram (EKG), blood pressure, and body temperature.

While I was engaged in astronaut life support research, Dr. Waggoner asked me to determine how the blood pressure measuring system (BPMS) which Garrett AiResearch had developed for use on Project Mercury astronauts during spaceflight might be adapted for medical practice. This BPMS consisted of a standard blood pressure cuff with a small piezoelectric microphone in it. The cuff was initially inflated and deflated with a rubber squeeze bulb, and later with an activated gas pressure source. The microphone detected the Korotkoff sounds created in the compressed artery under the cuff as indicators of systolic and diastolic blood pressure levels. Pressure and sound signals were integrated electronically to provide a digital blood pressure reading. After I discussed the BPMS with engineers who had developed it, I proposed that Garrett AiResearch adapt it for general medical use principally by automating the rates of cuff inflation and deflation to those recommended by the American Heart Association, and by limiting the maximum cuff inflation pressure to just above the systolic level identified during cuff inflation to prevent a false elevation of blood pressure due to the discomfort from cuff over-inflation. Then the thought came to me that the modified ABMS could be integrated into a system to control the rate of intravenous drug delivery for the management of blood pressure in intensive care patients. After I wrote proposals for an adapted BPMS for medical practice and its use in the management of blood pressure in intensive care patients, Dr. Waggoner and I discussed the design and patenting of these proposed systems with the Garrett AirResearch Patent Attorney. Unfortunately, he informed us that Garrett AiResearch had just decided to leave the field of biomedical engineering and that he could not consider submission of a patent application by Garrett AiResearch for either of these systems. These systems were subsequently designed and patented by other companies and put into widespread, effective use around the world.

While at Garrett AiResearch, I continued my work in emergency medicine during 12-hour shifts on weekends in local hospitals. As compared to the Lovelace Clinic, I attended many more patients with acute asthma, especially on smoggy days, and an increased number of motorcycle injuries and LSD (lysergic acid diethylamide, a potent hallucinogenic) overdose cases. The first emergency department in which I worked was in the Little Company of Mary Hospital in Torrance, a beachfront city at the base of the Palos Verdes Peninsula.

At the Annual Scientific Meeting of the Aerospace Medical Association in Bal Harbor, Florida in May of 1968, I took and passed the examination of the American Board of Preventive Medicine for the specialty of aerospace medicine. The examination had written core and specialty components, followed by an oral specialty component. The core component covered the basics of preventive medicine, including epidemiology, environmental health, and infectious disease. The specialty components covered areas specific to aerospace medicine, including pilot health maintenance, environmental physiology and toxicology, and pilot and passenger protection from stresses of flight. Questions in the oral specialty component were given by a three-member panel of aerospace medical specialists. Based on my being certified as a specialist in aerospace medicine and being engaged in the practice of it, I subsequently became a Fellow of the American College of Preventive Medicine.

3. As Director of Medical Services at Continental Airlines (Los Angeles, CA)

In the summer of 1968, I met A. E. "Shei" Sheihagen, a neighbor who was a B-707 captain for Continental Airlines, headquartered at the Los Angeles International Airport. When I told Shei that I was a specialist in aerospace medicine, he asked me whether an airline pilot with an elevated blood glucose and no associated symptoms should be "grounded" by the FAA. I replied by saying that FAA airman medical certification regulations did not allow any pilot to have a valid airman medical certificate to fly any type of airplane if the pilot must take an

MY EXPERIENCES

oral or an injectable medicine to control an elevated blood glucose. Then Shei told me why he had asked this question. He said that Continental's new Director of Medical Services, who was also a general surgeon and an FAA airman medical certification examiner in Hollywood, found that a Continental Airlines pilot had an elevated blood glucose not producing symptoms during the pilot's annual company health evaluation, and had grounded him pending determination of its cause by an endocrinologist. Shei said that because the medical director had reported the pilot's elevated blood glucose to Continental's flight management and the FAA without the pilot's permission, the pilots' union of Continental Airlines had filed a grievance against Continental Airlines for doing this. I did not comment on what Shei had just told me. Several days later, the Personnel Director in the Human Resources Division of Continental Airlines invited me to attend a meeting on both of these issues between several representatives of Continental's management and the pilots' union, which culminated in my being hired to replace Continental's medical director. Soon thereafter, I met with the pilot, the president of the pilots' union, Captain John Campbell, and the "medical representative" of the union, Captain Gilbert "Gil" Chase, and told the pilot what he would have to do to regain his flight status: have his elevated blood glucose level evaluated by an endocrinologist and show that he could control it with diet and exercise. Several days later, the pilot was hospitalized by his internist when his blood glucose reached an extremely high level, notably in spite of his not experiencing any symptoms of it. He was placed on injectable insulin for diabetes, resigned from Continental Airlines, and began to sell real estate in the rapidly-growing ski resort community of Breckenridge in Colorado. Years later, Captain Chase told me that the pilot was from an American Indian tribe which was known for many adult members developing very high fasting blood glucose levels with no symptoms, but followed by complications, such as blindness and kidney failure if their blood glucose levels are not controlled with insulin.

The medical department in Continental Airlines at the Los Angeles International Airport had replaced weekday medical services provided to Continental by the nearby Sepulveda Clinic. The department was well equipped, with a waiting room, separate offices for a physician,

DOUGLAS E. BUSBY

two registered nurses (RNs), an administrative assistant, two examination rooms, a laboratory, and an x-ray unit. It was used principally for the selection and annual physical examinations of pilots, flight attendants (called "hostesses," purportedly only by Continental), and directors of passenger service (best described as "onboard airline ticket agents"). It also treated occupational injuries in aircraft maintenance personnel and minor medical problems in flight crews, and vaccinated flight personnel and administrative staff for international travel. It had been placed under the Human Resources Division of Continental Airlines, headed by senior vice-president Harold Bell.

Soon after I became Continental's medical director, Mr. Bell decided to transfer my reporting relationship with him to the new personnel director and coordinator of contract negotiations with the various unions in Continental Airlines, Richard "Dick" Rogers. Later, Mr. Rogers told me that Mr. Bell's decision to have me report to him infuriated the pilots' union, which was still quite upset over the former medical director having released medical information on the diabetic pilot to the company through Mr. Rogers' predecessor. He said that the pilots' union then asked Mr. Bell to have me report to someone outside of the Human Resources Division to protect the pilots' medical records from Continental management's scrutiny, but Mr. Bell held firm on my reporting to him.

My work at Continental Airlines was certainly "interesting." Continental had a spurt of growth in late 1968 and 1969, as it added routes in the lower United States and to Hawaii. Therefore, I had to perform many pre-employment physical examinations on pilot and hostess applicants, in addition to annual health evaluations on pilots and hostesses. Interestingly, the president of Continental Airlines, Robert "Bob" Six, required that the airline only hire pilots who had flown air transport and fighter airplanes in the U.S. military services. His wife, actress Audrey Meadows, set strict physical standards for the employment of hostesses, including height and weight limits, no visual impairment requiring eyeglasses or contact lenses, no visible physical deformity or impairment, and no pregnancy.

This leads me to give some background on Mr. Six, who ran Continental Airlines with an "iron fist," and claimed sole responsibility

MY EXPERIENCES

for its spectacular growth and success. His father was a physician and hoped that Mr. Six would follow in his footsteps, but Mr. Six left home in his teens to become a barnstorming pilot, with his six-foot, six-inch frame barely fitting into the open cockpit of an airplane as he performed risky aerobatics and then took people on scenic rides at numerous airshows and carnivals being held across the United States. Eventually, he was employed by Varney Speed Lines, flying passengers in the southwest United States, and then became a part-owner of it and changed its name to Continental Airlines. The company grew and profited greatly during World War II from transporting U.S. military troops within the United States. Thereafter, it acquired a fleet of pressurized turboprop Vickers Viscount airplanes that flew out of Denver, Colorado, and became the first airline to use "continuous maintenance," which substantially reduced airplane downtime for maintenance. Consequently, all of the well-kept turboprops were sold at a profit and the airline became an all-jet fleet of Boeing B-707 and B-727, and Douglas DC-9 airplanes. Shortly before I joined Continental Airlines, it had moved its administrative offices to the Los Angeles International Airport while keeping its hub in Denver, and purchased Pioneer Airlines, which had been based in Texas. It had taken over the routes previously flown by Pan American World Airways in the Micronesian Islands in the eastern Pacific Ocean, flying Continental B-727s as Air Micronesia. And it had contracted with the U.S. military to transport troops between the United States and Viet Nam and between Viet Nam and rest and relaxation (R&R) areas in the South Pacific, and established a civilian passenger and supply operation, Continental Air Services, to support various U.S. Government operations in Viet Nam and Laos.

Although Mr. Six had been highly successful in business, his very short temper, often ignited by misperceived failings of others in supporting his wishes, led to a relatively short marriage to Broadway star Ethel Merman and many impulsive firings of Continental executives. Yet he tolerated a feisty Audrey Meadows and their close Hollywood friends, including John Wayne, Bob Hope, and Henry Fonda. Unknown to me when I joined Continental Airlines was Mr. Six's well-known dislike of physicians, an attitude which Mr. Bell attributed to the strained relationship that Mr. Six had with his father

DOUGLAS E. BUSBY

after he decided to fly airplanes rather than practice medicine as a career. Consequently, I occasionally experienced the ire of Mr. Six, such as when he angrily called me back to Los Angeles from the Annual Scientific Meeting of the Aerospace Medical Association in San Francisco, California, in May of 1969, because he had the sniffles and wanted to see me for a nasal decongestant spray to use during a flight to his ranch in Colorado. One of my nurses gave him a nasal spray out of the medical department's abundant stock, and when I reached the medical department within two hours to see him, he was already on his way to the ranch.

By far the most interesting pilot whom I met at Continental Airlines was Mira Slovak, when he rushed into the medical department in the fall of 1968 dressed in a white shirt, trousers, and sneakers, and asked me to examine him for return to work as a Continental pilot as quickly as possible because he did not wish to keep his Hollywood actress date waiting too long in his new Chevrolet Corvette. He was followed by a company guard, who asked him to move the car. This gave me time to determine that the medical department had no file on him and to call the Vice President of Flight Operations at Continental, Clayton "Red" Stubben, to ask why this pilot had been off work. Mr. Stubben said that in the spring of 1968, Captain Slovak had taken a leave of absence from flying a B-727 for Continental to fly a glider powered by a Volkswagen engine non-stop from Germany to the Santa Paula Airport in California, where he hangars his aerobatic airplanes. He stated that a downdraft forced the glider into a ditch just 20 feet from the end of this airport's runway, resulting in the glider being destroyed and Captain Slovak sustaining multiple serious injuries and losing consciousness for nine days. Finally, Mr. Stubben pointed out that Mr. Six and Continental's flight management were concerned with Captain Slovak's ability to work safely as an airline pilot in light of his recent near-fatal injuries in the glider crash, along with any chronic medical problems from other near-fatal injuries that he sustained when he was a national champion speedboat racer. When Captain Slovak returned from parking his car, I informed him that I needed to see all of the final medical reports of the physicians who managed his injuries from the glider accident, after which I would give him a thorough medical evaluation and Mr.

MY EXPERIENCES

Stubben would give him a comprehensive B-727 flight test to determine his fitness to return to work as an airline pilot. He complied with this process and was reinstated as a B-727 Continental Airlines captain.

A few weeks after Mr. Stubben and I returned Captain Slovak to work, Captain Slovak invited us to visit him on a Sunday afternoon in his hangar at the Santa Paula Airport. He showed us where his glider had crashed and a surviving piece of its tail with the Continental Airlines' logo on it (Mr. Stubben commented to me that he was glad that Mr. Six was not with us!). Then he showed us his newest airplane, a Bucker Jungmann acrobatic biplane, which he would use for many years in airshows. As we drove home, Mr. Stubben described Captain Slovak's remarkable life in aviation. I learned that in 1953, he was a young captain in Czechoslovakian Airlines who escaped from Czechoslovakia and communism by hijacking a DC-3 with some friends to West Germany. After several months of being interrogated in West Germany and then the United States, he remained in the United States, and the FAA was allowed to issue him a pilot's license. He became a pilot for William Boeing, Jr., the son of the aviation magnate, and soon became a member of the Boeing Unlimited Hydroplane Speedboat Racing Team and subsequently won three national championships for Boeing. Over the years, he was also a crop duster, an acrobatic pilot, and an air races competitor. In the four years after I returned Captain Slovak to work at Continental Airlines, I met and watched him perform at several airshows in the Los Angeles area, where he was known particularly for performing an end-over-end airplane maneuver called the *lomcovák*, (Czech word for headache), and flying an open-cockpit airplane upside down at an altitude of 50 feet with both of his hands dangling overhead. At the last airshow that I attended before leaving California, he did a vertical figure-of-eight maneuver in a glider, landing it gracefully in front of a cheering crowd.

Unforgettable Memories: Visit to Continental Air Services in Viet Nam and Laos

In February of 1969, Mr. Stubben received a request from the chief pilot of Continental Air Services, Ed Dearborn, that I visit its operations in Viet Nam and Laos to investigate allegations that the company's

DOUGLAS E. BUSBY

pilots in Viet Nam and Laos were being served poisoned food in its cafeterias, that two of its pilots in Laos had recently exhibited unusual behavior possibly due to the poisoned food, and that its employees in Laos were reporting poor health care there. Mr. Bell and Mr. Rogers approved the request. I flew from Los Angeles to Hawaii on a Continental Airlines B-707, sitting in the cockpit "jump seat" behind the captain, and then from Hawaii to the island of Guam in Micronesia on an Air Micronesia B-727, sharing the center cockpit jump seat and a seat in first class with an FAA flight inspector. The 22-hour flight from Hawaii to Guam made passenger and refueling stops on Johnston Atoll, and the islands of Majuro, Pohnpei, and Chuuk Lagoon (previously Truk Atoll). On Johnston Atoll, which was under the control of the U.S. military, everyone on the airplane had to get on a bus with covered windows and be taken to a secure location under armed guard. This experience contrasted with the other stops on the islands, where we were invited to get off the airplane to meet the local native people who had been waiting to sell us the local food and handicrafts. Although Air Micronesia provided separate food for the captain and first officer as a safety precaution against their being incapacitated by accidental food poisoning, I observed that the captain and first officer were eating locally-prepared hot dogs at one of the stops, and reminded them of this risk, which they gratefully acknowledged and then finished their hot dogs with a smile. Most striking to me on this long trip was the seemingly-endless blue ocean dotted with numerous islands, most surrounded by a beautiful reef. An astounding view was a large fleet of clearly-visible, sunken Japanese ships, including an aircraft carrier, under our approach to Chuuk's tiny airport.

While on Guam, I stayed in a modern hotel owned and operated by Air Micronesia. The first evening, I joined the crew and FAA inspector for dinner at an out-of-the-way but excellent Mexican restaurant. The next day, the Continental Airlines' station manager for Micronesia took me on a tour of the nearby Guam Adventist Clinic and Guam Memorial Hospital, after which we agreed that the clinic was well equipped and staffed, but the hospital's facilities were so outdated and understaffed that, if possible, arrangements should be made for company employees to be hospitalized in the new U.S. Naval Hospital on Guam. Later, I walked past several caves that Japanese

MY EXPERIENCES

soldiers had dug into the rock along the beach near the hotel and imagined the carnage there during the Second Battle of Guam in 1944. During my second evening on Guam, the station manager and his wife hosted a dinner for the flight crew and me to celebrate the first officer and a hostess having been married early that morning while working on a round-trip flight north to the island of Saipan.

Very early the next day, I rode in the jump seat behind the captain of a Seaboard World Airlines DC-8 cargo airplane flying from Guam to the Philippine islands, from which I would take a Continental Airlines flight to Viet Nam. This flight was quite memorable. The DC-8's flight crew included a navigator, who sat at a small desk behind me. As soon as we reached cruising altitude, the captain taped black photographic paper over all of the windows on his side of the cockpit to darken it and went to sleep. For the following three hours, the navigator periodically passed flight information through me to the first officer, and a few times I had to awaken him. This flight ended at the Clark Air Base, which was the Philippine Air Force base out of which the USAF was operating in the Southwest Pacific, with the hardest landing I have ever experienced. No wonder!

When I arrived at the Clark Air Base, I was met by the Continental Services station manager for the Philippines. He said that my departure for Viet Nam would be in two days, so he planned to show me the area around the Clark Air Base that day and, if I wished, for us to play a round of golf on its picturesque golf course the next day. That day, we visited the Naval Station Subic Bay, which was the forward base of the U.S. Seventh Fleet for ship repair and replenishment and a major operating center for the U.S. Military Sea Transportation Service during the Viet Nam War. In the harbor and shipyard were over 50 war and cargo ships being repaired and resupplied. Then we toured a village of American-style prefabricated homes that the U.S. Government had built for the Negritos on the island. The Negritos are an ancient group of dark-skinned, hunter-gatherers of small stature spread about the Pacific islands and Southeast Asia. They had not been adapting very well to their new homes and had been tearing them down for materials to make their traditional, circular huts. Aside from continuing to fish and hunt, the Negritos had developed quite a tourist industry focused on demonstrating their hunting accuracy with a long blowgun, and selling their fine-woven bamboo baskets. While in the Philippines, I stayed at an aging motel very close to the Clark Air Base. The station manager warned me that my room would be co-occupied at night by a veritable army of bugs and small lizards called geckos, unless I left a light on in the room.

About 3:00 a.m. on the day of my departure for Viet Nam, I joined cockpit crews from Continental Airlines and several other U.S. airlines for a briefing on flight conditions over Viet Nam and around Saigon's huge Tan Son Nhut Air Base where they would be landing that morning. The briefing focused on the enemy's use of radio navigation signals intended to lead airplanes off course and crash into a close-by mountain range, and the need to make landings and takeoffs at the airbase as steeply as possible to stay away from the enemy ground-to-air fire just beyond the perimeter of the base. Our flight to Saigon, which was carrying marines who had just been on R&R in Hawaii, was uneventful. I sat in the jump seat behind the captain, the hostesses served breakfast to everyone including the crew and me, and then the cabin became very quiet as the marines slept, wrote letters, or read.

When I got off the airplane at the Tan Son Nhut Air Base, I was surprised to see that it had been parked between a Lockheed C-5 Galaxy, the USAF's largest transport airplane just placed into service, and a large number of caskets that had just arrived on a Flying Tiger Line DC-8. As we started to walk towards the airport terminal, one of Continental's hostesses, who knew a USAF nurse on the C-5, invited me to walk with her up the rear ramp of the C-5 into its vast cargo bay to meet the nurse. Inside the C-5, I was exposed for the first time in my life to the carnage of war. I saw at least 400 wounded soldiers on stretchers, with most receiving intravenous fluids or blood, and most were bound in bandages and immobilized by splints. Some soldiers were groaning and writhing in pain or simply staring into space; some were semi-conscious or sleeping. The nurse told me that the soldiers had been wounded during a surprise simultaneous attack on their bases at Long Binh/Bien Hoa and Da Nang, north of Saigon, in what appeared to be a second Tet offensive. Consequently, evacuation hospitals in the area had been overrun with casualties, leading to the evacuation of the more seriously-wounded soldiers out of Viet Nam.

MY EXPERIENCES

Then she predicted that one-third of the evacuees would not survive the flight from Viet Nam to the Philippines or Hawaii.

Lockheed C-5 Galaxy

As I entered the main terminal of the Tan Son Nhut Air Base, a Vietnamese immigration officer looked at my Canadian passport and U.S. immigration green card, and without saying anything to me, ushered me into a small room containing only a short bench with an old tattered Time magazine on it. After an hour or so, Ed Dearborn came into the room with the immigration officer and informed me that I was being detained by the Vietnamese out of spite because Canada had just agreed with Communist China to export Canadian-grown wheat to it. Out of the blue, the idea came to me to show the immigration officer my USAF Reserve identification card. The immigration officer glanced at it, smiled, and said I could leave.

Ed Dearborn introduced himself to me as a pilot and soldier of fortune who had previously flown for Air America and in various military operations around the world before becoming the Chief Pilot of Continental Air Services. Although Continental Air Services was funded by the U.S. Agency for International Development and Air America was owned by the U.S. Central Intelligence Agency, both supplied and supported covert activities in Southeast Asia during the Viet Nam War. He was a very strict flight manager who, as one of his pilots later told me, was known for using his large fists in reprimanding his pilots. After we left the main terminal at the Tan Son Nhut Air Base, Ed took me to the heavily-guarded area of the base from which these Continental Air Services and Air America were operating a great variety of passenger and cargo airplanes. Ed pointed to a line of parked Continental Air Services airplanes being serviced and loaded, including the DC-3, Short SC.7 Skyvan, Cessna 180, Pilatus PC-6 Porter, de Havilland Canada DHC-6 Twin Otter, and even a Piper Cub. Then we went to his private office in Continental Air Services' hangar, to discuss the reasons for his request that I visit the Continental Air Services' facilities in Viet Nam and Laos.

Ed stated that Continental Air Services' employees in Viet Nam and Laos were concerned that food in Continental Air Services' cafeterias was being poisoned, even though specific cases of poisoning by food from either of these cafeterias had not been reported. He indicated that this concern in Viet Nam could be attributed to the cafeteria being operated under contract with a local food service company owned by a former Miss Hanoi. He said that because Air America uses the same cafeteria, he had repeatedly discussed the food-poisoning issue with Air America's management and been assured that its employees had not reported any symptoms that would suggest poisoning of the cafeteria food. Later, I did a walk-through of the cafeteria and found that it was being operated and inspected under American food hygiene standards, with no apparent violations of them. Then, Ed said that the concern for cafeteria food poisoning in Laos stemmed from two recent, unrelated incidents which, after he described them to me, did not indicate to me that systemic food poisoning was occurring in the Continental Air Services' cafeteria there. In one incident, a Pilatus Porter had struck a utility pole while landing on a narrow road being used as a runway in Laos, with its two physicians on board being killed and its pilot being seriously injured and subsequently hospitalized in Thailand. Ed pointed out that the Continental Air Services station manager for Laos had reported that the pilot was quite familiar with the runway and the weather did not appear to be a factor in the crash. However, in a several-day period before the accident, the pilot had become so paranoid that he checked and often rechecked Continental Air Services' airplanes and his car for explosive devices before getting into them, which indicated possible development or resurgence of a psychotic disorder. In the other incident, a Continental Air Services pilot in Laos began to exhibit impulsive behavior from suspected opium use, and drove his motorcycle through a war memorial in the capital of Laos. This serious infraction of Laotian law led to the pilot being fired by Continental Air Services and leaving Laos to avoid arrest and incarceration by the Laotian authorities. Finally, Ed verified reports that Continental Air Services' employees in Laos were receiving poor health care, which I would be looking into, adding that excellent health

MY EXPERIENCES

care of the Continental Air Services' employees in Viet Nam was being provided by the USAF clinic located on the **Tan Son Nhut Air Base**.

Ed then drove me to the Continental Air Services "compound," where I would be staying while in Saigon. On the way, I was fascinated by most of the road traffic being small motorcycles and scooters which, as Ed noted, create a spectacular, gray cloud of toxic exhaust whenever a group of them begin to move along together, such as pulling away from a stoplight. The motorcycles were often occupied by two or more people, even entire families, and loaded with a variety of items, some quite large. I was also fascinated by the high percentage of young people on the road. Most of the men were wearing white shirts and black trousers. Most of the women were wearing an ao dai, which is a traditional long tunic with side slits, worn over wide trousers.

The compound was located in central Saigon. It consisted of a large home surrounded by a high, gated wall. Ed pointed out that it and numerous others like it were built during the French colonization of Viet Nam, Cambodia, and Laos. Most of the homes appeared to have three spacious levels with porches and balconies, shuttered windows, rooms with high ceilings and tile floors, and servants' quarters. After I settled in a bedroom on the third floor of the home, I decided to catch up on my sleep. Soon, I was awakened by several loud bangs in rapid succession, and immediately assumed that I was hearing the sound of exploding missiles being fired into the city. (My assumption was correct, for I was subsequently informed that one of the missiles had struck a nearby home, instantly killing two Roman Catholic priests who were sleeping on its third floor). Then a nearby air raid siren went off for several minutes. I initially reacted to the noise by pulling the top bedsheet up over my head, and then by rushing down to the first floor to ask the housekeeper where I should go for protection. She and her daughter had taken shelter under the large staircase from the first to the second floor, and invited me to join them. She then described her life in war-torn Saigon, in French, as I had learned in high school in Canada, and as she had learned as a youngster in Viet Nam.

Later, a second, startling incident really made my day! By way of background to it, several highly-publicized bombings had been occurring in Saigon restaurants. However, Ed felt that this problem had been brought under control when we went to a popular restaurant for dinner that evening. Unnoticed by me while we talked, a small orchestra had set up close to us. Then, without warning, the orchestra's drummer announced its presence by suddenly "banging" on his drums and cymbals. I responded by heading for the floor under our table until Ed stopped me. My elevated heart rate from this scare took a while to slow down.

The next day, I had breakfast in the cafeteria for Continental Air Services and Air America employees on the Tan Son Nhut Air Base, and then joined Ed at a Skyvan that was being loaded with several civilian construction workers to transport them up the Mekong Delta to a small military base, and then return to Saigon with several civilian construction workers who were there. As I would soon observe, the Delta is comprised of a vast network of mainly-navigable tributaries of the Mekong River after it leaves Cambodia and crosses southwest Viet Nam.

Ed asked me to sit in the copilot seat of the Skyvan, and briefed me on the handling of a loaded Browning 9 mm pistol and several grenades that he kept in a canvas bag on the floor of the airplane between us should he have to land the airplane in enemy territory. The Skyvan, nicknamed the "flying shoebox," is a British 19-seat all-metal aircraft that was manufactured by the Short Brothers of Belfast, Northern Ireland. Its twin Garrett AiResearch turboprop engines were distinctively high-pitched and loud, so we had to ear special noise-dampening earphones. A large rear door under the fuselage allowed its quick unloading and loading.

Short SC.7 Skyvan

As we left the Tan Son Nhut Air Base, the ravage of war became evident in the numerous bomb craters dotting the landscape and the defoliation of forest areas and vegetation around rivers and roads by

MY EXPERIENCES

the chemical, Agent Orange. Ed flew the airplane at a higher-than-usual altitude because of reported hostilities in an area along our route. Below us, we could see four U.S. Army helicopters below us firing rockets into a village, setting it into flames. Ed put the Skyvan in a steep approach to our destination airport and landed it on a very short runway of perforated steel matting. He kept the Skyvan's engines at well above idle during the quick exchange of workers, then turned the Skyvan around for a steep departure in the direction opposite to its landing. While we returned to the Air Base, Ed let me fly the Skyvan at cruise altitude. When we arrived at the Tan Son Nhut Air Base, he received a message that just after we left the destination airport, a military cargo airplane about to land on the same runway that we had used was hit by a missile and crashed, with loss of its crew.

After my experiences in Viet Nam, I flew from Saigon to Vientiane, the capital city of Laos, on a Continental Air Services Douglas DC-3 (C-47). The DC-3's pilot was Ed's assistant, Larry Douglas, who appeared very tired. Consequently, I asked Larry who his copilot would be, and he laughed and replied, "You!" and invited me to sit in the copilot's seat. As soon as possible after takeoff, Larry flew the DC-3 southeast to the South China Sea to be clear of South Viet Nam. He taught me how to use the airplane's archaic radio navigation system and how to keep the DC-3's two engines trimmed, and then asked me to replace him in the pilot's seat as he went back to the passenger area to rest.

Douglas DC-3 (C-47)

My pilot's logbook shows that I flew the DC-3 for over five hours, during which Larry briefly came forward to tell me to increase our distance offshore from Cambodia's naval base, because Cambodia had just impounded a U.S. flagged merchant vessel (Columbia Eagle), creating a tense relationship with the United States. (The ship was carrying napalm bombs to Thailand for the USAF to drop in Viet Nam when it was hijacked to Cambodia by two American crewmembers to protest the Viet Nam War.) We could see the ship in the harbor, but fortunately, no one below made a move upwards to greet us. After we crossed the South China Sea and the Gulf of Thailand as far as Bangkok, the capital of Thailand, we turned north to fly over Thailand into Laos and land at the Vientiane airport.

Immediately after we arrived in Vientiane, Larry and I checked into the Continental Air Services compound, a short distance from the Vientiane airport. The compound consisted of a modern, two-story building and a spacious courtyard surrounded by a high gated wall topped with barbed wire. Although it had a cafeteria, Larry decided to introduce me to Laotian cuisine that evening at the Settha Palace Hotel, built during the French colonial period. When we arrived at the hotel, we were invited to a birthday party for a representative from one of the countries stationed in Laos to support the International Agreement on the Neutrality of Laos, which had been signed by 14 countries in Geneva in 1962. I recall meeting representatives from Canada, the United Kingdom, Poland, the Soviet Union, the People's Republic of China, and India. They seemed to be enjoying each other's company while knowing full well that the Agreement had been seriously violated by North Viet Nam when it constructed a military supply line, the so-called Ho Chi Minh Trail, through Laos and Cambodia to South Viet Nam, in order to support the surreptitious operations of its army and the Viet Cong in South Viet Nam.

At dawn the next day, I went to a nearby area of the Vientiane airport that was being used exclusively by Continental Air Services, Air America, and the Royal Laotian Air Force. I observed three Continental Air Services' DC-3s take off. A gentleman standing next to me said that the DC-3s were headed for northeast Laos to make low-level drops of bags of rice to the indigenous Hmong people in gratitude for their getting American fighter pilots to safety when their airplanes were disabled in missions over North Viet Nam and had to eject from them over Laos. The bags of rice would be thrown or pushed through an open cargo doorway in the side of the DC-3 by Hmong "kickers," many of whom had been making the fatal mistake of refusing to wear their safety harnesses. Later, I learned that DC-3s frequently returned with bullet holes in the wings and fuselage and that one had recently

MY EXPERIENCES

crashed with the loss of its flight crew and kickers from an unanticipated hail of bullets from the ground during a drop. Immediately after the DC-3s departed, I observed a squadron of armed North American Aviation T-28 Trojans of the Royal Laotian Air Force take off. Given that Laos was a supposedly-neutral country, I introduced myself to a man standing next to me and asked him if he knew what the planes were going to do. He said they would probably head north to conduct an airstrike against the communist Pathet Lao, a group allied with North Viet Nam during the Viet Nam War. Later, I was told that the man I spoke to was Edgar M. "Pop" Buell, a "farmer from Indiana" who came to Laos in 1960 as an agricultural adviser and then conducted relief work among the Hmong people and coordinated logistical support for the Central Intelligence Agency's so-called "secret war" against the Pathet Lao. I subsequently read that few Americans know that in nine years, the United States dropped more than two million tons of explosives on northern Laos during 580,000 bombing missions, making Laos the most heavily bombed country per capita in history.

I spent the rest of the day with the Continental Air Services station manager for Laos, trying to determine why company employees had expressed concern about the poor quality of their health care. He was reluctant to disclose the source, sources, or the nature of this concern, so I suggested that we visit the Australian Embassy Clinic and Mahosot Hospital, which the company was using for its employees. These facilities were quite outdated as compared to medical facilities in Bangkok and nearby Udon Thani, a Thai city just south of the border between Laos and Thailand. Later that day, I met the local physician with the U.S. Agency for International Development who orders the medical supplies needed to support the agency's activities in Laos. He agreed with me that the concern of Continental Air Services employees for the quality of their health care was a reflection of the primitive medical facilities in Vientiane, and because these facilities are unlikely to modernize in the near future, employees should go to the medical facilities in Udon Thani or Bangkok for the diagnosis and treatment of other-than-minor medical problems.

The following day, the Laos station manager gave me a brief tour of Vientiane before I flew to Bangkok. He took me past the large compound of the U.S. Agency for International Development, with its wall topped with barbed wire surrounding numerous buildings bristling with antennas. He showed me Vientiane's wide main street, pointing to many buildings that dated back to French colonial times, to people selling opium on street corners, and to sparsely-clothed men fashioning pure gold jewelry under the watchful eyes of their employers in closed-off walkways between buildings. We went into one of many jewelry stores, where the hand-fashioned pure gold jewelry was being sold at less than $25 a troy ounce weight plus a minimal cost for workmanship when the international price for gold at that time was over $40 a troy ounce weight. Finally, he stopped at a warehouse to show me a large number of artifacts, particularly from ancient religious sites, which had been collected for Mr. Six and Audrey Meadows and would soon be shipped to them via Continental Airlines.

My flight to Bangkok as an airline passenger was on a Royal Air Lao Vickers Viscount. About midway in the flight, the airplane landed on an airstrip with no terminal, hangars, or other airport facilities that I could see, and several very small and heavy crates were transferred by men in military-style uniforms from a military-style truck to the airplane's cargo compartment. Very suspicious indeed!

In Bangkok, I was met by the Continental Airlines station manager for Bangkok, who said that in two days I could take a Continental flight to Okinawa, Japan, and go home from there on another Continental flight. He had already arranged for us to visit the hospitalized Continental Air Services pilot, and for me to see some of Bangkok's numerous tourist attractions. As he drove from the airport into Bangkok, I was fascinated by it being both modern and antiquated, with high-rise buildings and colonial-style homes, broad avenues and narrow streets, shopping centers and open-air markets, parks and waterways, and many beautiful Buddhist temples and statues. Several American servicemen on R&R and I were among the first to stay at Bangkok's newest hotel, the Dusit Thani, which had every comfort imaginable, including a large movie theater. The next morning, I visited the Continental Air Services pilot, who had been in the intensive care unit of the Bangkok Adventist Hospital for over two weeks since the fatal Pilatus Porter crash. He was being treated principally for a serious head injury, multiple rib fractures, and a fractured femur. He

MY EXPERIENCES

had been semi-conscious since the accident and was unable to remember anything about it or even the name of his company or the type of airplane he had been flying at the time of the crash. His attending physicians believed that even if he regained full consciousness, he would have significant mental and neurological impairment, and a high risk of epileptic seizures due to his brain injury, and consequently, they predicted that he would never be able to fly an airplane again. Later, I learned that they were correct.

That afternoon, I took a guided tour of Bangkok that included observation of the heavy boat traffic on the river and ancient network of canals, or klongs, and the floating market, where women were selling produce and handicrafts from their long, narrow boats. Then the tour went through the colorful Temple of the Emerald Buddha, which is the most sacred Buddhist temple in Thailand, the Grand Palace, the white Temple of the Dawn, and the Temple of the Reclining Buddha with its gold-plated 151-foot statue of the Buddha reclining on his side. The tour ended with a second opportunity to see the waterways in action, especially the great number of water taxis, most being very narrow with a single row of seats and propelled and steered by an engine with a long propeller shaft, with the engine resting on the operator's lap. (The water taxis have since morphed into wider and larger boats driven by inboard motors.) I should point out that then, as now, a well-known, distasteful feature of the river and klongs was their pollution from dead animals to human waste to just plain daily household garbage. Returning to the beauty of Bangkok, the station manager and I had a Thai dinner followed by a performance of Thai classical and folk dance, an art form that dates back over 500 years. The costumes worn, including tall headdresses, were quite colorful and, as I was told, sections of a costume are placed over the dancer and sewn together just before a dance is performed. The dancing was heavily choreographed and quite expressive, with much movement of the arms out to the fingers and legs down to the toes while the torso is slowly twisted and turned. Most of the dances depicted different important events in the history of Thailand, with Asian flute, lute, dulcimer, and percussion instruments being synchronized with the movements of the dancers.

DOUGLAS E. BUSBY

The next morning I sat in the jump seat behind the captain of a Continental Airlines B-727 flight carrying marines from their R&R in Bangkok to Okinawa. There, I immediately boarded a Continental B-707 flight carrying marines from the Viet Nam war, again sitting in the jump seat behind the captain, for a non-stop flight to the Marine Corps Air Station El Toro, just south of Los Angeles. I sent a brief report of my trip to Mr. Bell, Mr. Rogers and Mr. Stubben, providing my recommendations for improving the quality medical care of company employees in Guam and Laos, documenting my inability to identify poisoning of food in the cafeteria for the employees of Continental Air Services and Air America at the Tan Son Nhut Air Base in Viet Nam, and describing my observations of the condition and care of the Continental Air Services pilot who had been injured in the Pilatus Porter crash in Laos. Mr. Bell sent the report to Mr. Six, who became furious over his not having been allowed to deny the request for me to make the trip. Finally, I remember that a few days after I returned from the trip, the two RNs in Continental's medical department told me that in my absence, Mr. Bell had tried unsuccessfully to talk them into letting him have a confidential look at Captain Campbell's medical file. Since he had ordered them not to tell me about this request, I decided not to discuss it with him.

In the summer of 1969, I received a telephone call at Continental Airlines from a person who introduced himself as Dr. Edward Condon, a professor at the University of Colorado in Boulder, Colorado who had been contracted by the USAF to review prior studies of UFOs. He asked me if I still had the pictures of UFOs that Paul Villa had given to me while pointing out that I could be in trouble with the USAF for not having turned them over to the USAF. I replied that I had indeed given them to the USAF through Dr. Schwichtenberg and that they were returned to me through him as reportedly being considered fake. Dr. Condon said that he wanted to examine the pictures, and set a date for me to meet with him for lunch and to obtain the pictures from me. When we met, our conversation covered how I received the pictures and Dr. Schwichtenberg's purported submission of them to the USAF. It then became casual as Dr. Condon described another reason for his being in the Los Angeles area. He said that a telephone lineman had witnessed a saucer-shaped object rapidly ascend from a large field,

MY EXPERIENCES

and in trying to get a picture of it with a Polaroid camera, had photographed only the dust pattern supposedly created by the UFO. Dr. Condon described how a surveyor, a photographer and he were planning to recreate the dust pattern in an attempt to estimate the diameter of what created it. When we parted, Dr. Condon assured me that he would return Paul Villa's pictures to me. I contacted his office about a year later and Dr. Condon's secretary said that Dr. Condon had no recollection of having visited me or of receiving any pictures from me. In retrospect, I should have asked "the" Dr. Condon with whom I met for personal identification, especially after I subsequently learned that Dr. Condon had submitted the report of his negative review of prior studies of UFOs to the USAF several months before I assumedly met with him. Interesting!

In late 1969, the industrial hygienist at Continental Airlines, who also reported to Mr. Rogers, asked me to help him improve the hearing protection program for Continental's ground and ramp-service agents and airplane mechanics. Up to that time, most of these employees had been protecting themselves from noise-induced hearing loss haphazardly with earplugs provided by the company or ear muffs purchased on their own. Coincidentally, the Airline Medical Directors Association, of which I was a member, had just discussed a growing number of workers' compensation claims for this form of hearing loss. As the first step in improving Continental's hearing protection program, I suggested that we look at the programs of other major U.S. airlines, and for this offered to visit my counterparts at United Airlines in Chicago and Trans World Airlines in Kansas City. With Mr. Rogers' permission, I flew on Continental to Chicago and met with Dr. George Kidera, Vice President and Director of Medical Services of United Airlines, who showed me the hearing protection devices that United was providing to its employees and how its employees were being trained on their use. Our meeting lasted so long that I missed the evening Continental flight back to Los Angeles, so Dr. Kidera insisted that I make the trip as a guest of United. The next day, I reported on what I had learned about United's hearing protection program in a memo to Mr. Rogers and the industrial hygienist. Mr. Rogers was so pleased with the content of the memo that he copied it to Mr. Bell, who copied it to Mr. Six, who became so angry with it that he ordered Mr. Bell to fire me. However, Mr. Rogers came to my rescue by saying that he had authorized the trip for the good of the company. Then, in an off-site dinner meeting together, Mr. Rogers told me about Mr. Six's longstanding feud with the president of United Airlines, and suggested that I not visit the Medical Director of Trans World Airlines. Fortunately, my afternoon with Dr. Kidera had a positive impact on Continental Airlines, in that Continental's ground and ramp-service agents and airplane mechanics were provided appropriate noise-attenuating ear muffs and earplugs to wear whenever exposed to airplane engine noise, notably at no cost to them.

In May of 1970, Continental Airlines received its first B-747, a new large, two-aisle, long-range airliner. Before the B-747 could carry passengers, the FAA required that Continental perform a full-scale simulated emergency evacuation of a flight crew and "volunteer" passengers using 50 percent of its exits and slide systems, in 90 seconds or less. First, all of the window shades in its passenger cabin were pulled down so that the cabin would be dark except for use of emergency lighting during evacuation. All of the airplane's doors were initially closed, with the crew and volunteer passengers not knowing which exits would be opened. The volunteer passengers received the evacuation briefing for the B-747 just before the evacuation began. I was responsible for medical care if injuries occurred, standing by with the two RNs and emergency medical supplies from Continental's medical department, and an ambulance with staff on each side of the airplane. The emotional tension was high among the medical among other company personnel, for during a full-scale simulated emergency evacuation just conducted by Pan American World Airways on its first B-747, an evacuation slide partially detached from the airplane and tipped, with an elderly volunteer passenger falling off the slide to the ground and sustaining fatal injuries. Continental's evacuation went quite well until most of the hostesses, who were last to evacuate, sustained painful friction burns on their thighs and buttocks from their nylon stockings being in contact with the slides during their rapid descent on the slides. Many of the hostesses did not wish to be evaluated and treated on-site and were either taken by the ambulances to the emergency department in the nearby Daniel

MY EXPERIENCES

Freeman Memorial Hospital or driven by car to the Sepulveda Clinic. The time for Continental's evacuation test was over 90 seconds, so the FAA ordered the evacuation repeated with new volunteer passengers. The repeat evacuation was performed in less than 90 seconds without injury; the hostesses wore slacks for it.

In the summer of 1970, I became involved with two incidents that occurred with Continental Airlines' hostesses. The first incident began on a Sunday afternoon, with a telephone call to me at home by a woman who said that she was a hostess for Continental, had been injured at work, intended to kill me, and abruptly terminated the call. I immediately contacted the local supervisor of the Continental's domestic hostesses, who said that during a recent airplane evacuation refresher training session for hostesses at Continental, the hostess who called me did not follow instructions to leave the airplane by jumping onto the evacuation slide. Instead, she jumped onto airplane's door sill and fractured her coccyx (tailbone). The supervisor stated that screaming in pain, the hostess was immediately driven to the Sepulveda Clinic, where the fracture was diagnosed and treated, and she was told to stay off work and given the name of a local orthopedist for follow-up care. The next morning, I intended to meet with a representative from the workers' compensation insurance company used by Continental, to suggest that the hostess be evaluated for a mental health issue possibly generated or aggravated by her injury. Instead, both the hostess's supervisor and I met with the representative, who informed us that the previous evening, the hostess stepped off a curb in Washington, DC, and was instantly killed by a passing car.

The other incident occurred a few days later. While the company's industrial hygienist and I were giving a talk on hearing protection in Continental Airlines' airplane maintenance department, I was interrupted by a message from the local supervisor of the company's international hostesses, asking me to come immediately to her office. She said that one of Continental's senior hostesses had just arrived at this hostess's apartment in Los Angeles from working on a military flight transporting troops from Okinawa and, in front of her apartment roommate, was threatening to commit suicide with a gun that she was holding on her lap. The cause of this scene was a "break-up" letter that she had just received from a married Continental captain with whom she had been having an affair during the company's military flights to Asia. I decided not to talk with the hostess over the phone or personally, but suggested to her roommate that she be taken to a nearby hospital emergency department for psychiatric care. Subsequent negotiations for this involved several of her friends, while she consumed a great deal of wine. Finally, she put the gun down, asked everyone to leave her alone, took her clothes off, and ran around naked in the traffic outside of the apartment until the local police arrived and arrested her for drunkenness and indecent exposure. When I arrived home that evening, I was unable to reach Mr. Rogers by telephone to describe this incident in advance of it possibly being reported in the local newspapers. However, I did talk on the telephone with Mr. Bell, who was at dinner in a local restaurant with his wife and another couple. I clearly remember our conversation, which included Mr. Bell agreeing with my decision to ground the hostess until she has a psychiatric evaluation clearing her, or not, to return to work. Three days later, I was having lunch in Continental's cafeteria when the hostess walked by me dressed in her hostess uniform and carting her flight luggage. I immediately went to her supervisor, who said that Mr. Bell had cleared her for work, and then to Mr. Bell, who stated that he had allowed the hostess to continue working because all of the executives except him had likely been intimate with her at some time or another, and out of spite for being grounded, she could reveal this to the executives' wives. I indicated to Mr. Bell that I would be willing to compromise on his clearing the hostess for work if he would agree to my referring the hostess for a psychiatric evaluation while she continued to work and meanwhile had no contact with the captain on military flights to Asia. Then Mr. Bell loudly accused me of fabricating my telephone call to him in the restaurant and his agreeing with my decision to ground the hostess during the call – and ordered me to leave his office.

The fall of 1970 did not go well for me as the Medical Director of Continental Airlines. One morning, my arrival at work was delayed for the first time, because I stopped at an automobile accident for 18 minutes to determine if anyone had been injured in it. I had just entered an examination room in Continental's medical department

MY EXPERIENCES

when Mr. Rogers called me on the telephone and ordered me to immediately write "an essay" for Mr. Six and Mr. Bell, telling them why I was late for work that day. I never received a response to the essay. On another morning, Mr. Rogers arrived at his office to find all of his personal items boxed and a letter from Mr. Six on his desk saying that he was fired. Although no reason was given for his firing, he later told me that contract renewal negotiations with the Continental's pilot and airplane mechanics unions had not been progressing to Mr. Six's satisfaction. Soon after Mr. Rogers left the company, I played a very slow round of golf in the fog on the top of Palos Verdes Peninsula with Dr. Leo Leonelli, who had recently completed The Ohio State University residency in aerospace medicine and was working in the emergency departments of local hospitals. As we were about to tee off on the first hole, two Continental pilots asked us if they could join us in negotiating through the fog. The next day, Mr. Bell asked me to come to his office and close its door behind me, after which he loudly berated me for associating with Continental pilots during contract negotiations with their union, as reported to him by the manager of aircraft maintenance who saw me golfing with the two pilots. Needless to say, Mr. Bell would not let me respond to his highly-unprofessional scolding, and in light of this and the international hostess incident, I began to wonder if he was deteriorating mentally from the stress of his position, which now included his coordinating union contract negotiations for the company until Mr. Rogers' successor was hired. A few days later, Mr. Bell's secretary came to my office to express her concern to me about a recent change in Mr. Bell's behavior, with his having frequent hostile verbal outbursts directed at her and throwing sharpened pencils upwards at a picture of the president of the company's airplane mechanics union attached to a ceiling tile in his office. Immediately after she left my office, I had an urgent meeting with Mr. Alexander Damm, the General Manager of Continental, to inform him of Mr. Bell's aberrant behavior and apparent need for psychiatric care. Mr. Damm stated that he was already aware of this, would be meeting with Mr. Bell on it. Several hours later, I was told by the acting personnel director that Mr. Bell had been fired by Mr. Six and did not have the opportunity even to say goodbye to his staff.

DOUGLAS E. BUSBY

While I worked at Continental Airlines, I continued to serve as a USAF reservist in the outpatient clinic in the nearby USAF Space and Missile Systems Center, and worked a 12-hour shift on weekends in the emergency departments of local hospitals. I purchased a new Cessna 182 Skylane for recreational use with my family and for rental to pilots by a fixed-base operator at the Torrance Airport nearby our home.

Cessna 182 Skylane

In 1968, and for the following three years, I gave a course on aerospace physiology and human factors to graduate students obtaining a Master of Safety Engineering degree from the Institute of Aerospace Management and Safety at the University of Southern California (USC), on the USC campus, at the Marine Corps Air Station El Toro and in Las Vegas, Nevada. In 1969, I edited a book containing the scientific papers presented that year at the XVIII International Congress of Aviation and Space Medicine in Amsterdam, Holland. This project was complicated by my having to ghostwrite a scientific paper for the book on medical experience in the Apollo 7 through 11 manned spaceflights, from the notes and slides which Dr. Chuck Berry used in his keynote presentation at the Congress. And much to the chagrin of the publisher of the book, the paper was published in "Aerospace Medicine," the journal of the Aerospace Medical Association, without the publisher's permission or acknowledgment of the work I did on it. In 1970, I wrote a comprehensive article on aerospace medicine for a new edition of the Encyclopedia Britannica, for which I received a small stipend and, more importantly, a new encyclopedia that became a valued reference source for my three daughters while they were in high school. And in the fall of 1970, I attended classes and took the written and oral examinations to

MY EXPERIENCES

become a citizen of the United States, which I did on November 20, 1970, proudly wearing my USAF Reserve Officer's uniform.

In early 1971, I realized that my work beyond Continental had become more fulfilling professionally for me, so when the new Torrance Memorial Hospital asked Dr. Leonelli and me to co-direct its new emergency department, I decided to leave Continental and join Leo in this new venture. My departure from Continental Airlines was cordial. The company hired an executive search firm, which identified several candidates, including some fellow specialists in aerospace medicine whom the company invited me to interview. Interestingly, one was the USAF officer, recently retired as a colonel, whom I had visited in Washington, DC, in the fall of 1960 to get information on how I might become an aerospace medicine specialist in the USAF; he did not remember me. Another was a longstanding friend, Dr. Lawrence "Larry" Marinelli, who became my successor at Continental.

4. As Co-Director of the Emergency Department at Torrance Memorial Hospital and as a Consultant in Aerospace Medicine (Los Angeles, CA)

During the summer of 1971, Leo and I became co-directors of the emergency department of Torrance Memorial Hospital. We also set up an office on Palos Verdes Peninsula for us to conduct FAA airman medical certification examinations and executive health evaluations, and for me to provide consultant services in human factors to the aerospace industry.

The emergency department had been well designed for its anticipated patient load, with six screened-off cubicles and two private rooms. One room was to be used when privacy would be necessary, such as for the management of cases involving the presence of police, and the other room was to be used only for CPR, especially of patients with ventricular fibrillation and cardiac arrest. The CPR room was equipped with the latest equipment for cardiac monitoring, defibrillation and pacing, pulmonary ventilation, and mechanical chest compression. It also had a well-stocked cardiac arrest "crash cart" with injectable cardiovascular drugs and supplies for defibrillation, venous cut-down, and drug and intravenous fluid administration. We trained all of the emergency department nurses in CPR, and helped them to maintain their proficiency in CPR with simulated cardiac emergencies.

I was on duty when the CPR room had its first patient, a policeman who had briefly experienced pain in his chest while performing his regular morning exercise routine at home. Even though his vital signs and EKG were normal when he arrived in the CPR room, I kept him there on continuous cardiac monitoring. Several minutes later, his heart suddenly fibrillated and he lost consciousness and stopped breathing. He was "dead" for several minutes as two nurses and I gave him CPR, which required several external electrical shocks of increasing intensity from the manual defibrillator to return his heart to a normal rhythm. Thereafter, he had a rapid recovery, apparently with no mental or physical effects from this cardiac event. However, he later recalled to me with some delight everything that the nurses and I had said and done while we were attempting to resuscitate him. He stated that immediately after he lost consciousness, he left his body and heard and saw everything that we did from a vantage point directly over his body and near the ceiling in the CPR room.

While co-directing and working in the emergency department of Torrance Memorial Hospital, I continued to teach in USC's Institute of Aerospace Management and Safety and was a consultant to three local aerospace companies. Wyle Laboratories in El Segundo asked for my opinion on why many helicopter pilots who were testing its new helicopter simulator were becoming disoriented and nauseated, some to the point of retching and even vomiting – a phenomenon which has since been called "simulator sickness." During a flight simulation, the pilot was seated behind a flight control column on an otherwise-open platform that could tilt in the pitch, yaw, and roll axes of flight. The pilot then "flew" a freely-suspended television camera over a detailed model of a city, with the images from the camera being continuously projected onto a large vertical screen above and behind the model. I had pilots "fly" the simulator with and without platform movement, and with and without head motion, but they still experienced

MY EXPERIENCES

simulator sickness. Then it occurred to me that pilots can develop a fear of height that does not exist when they are enclosed by a structure for reference, so I recommended that at the least, the framework of a helicopter cockpit be added to the simulator's moving platform. This substantially reduced the occurrence and degree of simulator sickness.

Then, North American Rockwell Corporation in Los Angeles asked me for help in the design of its B-1 Lancer long-range, multi-role, heavy bomber for the USAF. This large aircraft would carry four crewmembers, including a pilot, a copilot, and two combat systems officers. Because of this airplane's intercontinental flying capability, the USAF asked North American Rockwell to provide enough room on its flight deck for food storage and preparation, hygiene needs, and crew rest. This company's Corporate Medical Director, Dr. Toby Freedman, invited me to accompany him and B-1 design engineers on a tour of the B-1 mock-up to consider what changes might be made to the B-1's flight deck to accommodate the USAF's request. We suggested several changes, but had no follow-up on them.

Finally, Robert McCulloch, founder of Lake Havasu City in Southeast Arizona and owner of McCulloch International Airlines, asked me to conduct pre-employment physical examinations on pilot and hostess applicants, as well as annual health evaluations on pilots, for his fleet of Lockheed L-188 Electra turboprop, and B-720 and DC-8 jet airplanes based at the Long Beach, California airport. The primary service of his airline was flying prospective buyers of residential lots in Lake Havasu City from the Northeast and Midwest United States to Lake Havasu for a free mini-vacation. Leo joined me in providing the health evaluations in our office.

Leo and I each saw pilots in our office who had been denied an FAA airman medical certificate because of a medical condition that these pilots believed would not impair their ability to safely fly an airplane. We suggested to them that they write a letter to the Aeromedical Certification Branch of the FAA's Civil Aeromedical Institute (CAMI) in Oklahoma City, Oklahoma, requesting a medical waiver from the FAA to fly an airplane with a medical condition. We recommended that the letter be accompanied by a completed FAA airman medical certification examination form without our signing the form, along with medical records and current tests pertaining to the condition. We would also include a letter summarizing the management and status of the condition, the latter including related functional capabilities. One pilot who came to me to determine if he could obtain an FAA airman medical certificate was the producer and director of a popular television show, who had developed permanent atrial fibrillation without symptoms or identifiable cause. While we gathered the information necessary for the FAA to make a waiver decision, I telephoned Dr. Audie Davis, Chief of CAMI's Aeromedical Certification Branch, to discuss this seemingly-unique case. Dr. Davis indicated that medical waivers had already been given to several other pilots with permanent atrial fibrillation. The pilot received the medical waiver. Subsequently, Dr. Davis and I published a scientific paper on the medical certification of pilots to fly with permanent atrial fibrillation without symptoms or identifiable cause.

At the end of our conversation regarding the FAA's position on medical certification of pilots with atrial fibrillation, Dr. Davis mentioned that the position of Chief of CAMI's Aeromedical Research Branch had recently opened, and suggested that I contact Dr. J. Robert "Bob" Dille, Director of CAMI, if I might be interested in applying for it. A few days later, I was invited by the head of the Department of Preventive Medicine at the Mayo Clinic to come to the Clinic in Rochester, Minnesota be interviewed for a medical staff position in his department. He said that in this position I would be performing executive and pilot medical evaluations, the latter principally for Northwest Airlines, and if I wished, I could conduct research in aerospace medicine at the Clinic. I was offered a wonderful future at the Mayo Clinic, but my wife refused to move to Rochester. Soon thereafter, I telephoned Dr. Dille, who said that he was hoping that I would apply to be the next Chief of CAMI's Aeromedical Research Branch, but a U.S. Government freeze in hiring prevented him from

MY EXPERIENCES

filling it. About that time, my wife became increasingly concerned about the exposure of our daughters to the growing drug culture around our home, and we began to discuss our return to Canada. However, we decided to "stick it out" on Palos Verdes Peninsula and even replaced our four-seat Cessna 182 airplane with a six-seat Piper PA-32-300 airplane so that all five of us could periodically fly away from the area.

Piper PA-32-300

5. As Head of the Civil Aviation Medicine Unit in Canada's Defense and Civil Institute of Environmental Medicine (Toronto, ON)

At the Annual Scientific Meeting of the Aerospace Medical Association in Bal Harbour, Florida in 1972, Dr. Ian Anderson, Director of the Aviation Medicine Division in Health and Welfare Canada in Ottawa, asked me if I might be interested in returning to Canada as a full-time "consultant in aerospace medicine" in the Aviation Medicine Division, to develop and head a Civil Aviation Medicine Unit in Toronto. He said that the unit would be an extension of the Aviation Medicine Division and would be located at the former RCAF IAM unit on Avenue Road in Toronto which, along with the IAM facility at the RCAF Station Downsview, had been renamed the Defense and Civil Institute of Environmental Medicine (DCIEM). Dr. Anderson said that a major responsibility of the Civil Aviation Medicine Unit would be to coordinate the evaluation of civilian pilots with health problems for the Transport Canada Aviation Medical Review Board in Ottawa to decide whether airman medical certificates should be issued to them. He added that the unit would also be responsible for developing

DOUGLAS E. BUSBY

materials to be used by Canada's regional flight surgeons in training civil airman medical certification examiners and pilots in Canada, for designing a new civil airman medical certification examination form for use in Canada, and for coordinating and conducting civil aviation medicine research in DCIEM. In retrospect, the excitement of my family over the prospect of our returning to Canada led me to accept Dr. Anderson's offer of this position based on his description of the position. I simply gave no thought to asking Dr. Anderson if DCIEM had existing educational and research functions in civil aviation medicine and if so, how the unit would relate to them. Moreover, I failed to ask him whether someone was presently coordinating the evaluation of civilian pilots with health problems for the Transport Canada Aviation Medical Review Board.

We moved back to Canada in the mid-summer of 1972. This time, I had to obtain an Immigration Canada certificate even though, as I subsequently discovered, I was actually a dual citizen of Canada and the United States. I also learned two years later that during the move, CAMI's director, Dr. Dille, tried unsuccessfully to reach me by telephone to say that the U.S. Government had temporarily lifted its freeze on the position of Chief of CAMI's Aeromedical Research Branch. We purchased a home on Tanglewood Drive in the country near the village of Caledon and the Town of Orangeville, about 25 miles north of the Toronto Pearson International Airport and 45 miles from the DCIEM facility on Avenue Road in Toronto. This move was to create quite a change from living in the Los Angeles area, for we would be living in farmland, with its rabbits, deer, and groundhogs, and again enjoy four distinct seasons, especially winter with snowmobiling in the fields around our home. Orangeville had a small general hospital where I worked in its emergency department during a 12-hour shift on weekends, which extended to other in-hospital activities such as performing intake medical evaluations of hospital patients, assisting in surgery, and delivering babies. Another pilot and I flew our Piper PA-32-300 airplane from the Torrance Airport to the Waterloo-

MY EXPERIENCES

Wellington Airport, which was 35 miles further away than the Orangeville Airport from our home, but had much longer runways.

On my first day at the DCIEM facility on Avenue Road, Dr. Anderson came from his office in Ottawa to Toronto to show me the Civil Aviation Medicine Unit, which consisted of two private offices off of a common area for a secretary and visitors. Dr. Anderson was a successor to Dr. Morris Fraser, with whom I had worked at the Lovelace Foundation. He had graduated from the Medical School at the University of Aberdeen, and served as a physician in the Royal Air Force and then the RCAF, ending his RCAF career in 1970 as a specialist in aerospace medicine and Commanding Officer of the RCAF School of Aviation Medicine at the RCAF IAM in Toronto. He then became Director of the Aviation Medicine Division of Health and Welfare Canada, located in the Transport Canada Headquarters in Ottawa. As Dr. Anderson and I began to discuss the responsibilities of the unit, Major Jack Soutendam, an aviation physiologist who was Commanding Officer of the on-site Canadian Armed Forces (CAF) School of Operational Medicine, came by to meet me. He immediately asked Dr. Anderson and me whether the Civil Aviation Medicine Unit would be taking over existing civil aeromedical education and research functions of DCIEM, specifically the aeromedical education of civil airman medical certification examiners and pilots currently being conducted by the CAF School of Operational Medicine. To my surprise, Dr. Anderson told Major Soutendam that he had not yet discussed who would be responsible for these functions with the military and civilian authorities in DCIEM and Ottawa, and stated that the unit had already been assigned tasks that did not conflict with what DCIEM was doing in civil aviation medicine.

Later that day, Dr. Anderson took me to the DCIEM facility in Downsview, to meet Dr. Romney Lowry, the Director-General of DCIEM. Needless to say, my first and subsequent encounters with Dr. Lowry were quite antagonistic on his part. Immediately after Dr. Anderson introduced me to him, Dr. Lowry asked me what an "American" physician expected to accomplish at DCIEM. In reply, I

DOUGLAS E. BUSBY

summarized the responsibilities of the Civil Aviation Unit that Dr. Anderson had described to me when he invited me to head the unit. Seemingly unsatisfied with this response, Dr. Lowry echoed Major Soutendam's earlier question regarding the unit taking over existing civil aeromedical education and research functions of DCIEM, and Dr. Anderson replied that an answer to his question had had not yet been determined. Then Dr. Lowry abruptly dismissed us from his office, stating that he would soon visit the Civil Aviation Medicine Unit to get the answer from me.

I should provide some background to my uncomfortable encounter with Dr. Lowry that day. I had never met him personally and did not know that I would, in a sense, be reporting indirectly to him as the director of DCIEM. I initially heard of Dr. Lowry during my summers as a URTP cadet at the RCAF IAM, and Dr. Nelson had suggested that I contact him about the potential for my having a career in civil aerospace medicine in the United States. I was told that in the late 1950s, he had been an RCAF medical officer posted to Washington, DC, and while there had resigned from the RCAF to manage the Space Medicine Branch in The Boeing Company in Seattle, WA. I subsequently had a very brief telephone conversation with Dr. Lowry on career opportunities in civil aerospace medicine in the United States, and he emphatically and as I later learned, incorrectly, told me that such opportunities did not exist for a "Canadian physician." While I was at the Lovelace Foundation, Dr. Schwichtenberg said that as a consultant to the Boeing Company, he had heard that Dr. Lowry mistakenly showed the success of research on recycling urine into potable (drinkable) water to a group of visitors, by having a technician drink some urine reportedly converted into pure water. The technician experienced near-fatal acute renal (kidney) failure from normal, toxic chemical material that had been incompletely removed from the urine during the conversion process. Dr. Schwichtenberg stated that Dr. Lowry left Boeing shortly after this incident and was subsequently appointed chief of the Research and Education Division in the FAA's Office of Aviation Medicine in

MY EXPERIENCES

Washington, DC When I was the medical director of Continental Airlines, Dr. Lowry generated considerable controversy at the FAA, as reported at a meeting of the Airline Medical Directors Association. At the direction of the temporary Federal Air Surgeon, USAF Major General Samuel ("Sam") White (not Dr. Sam White at the Lovelace Foundation), Dr. Lowry had written an investigative report which concluded that over 100 scientists and specialized technicians staffing the recently-opened FAA Civil Aeromedical Research Institute (CARI), later called the Aeromedical Research Branch of the FAA Civil Aeromedical Institute (CAMI), in Oklahoma City were engaged in aeromedical research projects that had little-to-no relevance to civil aviation pilot performance, and pilot and passenger safety. The furor that the report created among CARI's researchers and the wider aviation medicine community led to Dr. White being transferred back to the USAF and to Dr. Lowry's resignation from the FAA.

After we visited Dr. Lowry, Dr. Anderson assigned the first projects to the Civil Aviation Medicine Unit. I was to develop civil aeromedical education materials, including a handbook and slides, to be used by regional flight surgeons in training airman medical certification examiners and airmen, and to design a new airman medical certification examination form. Dr. Anderson authorized me to hire a secretary who had experience in medical transcription, and arranged for me to use the graphic arts department in the CAF School of Operational Medicine to create aeromedical education illustrations and convert them into slides. Two weeks after I arrived in the Unit, Dr. Lowry unexpectedly walked into it and immediately asked me what had been decided regarding the Unit taking over the existing civil aeromedical education and research functions of DCIEM. I suggested that he contact Dr. Anderson regarding this and he departed without further conversation. Dr. Lowry returned at least once a month with the same question, to which I gave the same answer. I reported these encounters with Dr. Lowry to Dr. Anderson, and to my knowledge, Dr. Anderson never followed up on them.

DOUGLAS E. BUSBY

After my first month in the Civil Aviation Medicine Unit, Dr. Anderson asked me to attend the twice-monthly meetings of the Transport Canada Aviation Medical Review Board in Ottawa. At my first meeting, I learned that in Canada, airman medical certification decisions, especially on pilots with heart problems, were taking into account data on the risk of a medical problem causing impairment of flying ability, in addition to the medical history and existing health of the pilot related to the problem. I also discovered that a physician in Dr. Anderson's office, Dr. Roy M. Stewart, had been coordinating the evaluation of pilots with health problems for the Transport Canada Aviation Medical Review Board. When I asked Dr. Anderson how this function under Dr. Stewart would relate to a seemingly-identical function that Dr. Anderson had described to me for the Civil Aviation Medicine Unit, Dr. Anderson replied that tell me, but never did.

In the fall of 1972, Dr. Anderson invited me to be his guest at a meeting of the National Research Council of Canada, held in Ottawa. When he began to introduce me as a possible new member of the council, Dr. Lowry interrupted him, stating that I was an American and "could not be trusted." Several meeting attendees, but not Dr. Lowry, later apologized for the insult. After this meeting, I informed Dr. Anderson that as long as Dr. Lowry was a member of the council, I wished not to be a member of it. A few days later, Major Soutendam made some unkind remarks about me to his staff after I had been interviewed on "CBS This Morning" on the success of a Russian Soyuz spaceflight, and had lectured on human factors in flight to an engineering class at York University in Toronto. And even though Major Soutendam subsequently told the graphic artist in the CAF School of Operational Medicine that the school did not have to support the Civil Aviation Medicine Unit, I was able to get enough assistance from an artist in the School to complete a set of slides so that along with a new handbook, the regional flight surgeons had the necessary materials in aviation medicine for training airman medical certification examiners and airmen. Then I developed a new airman medical examination form and submitted it to Dr. Anderson.

MY EXPERIENCES

In June of 1973, I took stock of my professional life in Toronto. Dr. Anderson was still reluctant to determine the relationships between the Civil Aviation Medicine Unit and DCIEM. He had not yet clarified how the Unit would be coordinating the evaluation of pilots with health problems for the Transport Canada Aviation Medical Review Board, when Dr. Stewart appeared to be managing this function effectively. The handbook and slides for the regional flight surgeons to use in training airman medical certification examiners and airmen and a draft new airman medical examination form had been completed. About that time, I realized that there was potential for me as a consultant in aviation medicine in and beyond Toronto, so I decided to leave Health and Welfare Canada to work in aviation medicine as a solo practitioner, even though aviation medicine was not yet considered medical specialty in Canada.

6. As a Consultant in Aviation Medicine in Canada (Toronto, ON)

In July of 1973, I opened a consultant office in aviation medicine near the Toronto International Airport. The office was equipped for conducting airman medical certification and other physical examinations, resting and exercise stress EKGs, and several automated health-screening laboratory tests. With the support of Captain R. L. "Bob" Dodds, Chair of the Aeromedical Committee of the Canadian Airline Pilots Association (CALPA), I was soon being visited by airline pilots with airman medical certification problems, conducting airman medical certification examinations on professional and private pilots, and assisting the Winnipeg-based airline, Transair, in identifying possible medical causes of flight errors being made by its pilots. I also did some consultant work in occupational medicine for companies on repetitive strain injuries, such as carpal tunnel syndrome in employees assembling protective helmets for hockey players and constructing wire grocery carts, and for Canada Post on "suspicious," workers' compensation claims that were occurring especially among its immigrant employees. Finally, I substituted for

DOUGLAS E. BUSBY

Dr. Doug Warren, Medical Director of Canadian Kodak, while he taught a class on occupational medicine at the University of Toronto, went on vacations, and worked with colleagues on developing the specialty of occupational medicine in Canada. Doug trained me on how to identify occupationally-related and other lung diseases in chest x-rays.

Transair was operating daily Boeing B-737 and Fokker F28 flights between Winnipeg and Toronto, with intermediate stops, and B-737 and B-707 charter (so-called "snowbird') flights from Canada to Florida, the Caribbean, and Mexico. In a several-month period, this airline had had three remarkable events due to poor pilot performance, and its flight manager to ask me to assess them from the perspective of a specialist in aviation medicine.

The first event occurred when Transair's chief pilot failed a check ride on its new B-707. Just before he flared the airplane for landing, he asked his copilot to take over control of the airplane because of his "poor eyesight." I suggested that the flight manager ground the chief pilot pending his eyes being examined by an ophthalmologist in Toronto, who is experienced in assessing pilot vision. The following day, the ophthalmologist found that the chief pilot had wet macular degeneration with significant and irreversible loss of central vision in both eyes. The chief pilot subsequently admitted to the flight manager and me that he had memorized the eye chart in his aviation medical examiner's office, and the aviation medical examiner had not checked his near vision for some time, so that he could have a medical certificate to fly. Transair fired the senior pilot, and I reported the incident and the aviation medical examiner's shortcomings to Dr. Anderson.

The second event occurred when the captain of a Transair B-737 was cleared by Canadian air traffic control to land as scheduled at the Sioux Sault Marie (Ontario) Airport, at night and during a snow shower. Instead, he landed the airplane at the Sioux Sault Marie (Michigan) Airport, which also had a snow shower. When the captain and the first officer saw that the taxiway off the runway on which they

MY EXPERIENCES

had landed was not where it should have been and heard the control tower at the Sioux Sault Marie (Ontario) Airport ask where they were, the captain immediately turned the airplane around and flew it to the Sioux Sault Marie (Ontario) airport. The kerfuffle that these pilots created involved U.S. Customs and Immigration, the FAA and Transport Canada, and the U.S. State Department. I was asked to determine whether pilot impairment was a factor in this incident – after the pilots had flown the airplane on to Toronto! I interviewed and examined each of them, and found no evident medical cause of the incident. I thought that Transair might have an airline cockpit management problem, which could be corrected with a program recently developed by Dr. Charlie Billings at The Ohio State University, and already being used by several airlines in the United States.

A third event a few weeks later further pointed to inadequate cockpit management, in this case, a checklist error. While landing an F28 at the Red Deer (Alberta) Airport at night and during a snow shower, the captain did not reset the airplane's Kollsman window to local atmospheric pressure, which he would have checked and acknowledged when the landing checklist was read to him by the first officer. (This window in an airplane's altimeter allows a pilot to set the altimeter to local atmospheric pressure. However, when flying above 18,000 feet mean sea level [MSL], all airplanes must have their Kollsman widows set to a common atmospheric pressure setting of 29.92 inches of mercury, which is the atmospheric pressure at MSL.) Consequently, the captain's approach to the airport was too low, recognized by the pilots when the airplane bumped into the tops of tall pine trees along the approach path to the airport. Fortunately, the pilots recognized what was happening and their approach was corrected. When I saw the airplane the following day, its undersurface was quite scratched and pine boughs were sticking out of its wheel fairings (pants). This time, I talked with the pilots without examining them. The pilots had already admitted the error, and I reminded Transair of a possible cockpit management problem. Interestingly, I was subsequently in the jump seat behind the captain of one of the company's B-737s during a late-night landing at the Toronto International Airport, when I observed that the captain had missed the Kollsman reset callout by the first officer and recognized that the airplane was below a safe glideslope.

Unforgettable Memories: Crash of our Piper PA-32-300 Airplane

On a very warm and humid Saturday afternoon in August of 1973, I crashed our Piper PA-32-300 airplane, proving the hard way what I had been teaching for years in human factors classes: "airplane accidents are often foreshadowed by one or more events that increase the probability of their happening." Although several events preceding the accident that day could have contributed to it, I believe the most significant one occurred in the spring of 1973, when the owner of the Orangeville Airport, Fred Brundle, convinced me that the airport's 1,900-foot north-south grass landing strip was more than long enough for safe takeoffs and landings in either direction with my airplane. (A paved runway crossing the grass strip at a 90-degree angle was far too short for the safe operation of the airplane.) Consequently, I decided to move the airplane from Waterloo-Wellington Airport closer to our home near the Orangeville Airport. Over the following several months, I found that a line of tall trees at the south end of Orangeville Airport's grass strip substantially shortened usable takeoff and landing distances. I gave thought to moving the airplane back to the Waterloo-Wellington Airport, but decided to keep it close by until it was painted with new, Canadian identification numbers and sold. Then, for our last trip with the airplane, we decided to fly to Denver, Colorado, for a one-week vacation. On the way to Denver, I commented to my family that the airplane seemed to resent being sold, after I had to make a forced landing at a private airport in Nebraska when the tachometer cable broke so that I had no indication of how fast the propeller was turning, and the oil dipstick access door unexplainably flipped open as we approached the Denver airport.

MY EXPERIENCES

Our return to Canada that Saturday was fraught with more serious events, beginning with our approach to landing at the Windsor Airport to clear Canadian Immigration and Customs. As we entered the traffic pattern to land, an air traffic controller in the airport's air traffic control tower cleared me to land on the active runway, even though it was occupied by an Air Canada DC-9 taxiing to its takeoff position. When I realized what was happening, I asked the controller for an alternate runway on which to land, and he replied, "Wind calm; land on any other runway you wish." I landed the airplane on a much shorter runway and taxied it to a shaded area on the tarmac outside of the immigration and customs office. Inside, I found the Immigration and Customs officer sound asleep in his tilt-back chair, with his feet on his desk. I awakened him, and as soon as I told him why I was there, he said that we could continue to our flight into Canada and went back to sleep. When I returned to our airplane, two obviously-annoyed Air Canada pilots were waiting for me. They demanded that I immediately file a complaint against the air traffic controller who had given me clearance to land on a runway occupied by the DC-9. After I assured them that, I had already decided to do so the coming Monday. I thanked them for their concern, got back into the airplane, and at the request of my now very warm and thirsty family, taxied it across the airport to an airplane maintenance facility that had a snack bar.

As I left the airplane to get soft drinks, I asked the aviation gas attendant to fill the airplane's two fuel tanks, one in each wing. When I returned, I was horrified to see that he was filling the first tank with low-octane gas – with his hand holding the fill nozzle over a placard on the wing, saying "high-octane gas only." Surprised by this error, I rather loudly ordered him to "stop" what he was doing. I then had a tense meeting with the owner of the maintenance facility, who was also a pilot. Together we calculated that the fuel in one tank would be about one-third low-octane gas and the fuel in the other tank would be entirely high-octane gas, and he assured me that I should not notice a loss of engine power while subsequently drawing gas equally from both tanks.

DOUGLAS E. BUSBY

I had hoped that the flight from Windsor to Orangeville would be pleasant, as the air was calm, albeit still quite warm and humid, and the visibility was unlimited. I decided to fly the airplane over London to show our daughters where they were born and I was trained in medicine, and then over Kitchener-Waterloo and Guelph to the Orangeville Airport.

As we approached London, I notified air traffic control that the airplane would be entering the air traffic control zone from the west and pushed the airplane's transponder button so that air traffic control could identify it. When the airplane was about a mile from the eastern edge of the control zone, it nearly collided with a glider flying illegally within the control zone. At the time, my gaze was directed downwards, routinely scanning the airplane's instrument panel, but my wife and daughters saw one of the glider's wings pass in front of the airplane, casting its shadow into our cockpit. I immediately informed air traffic control of the "near miss," and a controller said he would give me a communication channel on which to report the incident. However, I did not hear back from him.

Orangeville Airport did not have a control tower or radio communication to advise aircraft on take-off and landing. As we approached the airport, I noticed that its short runway had been repaved and that some of the grass landing strip appeared to have been graded and replaced with crushed stone. I made a low pass over the grass strip, then descended for landing over the tall trees at its south end. I used a steep and slow descent with full flaps, but my approach to touchdown was too fast, so I aborted the landing. I again tried to land, but just before touchdown saw an airplane begin to take off east-to-west on the short, repaved runway. I aborted that landing, in doing so closely passing over the other airplane at the intersection of the grass strip and paved runway. At this point, I decided to land the airplane at the Waterloo-Wellington airport after attempting one more landing at the Orangeville Airport.

I placed the airplane again in a steep and slow descent with full flaps. The airplane touched down on the grass landing strip, and soon rolled onto unpacked, crushed stone which made an enormous racket

MY EXPERIENCES

as it was thrown backward by the landing gear tires against the fully-lowered flaps. As I raised the flaps out of concern for their being damaged by the stones, the right landing gear went over a pile of stones, giving us quite a jolt as it came back down. At this point, I decided to abort the landing, applying full throttle, lowering the flaps again, and pulling back hard on the yoke. The airplane barely cleared a woven log fence along the north end of the airport as its propeller struck the fence and was extensively chipped. Moreover, its left landing gear was torn out of the wing by a tall post aligned with the center of the grass landing strip and, as my daughter, Sharon observed, momentarily swung back and forth on its hydraulic line before separating from the line and falling into the farmer's field beyond the fence. (Later, I learned that the farmer who owned this field beyond the north end of the airport had wired the fence logs together and placed the post to deter pilots from landing on his property.) Then the left hydraulic line separated from the airplane and wrapped momentarily around the airplane's rudder, forcing the airplane into a left turn between two large trees along the road adjacent to the airport. With the hydraulic line now off of the rudder, I had full directional control over the airplane.

For the following two hours, I communicated on an assigned radio frequency with the Toronto International Airport Air Traffic Control Center. A passing pilot assessed the damage to the airplane, and reported that the nose and right landing gear were intact and the leading edge of the left horizontal stabilizer was extensively damaged. I was assigned an airplane holding pattern just north of the Toronto International Airport, where I decided to dump most of the airplane's fuel to prepare for an engine-out landing at the airport. Before I made the dump-fuel decision, my wife and I read the fuel management section of the PA-32-300 Operator's Manual, finding that no mention was made of in-flight fire risk from using the airplane's fuel system drain lever in flight. (We did not know that the airplane's exhaust pipe was bent during the airplane's contact with the fence, so that the exhaust pipe opening was just behind the dump fuel exit!) When the fuel tanks were just about empty, I notified the Air Traffic Control Center that I wished to make a straight-in, gliding approach to a runway to be foamed for the airplane to touch down, initially on its right landing gear, then on its nose gear, and finally on the tip of its left wing. After the Center approved the approach and foaming, my wife and I took a few moments to tell our daughters when and how to position themselves for a crash landing, dictated a brief "last will" to relay to my mother and stepfather should we perish in the crash, and along with our daughters, said The Lord's Prayer. As we got closer to the end of the runway, I saw that our airplane would be passing directly over a tall blast fence and a visual guidance system mounted on a large block of cement. Just after the airplane cleared the blast fence, I shut off the airplane's fuel, fuel mixture, and engine power switches as recommended for an emergency landing, while intending to guide the airplane over the visual guidance system to the foamed runway just beyond it. However, the airplane was no longer able to sustain flight at its safe glide speed due to damage to its flight surfaces and then rapidly descended from an altitude of about 75 feet. I guided the airplane to the right of the visual guidance system, and it pancaked onto the grass to the right of the end of the runway. It skidded to a stop in 80 feet while turning counterclockwise about 135 degrees.

With the help of the Toronto International Airport's Fire Department, we were able to get out of the airplane in a few seconds. At the time, the only injury was a small bite wound on my daughter Stephanie's tongue. A few days later, I realized that I had temporarily sprained my right thumb while holding onto the airplane's yoke during the crash, with its shaft being bent about 45 degrees to the right during the crash. And for several months, a thin bright circle of light would appear in my field of vision whenever I looked at a dark or cloudless sky, or a blank wall. This visual phenomenon was created by the reflection of sunlight by a deep chip in the propeller when the airplane flew towards the sun in the holding pattern.

Not a good day!

MY EXPERIENCES

After we removed our luggage from the airplane, we were taken to a hangar where the airplane would be stored until cleared by Transport Canada for its repair or salvage. Two aircraft accident investigators from Transport Canada interviewed me in detail about how our airplane ended up at the Toronto International Airport rather than at the Orangeville Airport. At one point, we were interrupted by two airport policemen who had just detained two American Airlines' airplane maintenance workers with radio and navigation equipment that they had stolen from the airplane. The policemen wanted to know whether I wished to have the workers arrested for burglarizing our airplane. I recall telling the police that I had been through enough stress for the day, and to let the maintenance workers go free after they replaced the equipment.

From the day of the crash, the potential for our daughters suffering from post-crash anxiety was of concern to my wife and me. At first, the family took time every day to discuss the crash and our feelings during and after it. About a month after the crash, my wife felt that taking our three daughters to a local air show while I was at work in the emergency medicine department of the Orangeville Hospital might be anxiety-preventing for them. They decided to leave the show just before it ended, and as they were walking along a path to the parking lot, a Pitts Special aerobatic biplane made an emergency landing, hit a ditch, and flipped upside down just a few yards from them. Fortunately, the pilot was not injured and even waved to them, apparently to show them so, as he got out of his airplane. Then, about two months after the crash of our airplane, our daughters were riding home on their school bus when it had to stop for passing emergency vehicles in the vicinity of the Orangeville Airport. They saw that an airplane had just crashed through the same fence as our airplane had done, but instead had ended its flight in the farmer's field. That evening, we were pleased to learn that no one was injured in that accident. Discussions of our crash and the two no-injury accidents so close in time to ours seemed to have a dissipating effect on the whole family's post-crash anxiety. But I never flew an airplane again without an expert copilot beside me.

DOUGLAS E. BUSBY

A few days after the crash, our airplane was purchased "as is" by a local aviation company. Then its wings were removed and it was taken by truck to California for its restoration and use as an air taxi in the Toronto area. Nothing came about from the incidents at the Windsor Airport and in the London air traffic control zone.

Finally, I recall that on Monday morning after the accident, the two Transport Canada airplane accident investigators who had interviewed me immediately after the crash flew a single-engine airplane into Orangeville Airport to get a better idea of what had occurred during my failed attempts to land there. They were also unable to make a safe landing on the grass strip while approaching it over the tall trees at its south end and determined why. They measured the functional length of this runway and found that it was 1,500 feet - 400 feet shorter than the 1,900-foot length, as Mr. Brundle had told me. The Operator's Manual for the Piper PA-32-300 states that this airplane needs 1,350 feet for take-off over a 50-foot obstacle, and 1,000 feet for landing over a 50-foot obstacle. Notably, these landing distances are substantially increased in warm and humid weather, as existed at the Orangeville Airport on the time of the crash.

In the spring of 1974, I was visited in my office by an Air Canada B-747 captain, whom I had met when I visited the glider club operating off of his farm near Orangeville. He had just returned from London, England as an Air Canada passenger because he had unexpectedly developed a "fear of flying" while piloting a B-747 passenger flight to London, and had to ask his first officer to land the airplane. First, I asked him many "screening" questions that I hoped would give me an indication of what caused this to happen, such as whether he had ever experienced fear of flying, had a medical problem of concern to him, or had taken any medication or used any drug before it occurred, or had recently experienced any mental or emotional strain in his professional or family life, and initially, all of them were answered negatively.

I then asked the captain to assume that fear of flying in a pilot usually stems from a life event, and to dig deeply into his mind for

MY EXPERIENCES

such an occurrence, no matter how minor, a day or so before his flight to London. Very slowly and at times quite reluctantly, he described several seemingly-relevant events, beginning with his departure from his home for the flight. He recalled that just before he said goodbye to his wife, she accused him of giving too much attention to a female pilot at a glider club party the previous evening, and then, would not kiss him and wish him a safe flight, as she had always done in their marriage. He said that while driving his just-purchased, new car to Toronto International Airport, its carburetor caught on fire, which a passing motorist extinguished and then drove him a short distance to the airport. He stated that when he arrived at the airport, he telephoned the automobile dealership that sold him the car to ask it to retrieve the car from the side of the highway, checked into the flight operations office for Air Canada, and went into the pilot lounge to relax until he could board the airplane. He then remembered that while paging through an aviation magazine in the lounge, he read an article on fear of flying. He stated that he flew the B-747 to Great Britain without difficulty until he looked downwards at the British countryside through the large cockpit window at his left, and suddenly experienced severe, sustained fear, which made him incapable of piloting the airplane, which he turned over to his copilot. He then voluntarily grounded himself in Great Britain. At the end of our visit, the captain expressed strong emotional relief from identifying one or more emotionally-stressful events that, in my opinion, appeared to have triggered his fear of flying. He was agreeable to staying grounded until he was evaluated for his emotional fitness to work as an airline pilot by an aeromedical psychiatrist in Toronto, in coordination with the Regional Medical Director of Air Canada. He soon returned to work at Air Canada, and several weeks later I was at his glider club when he flew a plane towing a glider in which I was a passenger.

In the spring of 1974, my wife started to express strong misgivings about our family having moved back to Canada. She believed that career opportunities would be greater in the United States than in Canada our daughters and her, and was giving thought to working on a master's degree in bacteriology or immunology if we could return to the United States.

At the Annual Scientific Meeting of the Aerospace Medical Association in Washington, DC in May of 1974, Dr. Dille informed me that the U.S. Government had again lifted its freeze on filling the position of Chief of CAMI's Aeromedical Research Branch, and that he was hoping that I would apply for it. My application was successful.

My consultant office in Toronto was taken over by an occupational medicine physician and aviation medical examiner who had been hoping to establish a similar office in the Toronto International Airport area. With fond memories, I left my work as a consultant in aviation in Canada and as an emergency department physician in Orangeville, and we sold our country home and regrettably, our snowmobile.

7. As Chief of the Aeromedical Research Branch in the FAA Civil Aeromedical Institute (Oklahoma City, OK)

In July of 1974, we moved from Canada to a newly-built home that we had purchased on Valley Ridge Road in Norman, Oklahoma. Our home was a short, "back-roads" driving distance to CAMI, located at the FAA Aeronautical Center at the Will Rogers Airport on the southern edge of Oklahoma City. As sung in the musical show, "Oklahoma," the wind really "comes sweepin' down the plain." Then too, there's high summer heat and humidity, and many winter ice storms and spring tornado warnings to make life interesting in a state with strong Native-American and African-American histories, diversified geography, and the unique "Okie" accent and dialect.

As Chief of CAMI's Aeromedical Research Branch, I was responsible for the work of over 90 scientists and staff doing research in aviation physiology, psychology, toxicology, and protection and survival, and providing technical, veterinary, and statistical support for the research. The laboratory for each field of research and the

MY EXPERIENCES

units conducting the research were each headed by a scientist. I remember that when I arrived at CAMI, units in the Physiology Laboratory were determining whether the type and degree of "stress" that air traffic controllers experience can be reflected in their stress hormone levels, whether various over-the-counter drugs can hurt pilot performance, whether a subtle difference in people's EKGs may point to an increased risk for heart attack, and whether the reading of digital-strip gauge is more efficient than the reading of analog gauge when both have the same functions in an airplane cockpit. Units in the Psychology Laboratory were determining the emotional and mental qualities of a safe and effective air traffic controller, what air traffic control tests should be used in the selection of air traffic controllers and to assess progress during their training, and what effects background noise and shift work might have on air traffic controller performance. Units in the Toxicology Laboratory were engaged in identifying alcohol and prescribed, over-the-counter, and illicit drug levels in blood and fluids taken from pilots and others killed in aviation accidents, and possible adverse effects of low radiation levels at high altitudes on mammals. One unit in the Protection and Survival Laboratory was simulating small airplane crashes with manikins to determine the safest locations for harness and seat belt attachments to the frame of a small airplane, and evaluating the effectiveness of child safety seats. Another unit was developing an artistic technique for reconstructing the human face for identification purposes.

The Aeromedical Research Branch had access to an impressive array of on-site research equipment, including a large and a small decompression chamber, a fresh-water pool in which the fuselage of an airliner could be completely immersed, a wind tunnel that could blow hot and cold air, and a mock-up of the coach section of a B-727 which could be tilted at various angles to simulate loss of nose and landing gear during a simulated passenger evacuation of it. The physiologists had a Link flight simulator, a fully-operational Beechcraft V-Tail Bonanza four-passenger airplane, treadmills and bicycle ergometers, a cardiovascular tilt table, several instruments for measuring vital physiological functions, and an automated device for analyzing various blood chemicals. The psychologists had several rooms for individual and group performance testing of all sorts using sophisticated light-canceling and other devices while monitoring subjects with electroencephalography (EEG), which measures electrical activity in the brain, and electrooculography (EOG), which measures eye movements electronically. The Toxicology Laboratory had the latest in forensic analytical equipment. The Protection and Survival Laboratory had a high-speed track for the deceleration and impact testing particularly of airplane seats and cockpits while being recorded by two ultra-high-speed cameras.

"Flying" the Link flight simulator

From an organizational standpoint, CAMI was made up of four branches: Aeromedical Certification, to which pilots apply through FAA airman medical certification examiners for their airman medical certificates and request reconsideration of denied certificates; Aeromedical Education, which conducts training seminars to qualify physicians to conduct FAA airman medical certification examinations, and trains pilots on aviation medicine in-flight safety; Occupational Medicine, which supports the national air traffic controller program and manages occupational health problems at the Aeronautical Center and in CAMI. The Aeromedical Education Branch was also responsible for maintaining a library of books, journals, and documents related to aviation and general medicine. While I was at CAMI, its Director was Dr. Dille, who reported to the Federal Air Surgeon at FAA Headquarters in Washington, DC. Well in advance of new fiscal year, the scientists in the Research Branch presented each of their research proposals to a three-member panel from OAM, as

MY EXPERIENCES

well as to Dr. Dille, their laboratory head, and me, for our review and initial approval.

In the fall of 1974, I was sent to the FAA Management School in Lawton, Oklahoma, for several weeks, as required for all new managers. Most of my classmates had been air traffic control supervisors or aviation safety inspectors who, in addition to my training at the school, provided me a great start in understanding how the numerous components of the FAA function and interact. I also received my first training in racial and cultural diversity in the workplace, which I soon put to use in serving on the Aeronautical Center's Upward Mobility Team. Much more management training would follow in three week-long sessions for FAA executives in Williamsburg, Virginia, and Menninger Foundation lectures during a white-water rafting trip in Colorado and Utah.

On New Year's Day in 1975, I received a telephone call from Dr. Dille, who said that I was to leave immediately on a flight to Miami, Florida, where I would join a "Blue Ribbon Committee" being formed to study whether Eastern Airlines' 12 fatal airplane accidents in the past a few years had any sort of common cause. I did not learn from him, or subsequently from anyone else, who had requested or organized the committee. The first meeting of the committee was held the following morning at the headquarters of Eastern Airlines. The committee had three pre-selected chairs - one from Eastern, one from the FAA, and one from the Air Line Pilots Association (ALPA). Likewise, it had several pre-selected, Eastern/FAA/ALPA three-person panels, each being assigned an area of airline operations in which to look for possible contributions to the accidents, including human factors, mechanical factors, air traffic control, flight conditions, and pilot training. I served on the human factors panel along with the Medical Director of Eastern Airlines and the Medical Director of ALPA. Although the President of Eastern Airlines, retired astronaut Frank Borman, was very concerned about organizational bias in this study of his company's fatal airplane accidents, much to his chagrin the committee chairs decided to go ahead with it. They distributed all of the accident reports to the panels, and over the following four days, the panels reviewed them and prepared preliminary reports of their findings.

About two months later, the committee met in Miami the second time, and over two days finalized its findings and developed recommendations for accident prevention in Eastern Airlines. About six months after the committee was formed, it met for a day in Washington, DC to review its final report and turn over all of its working materials to whomever had ordered the committee's formation. The committee was then disbanded, and to my knowledge, its final report was never published. I recall that two common causes of Eastern Airlines' 12 fatal airplane accidents identified by the Blue Ribbon Committee were deficiencies and inconsistencies in pilot training in cockpit management in and between Eastern's airline pilot training centers.

I spent over two years at CAMI as Chief of its Aeromedical Research Branch. During that time, its scientists were making several noteworthy contributions to aviation medicine. Measurement of hormone levels in air traffic controllers found that air route traffic controllers had higher levels of chronic work stress (of cortisone in the urine) and airport air traffic controllers showed higher levels of acute work stress (of adrenaline, or epinephrine, in the urine); this data was interpreted in light of the current issue of so-called "air traffic controller burnout." Differences were being discovered among individuals in their mental ability to gather information and respond to it and were beginning to be applied successfully in the selection of air traffic controllers. Animal experiments were showing that extremely-toxic gases are emitted from burning wool and other materials used in the passenger cabins of airplanes, leading to immediate measures by textile manufacturers to reduce this hazard in and beyond the aviation environment. Crash testing of child restraint systems were finding that several of these systems were ineffective, and proving that the most effective systems were backward-facing. The emergency evacuation of airline "passengers"

MY EXPERIENCES

with simulated handicaps through exits of the simulated B-727 coach section ere providing data for seating handicapped passengers in locations from which they can be rapidly evacuated without impeding the evacuation of non-handicapped passengers.

While I was at CAMI, the U.S. National Transportation Safety Board (NTSB) published its report of a rapid, severe decompression that had occurred in a DC-10 flying at 39,000 feet over Albuquerque, New Mexico. The report stated that resulting symptoms from hypoxia, including brief loss of consciousness from temporary exposure to high altitude without breathing supplemental oxygen were experienced mainly by flight attendants, possibly due to their tolerance to hypoxia being reduced by their physical activity before and during the decompression. Moreover, a more recent decompression incident with loss of consciousness among flight attendants was being investigated by the NTSB. From my experience in decompression research in the RCAF and review of subsequent scientific literature on high-altitude decompression, I had learned that the time of useful consciousness (TUC, or time to take useful action to prevent incapacitation from hypoxia) is reasonably predictable for a physically-inactive person, but had not been determined for a physically-active person. From the two high altitude decompressions investigated by the NTSB, the physically-active flight attendants appeared to need oxygen sooner than the physically-inactive passengers during and after decompression, and Dr. E. Arnold Higgins, physiologist, and I set out to prove this.

In our study, 10 male and 10 female volunteers representative of the flight attendant population were exposed in CAMI's large decompression chamber to the DC-10's decompression profile (6,500 to 34,000 feet in 26 seconds, then descent at 5,000 feet per minute) while at rest and performing light-to-moderate work on a bicycle ergometer. TUC was determined with a light-cancellation, reaction-time test. The average TUC for females decreased from 54 seconds at rest to 32 seconds while performing work, and the average TUC for males decreased from 54 seconds at rest to 34 seconds while performing work (TUC difference not significant). These results led to an FAA directive stating that in the event of a decompression, flight attendants are to immediately sit down and breathe supplemental oxygen for the period of the emergency. The results also led the FAA to have the airlines tell their passengers that in the event of a decompression, a passenger is to don the oxygen mask for his or her seat, before helping anyone else, including children, don their mask.

I found that being the Chief of CAMI's Research Branch has its very interesting incidents, with three coming to mind. The first incident involved a part-time technician in the Psychology Laboratory who somehow plugged a set of electrooculography leads from a volunteer subject into an electrical socket instead of a recording instrument. The subject said that he enjoyed a dazzling display of all sorts of colors during his momentary shock. Ophthalmological and neurological evaluation of the subject did not find any eye, brain, or other bodily damage. The second incident occurred when the blades in the exhaust system over a fume hood in the Toxicology Laboratory were reinstalled backward when the system was serviced. Consequently, the highly toxic gases from burning a sample of woolen airline cabin material were blown back into the lab, leading to an emergency evacuation of CAMI and noisy visits by local fire trucks and ambulances. No one became ill from the incident. The third incident stemmed from a scientist in the Toxicology Laboratory receiving Dr. Dille's permission to donate some healthy mice from a just-completed study to a local middle school, where a teacher used the mice to demonstrate conditioned animal responses, such as teaching a mouse to strike a lever for a food pellet, in a class on behavioral psychology. Then the teacher asked the students if anyone wished to have a mouse to keep as a pet. One boy knew that his mother would object to him having any sort of a pet, but took a mouse home and hid it in a shoebox under his bed. The next day, the boy's mother saw the box, opened it, and was bit on the thumb by a very startled mouse. Local media took great joy in reporting the incident, I should note, with considerable embellishment. CAMI had to retrieve all of the mice

MY EXPERIENCES

given to the school. Reportedly, the mother sued the FAA for her mouse bite. Dr. Dille was silent on the outcome of the suit.

Several months after I arrived at CAMI, its Education Branch, headed by an outstanding lay educator in aviation medicine, James, "Jim" Harris, placed me on the roster of speakers at its FAA aviation medical examiner training seminars. Six seminars were usually conducted annually across the United States using the Federal Air Surgeon or the Deputy Federal Air surgeon, senior staff of OAM and CAMI involved with FAA airman medical certification and aircraft accident investigations, and consultants to the FAA in psychiatry, cardiology, ophthalmology, otolaryngology, endocrinology, and addiction medicine. Initially, I lectured on aviation physiology and research being conducted in CAMI's Aeromedical Research Branch, and presented anonymous pilot medical certification cases to a panel of the medical consultants, with each case presentation being followed by, "Would you fly with this pilot?"

Jim was greatly interested in educating pilots about preventable causes of airplane accidents, particularly alcoholic beverages, fatigue, various medications, and in-flight disorientation. He encouraged me to write a popular four-article series on visual illusions in flight for a pilot magazine that was published by the FAA, as well as the chapter on medical facts for pilots for a manual on pilot training, also published by the FAA.

While at CAMI, I received my Oklahoma license to practice medicine through Oklahoma's reciprocity agreement with Ohio and worked a 12-hour shift on weekends in emergency medicine in the emergency department of the Norman Regional Hospital. During my first shift, I noticed a distinct lack in the quality of health care by an inexperienced staff that consisted only of a licensed practical nurse (LPN) supervisor and certified nursing assistants (CNAs). After the shift, I commented on this to the full-time medical director of the emergency department, who simply told me that the hospital was having difficulty finding experienced RNs to hire. This patient care deficiency became sadly apparent the following weekend when I treated an adult male who was having a severe episode of asthma. After I examined him and started therapy, I asked a CNA to observe the patient in bed while I sutured a laceration and to inform me if he was not responding effectively to treatment. About 20 minutes later, I went to the bed where I had left the asthmatic patient, and he was gone. I asked what had happened to him, and the CNA said that she had discharged him under the assumption that I would do so after seeing that his breathing had improved. I immediately asked the LPN supervisor to telephone the patient's family to get a status report on the patient's asthma, and she was told that the patient was in extreme respiratory distress, has just lost consciousness, and was being returned to the hospital by ambulance. When the patient arrived at the emergency department, he could not be resuscitated and died. The next morning, I reported this incident in a closed-door session with the hospital's administrator and the medical director of the emergency department. They intently listened to me without comment or discussion, and then fired me without explanation. I have nothing further to report about the incident except that the emotional shock of it led me to end many years of working in emergency medicine.

An interesting story led to our unexpected move to Washington DC in 1976. When I arrived at CAMI, an FAA proposal to routinely use the double Master's two-step exercise test to detect coronary artery disease (CAD) in airline pilots during their FAA airman medical certification examinations had already been debated for several years. This proposal stemmed from the crash of a Lockheed Electra while it was landing at the Ardmore, Oklahoma airport in April of 1966, with 83 of its 98 military passengers and civilian crew perishing. The airplane was owned by the American Flyers Airline, which operated under contract with U.S. Military Command, and was being flown by the President of American Flyers, Reed Pigman. It was subsequently learned that during his FAA airman medical certification examinations, Mr. Pigman did not disclose that he was being treated

MY EXPERIENCES

for CAD and diabetes, either of which would have disqualified him as a pilot. The U.S. Civil Aeronautics Board investigated the crash and concluded that its probable cause was pilot incapacitation by coronary artery insufficiency, and so the FAA Federal Air Surgeon, Dr. Peter "Pete" Siegel proposed use of the Master's two-step exercise test to detect this condition during FAA airman medical certification examinations of professional pilots.

When I was the Medical Director of Continental Airlines, I joined the other major U.S. airline medical directors in opposing the double Master's two-step exercise test, basically for two reasons. First, Master's and similar cardiac stress testing performed on seemingly-healthy airline pilots would produce a significant incidence of false-positive EKGs, and consequently their grounding pending coronary angiography. Second, the risk of cardiac-related incapacitation of airline pilots was quite low, and even if one of the two pilots in an airline cockpit would become incapacitated, the other pilot was trained to take over flight control and conduct an emergency landing of the airplane.

The FAA Administrator, John Shaffer, and Dr. Siegel supported the Master's two-step test proposal. In late 1973, Dr. Siegel was invited to the White House to meet with two prominent persons in President Nixon's administration - H. R. "Bob" Haldeman, the White House Chief of Staff, and John Ehrlichman, the White House Domestic Affairs Advisor – both of whom advised him to drop the proposal. On the way back to FAA Headquarters from the meeting, Dr. Siegel had a heart attack which led to his immediately having emergency coronary artery bypass surgery. Thereafter, Dr. Siegel took a clinical position in the U.S. Navy, in which he had been a reservist, and his deputy, Dr. Homer "Rick" Reighard, was promoted to Federal Air Surgeon. At the Annual Scientific Meeting of the Aerospace Medical Association in Bal Harbour, Florida in May of 1976, Dr. Reighard asked me to be his deputy, and I accepted. The Master's two-step proposal was dropped.

My promotion to the super grade (G-17) position of FAA Deputy Federal Air Surgeon required that the Federal Government conduct a

DOUGLAS E. BUSBY

thorough background security check on me and that I be personally interviewed for the position by the FAA Administrator, Dr. John McLucas. My visit with Dr. McLucas was very pleasant. He described how the new John F. Kennedy Memorial Center nearby was raising local interest in the performing arts, asked me a few questions about my past work in aerospace medicine, and finally expressed his hope that I would enjoy living and working in Washington. As I left his office, his secretary invited me to join a group of U.S. Government employees on the White House lawn while President Ford welcomed the Prime Minister of Sweden to the United States.

8. As Deputy Federal Air Surgeon at FAA Headquarters (Washington, DC)

My wife and I then looked for a home for our family close to good schools and within a reasonable driving distance of FAA Headquarters. Initially, we were attracted to the condominiums that had recently been converted from office and hotel suites in the famed Watergate Hotel, but out of concern for cost and high levels of environmental noise, we purchased a home on Timber Hill Lane in a quiet area of Potomac, Maryland. The homes in the area had been built in a forest with lots of wildlife, including large raccoons which seemed to enjoy opening trash can lids and looking through windows at night. I have fond memories especially of our visiting the United States Capitol, National Monuments, Smithsonian Institution, and National Cathedral, and walking along the towpath on the Potomac section of the Chesapeake and Ohio Canal.

In early September of 1976, I moved into the FAA Deputy Federal Surgeon's office in FAA Headquarters at 800 Independence Avenue SW in Washington, DC. The day began with Dr. Reighard introducing me to the staff of OAM, and then showing me the headquarters' boardroom and where he would sit at a large oval table during daily staff and other meetings with the FAA Administrator. I recall Dr. Reighard's advice that as his deputy, I would be entitled to speak on his behalf only when a question is directed to me by the administrator

MY EXPERIENCES

or his deputy, adding that my answers should be short and to the point. He then took me to the FAA's Emergency Operations Center, recalling the many hours that he had spent there during a spate of hijackings of U.S. airliners that had reached its peak in early 1969. He pointed to his station in the Center, equipped for communicating with medical counterparts in other emergency centers, with consultants to the FAA from many medical specialties, and with other OAM personnel. When we returned to his office, he asked me to close the doors to the outer office area and the meeting room between our offices, and firmly stated to me that as his *"alter ego,"* he expected me to express any concerns that I might have with his functioning as Federal Air Surgeon only to him behind closed doors. He then asked me to open the doors to his office and warmly welcomed me to OAM. Dr. Reighard and I would become very close associates, with our sharing virtually every moment of our workdays.

Dr. Reighard had received his medical degree from Temple University and his master of public health degree from Harvard University. In 1950, he entered the USAF to serve for two years as a flight surgeon, and in 1953, he joined the Civil Aeronautics Administration, the predecessor of the FAA. His many accomplishments in the FAA before he became the Federal Air Surgeon in 1975 included making the first major revision of the medical standards for airman medical certification in the United States since 1926, and serving as chair of the U.S. Task Force on Deterrence of Air Piracy. Reportedly, he was responsible for the suggestion by the Task Force that the media reduce its immediate, detailed reporting of all hijackings of U.S. airliners, the adoption of which was associated with a steep decrease in hijackings. And he was responsible for suggesting to the Task Force that it consider the use of magnetometer technology to screen airline passengers for weapons, after reading an article on other uses of magnetometers in his son's copy of "Mechanics Illustrated." Over the years, Dr. Reighard became a specialist in aerospace medicine and served in various positions in OAM, including many years as the Deputy Federal Air Surgeon. At the

DOUGLAS E. BUSBY

time that I became his deputy, he was implementing a multi-professional monitoring system for airline pilots who had been reinstated after being grounded and treated for alcoholism.

Four days after I began to work at FAA Headquarters, I received an unexpected telephone call from Dr. Reighard at home in the early evening. At the time, Dr. Reighard was speaking at an FAA airman medical certification examiner training seminar in Seattle, Washington. He said that a Trans World Airlines B-727 flying from New York to Chicago had just been hijacked and that I shouldt go immediately to the Federal Air Surgeon's station in the FAA's Emergency Operations Center, gather information on the person or persons who had hijacked the airplane, including the possible history of similar activity, and stand by with the FAA's consultant psychologist, Dr. John Dailey, to have a telephone conference call with him to determine how OAM might contribute to a favorable outcome of the hijacking.

When I arrived at the Operations Center, I learned that the airplane had been taken over by five "Fighters for Free Croatia," a group seeking Croatian independence from Yugoslavia. The hijackers claimed that they had bombs with them and had placed a bomb in a locker at the Grand Central Station in New York, wanted to appeal to the American People for Croatia's independence in five major U.S. newspapers, and had ordered the captain of the airplane to redirect it to Montréal, Canada. At this point in the hijacking, Dr. Reighard, Dr. Dailey, and I had a conference call and agreed that since the hijackers were not carrying hand-held weapons, the "bombs" in the airplane and locker were likely fake and that yielding to the hijackers' wishes would likely lead their surrendering to the authorities. I passed our thoughts directly to Dr. William Coleman, Jr., Secretary of Transportation, and Dr. McLucas, both of whom had just arrived in the Emergency Operations Center, as well as to others in the center. A few minutes later, we were informed that the locker bomb had just exploded while it was being dismantled, killing a New York police officer; later, the airplane bombs were found to be fake.

MY EXPERIENCES

The hijacked airplane was refueled in Montréal, then flown to Newfoundland, Canada, where 30 of the 86 passengers were released and the airplane refueled, and then to Iceland, where it was refueled again. Before the airplane arrived in Iceland, I made a telephone call to the medical commander of the USAF base there to discuss possible emergency medical support for the airplane's crew and passengers, and was assured that his medical facilities and staff would be ready should this support be needed. The airplane had to overfly Great Britain because the British government refused permission for it to land there. After tense negotiations with the French government, the airplane was allowed to land near Paris, France, after the hijackers dropped leaflets promoting Croatian independence over the Avenue des Champs-Élysées. The hijackers surrendered peacefully, and no injuries or deaths occurred as a direct result of the hijacking.

I had several major responsibilities as the FAA Deputy Federal Air Surgeon. One was reviewing the individual medical files of pilots who have a medical condition that resulted in their having been denied an FAA airman medical certificate, as required by Part 67 of the Title 14 of the Code of Federal Regulations. These pilots had already appealed unsuccessfully to CAMI's Aeromedical Certification Branch for reconsideration and were requesting an exemption to Part 67 to the Administrator of the FAA. Each file was prepared for the Federal Air Surgeon by the Medical Standards Division of the OAM. The file would contain all of the medical records pertinent to the pilot's medical condition, often including the report of a review of these records by a panel of medical specialists serving as consultants to the Federal Air Surgeon. And the file would also contain a letter of exemption or denial addressed to the pilot and signed by the Federal Air Surgeon (or, if he was absent, by the Deputy Federal Air Surgeon) on behalf of the Administrator of the FAA. This exemption system could have its failures, which OAM tried to identify by closely monitoring airplane incidents and accidents for probable medically-related causes. A possible failure occurred when a private pilot who was granted an exemption for Parkinson's disease reportedly controlled by the drug, levodopa, lost control of his airplane and crashed, killing his wife and him. An actual failure occurred when an exemption was based on incomplete or distorted facts. In December of 1976, a 33-year-old pilot was buzzing the Baltimore Stadium with a small rented airplane less than 10 minutes after the Pittsburgh Steelers beat the Baltimore Colts in an American Football Conference playoff game, when he crashed the airplane into the stadium's upper deck. Fortunately, no serious injuries occurred. The pilot had a long history of aberrant behavior, which led to his being grounded and reinstated with an exemption after the U.S. Aircraft Owners and Pilots Association (AOPA) had a well-known psychiatrist vouch for this pilot's sanity, which was soon disproven while the pilot now had an airman medical certificate. He was arrested a week before the game for using the airplane to drop rolls of toilet paper and a bottle on a restaurant owned by a former linebacker for the Colts, and two days before the game had used the plane to buzz the stadium and drop blue-and-white neckties on the playing field while the Colts were practicing.

My major responsibilities also included giving support to OAM operations. I worked closely with OAM's Administrative Officer and her staff in managing the budget for the FAA's aviation medicine program, preparing the annual budget, and maintaining so-called "backup books" of documents for use by the Federal Air Surgeon in answering questions on the program in Congressional budgetary and other hearings. A special project was helping Dr. Reighard to prepare his introductory statement and a backup book for a congressional hearing on the FAA's rule for the mandatory retirement of airline pilots at age 60. When Dr. Reighard was rushing out of the Rayburn House Office Building after being intensely questioned for an entire day of the hearing, he slipped on a marble stair and injured his lower back, and had to be immediately hospitalized for treatment of the injury. Consequently, I had to take his place the next day in a Congressional hearing on the FAA's budget in the same building. I recall many questions coming at me from the brilliant congresswoman

MY EXPERIENCES

with the iconic hat, Bella Abzug, who in particular wanted to know what the FAA was doing to prevent alcohol-related airplane accidents.

Yet another of my major responsibilities was conducting an overview of aeromedical research activities at CAMI. While I was at CAMI, I had participated in the review of annually-submitted research proposals by the scientists in its Research Branch, and Dr. Reighard asked me to continue to do so as the FAA Deputy Federal Air Surgeon. Moreover, he had me review all of the pre-publish reports of the scientists in the Aeromedical Research Branch at CAMI and OAM staff. Snce I was quite familiar with the research that the Toxicology Laboratory in the Aeromedical Research Branch at CAMI was doing on burning airplane interior materials, Dr. Reighard appointed me to represent him on the FAA's Special Aviation Fire and Explosion Reduction (SAFER) Advisory Committee.

During the three years that I served as Deputy Federal Air Surgeon, Dr. Reighard had me represent him at three international events. The first was the International Congress of Aviation and Space Medicine in Johannesburg, South Africa in 1976. I spoke at its opening session on advances being made in aerospace medicine. The session was attended by John Vorster, the prime minister of South Africa and a staunch supporter of apartheid, which had led to South Africa's exclusion from the global economy and the recent Soweto uprising. Consequently, I, among several attendees from the United States and other countries, did not stand when he entered the meeting room. To my knowledge, no comment was made on what we had done, but perhaps, as a form of retaliation, a reporter who was well known in South Africa for being confrontational, attempted to get me to make a negative, racially-charged comment about Dr. Coleman, the prominent African-American U.S. Secretary of Transportation.

The second event was Rehabilitation USA in Tokyo, Japan in 1977. Before I traveled to Tokyo to attend it, Dr. Reighard asked me to fly 14 hours non-stop from New York on a Pan American World Airways B-747SP (SP for special performance) which had been designed to fly at least 1,000 nautical miles further than a standard B-747. He had been told that B-747SP flight attendants and passengers on this flight were complaining of eye and respiratory tract irritation from cigarette smoke, possibly due to one or more of this airplane's air-conditioning "packs," which operate like jet engines, being shut down at cruise altitude to conserve fuel. I was welcomed by both of the flight deck crews who would operate this long flight, during which I sat in the jump seat behind the captain or in a passenger seat on the upper deck of the B-747. I made several walk-throughs of the passenger cabin during the flight and found that the accumulation of cigarette smoke bordered on intolerable for me in the aft section of the airplane when air-conditioning packs were shut down and many passengers were smoking cigarettes. Fortunately, the no-smoking rule for U.S. airline travel in the United States and abroad was soon to come into being.

Rehabilitation USA was held at the behest of the Japanese government to familiarize its government, industry, and social services with how the United States enhances the quality of life for people with disabilities. In a seminar at the U.S. Embassy, I spoke and answered questions about the study of the emergency evacuation of handicapped airline passengers that had been conducted at CAMI.

Speech at the U.S. Embassy in Tokyo

A highlight of the Tokyo event for me was meeting the Canadian-born actor, J. Harold Russell, who had lost both of his hands in an accidental explosion while he was teaching demolition during WW II. The epic film, "The Best Years of Our Lives" was based on his accident, and for starring in it he received an Academy Award for Best Supporting Actor and an honorary Academy Award. Mr. Russell served as chair of the Tokyo event, during which I was repeatedly amazed by his dexterity in

MY EXPERIENCES

operating hook mechanisms for his hands, especially in removing his reading glasses from a suitcoat pocket and putting them on.

The third event was the groundbreaking for the new U.S. Army Aeromedical Research Laboratory at Fort Rucker, Alabama in 1978. It was attended mainly by aerospace medical specialists from the other military services and the military services of other NATO countries. I participated in it as the representative of the FAA, speaking about the past and future contributions of the laboratory to civil as well as military aerospace medicine. The groundbreaking was followed by its attendees being given earplugs and seated in bleachers above a valley to watch a battlefield demonstration below. It started with dozens of well-camouflaged soldiers unexpectedly appearing throughout the valley and a Black Hawk helicopter suddenly rising beside the bleachers. The soldiers fired mortars and the helicopter fired rockets at several fake tanks in the valley. I heard that a few days later, a U.S. congressman asked the Army how it could justify spending so much taxpayer money firing weapons, to entertain a group of physicians!

I became involved in another U.S. airliner hijacking in October of 1977. A morning flight of a Frontier Airlines B-737 from Grand Island, Nebraska had been boarded by a man who bolted through the security checkpoint onto the airplane, brandishing a sawed-off shotgun and demanding to be flown to Atlanta, Georgia. The airplane had been refueled in Kansas City, Missouri, where the hijacker released 18 women and children, and a male heart patient, and had just arrived in Atlanta, when Dr. Reighard contacted me from the FAA's Emergency Operations Center and asked me to take a pair of special headphones to Atlanta. He said that if the hijacker would unknowingly use them instead of cockpit headphones in communicating with people on the ground, the special headphones could be remotely activated to send a powerful, incapacitating shock of electricity through the hijacker's head. Two FAA pilots, one of them a developer of the special headphones, and I immediately flew to Atlanta in an FAA airplane, my first ride in the new Beechcraft Super King Air 200. The Frontier airplane was parked at the far end of the

DOUGLAS E. BUSBY

Atlanta International Airport, about 150 yards from a small-aircraft terminal, surrounded by many police vehicles blocking the area from the media and sightseers. Inside the terminal lobby were special agents from the Atlanta Federal Bureau of Investigation (FBI) office and police officers from four local constituencies. A trained FBI "negotiator" was communicating with the hijacker from the terminal manager's office. So many loaded weapons had been placed against a lobby wall that the Atlanta FBI Special Agent-in-Charge had them placed in an empty office out of expressed concern that a weapon could fall over and accidentally discharge.

Soon after we arrived and everyone was gathering for a briefing on the hijacking, attention focused momentarily on the arrival of "Atlanta's coroner," dressed in a white jumpsuit with a black belt holding a matching pair of gleaming long-barrel pistols with mother-of-pearl handles, seemingly ready to take on the hijacker single-handed. In the briefing, I learned that the hijacker and his male partner, both gay, had recently robbed an Atlanta bank and been arrested for it. The hijacker had been released on bond and his partner until their trial, scheduled to begin the day after the hijacking.

From the time the hijacker boarded the airplane, he repeatedly demanded the release of his partner from jail, three million dollars, two parachutes, a variety of guns, and a commitment to fly his partner and him away from Atlanta. At the time of the briefing, 11 male passengers, two stewardesses, and the captain and first officer were still on the airplane. Although the captain of the airplane had repeatedly stuck his arm out of the left cockpit window to signal his need for a gun to shoot the hijacker, the FBI decided to use negotiations instead of force to end the hijacking. However, by late afternoon, the hijacker was becoming quite impatient. An FBI marksman was unsuccessful in aiming at the hijacker, who shielded himself with a hostage while he was in the airplane's doorway. Then the hijacker released the airplane's two stewardesses as a "gesture of good faith," after which two female FBI special agents dressed in Frontier Airlines stewardess uniforms started to walk towards the

MY EXPERIENCES

airplane to be replacements for them, but had to stop and return to the terminal when the hijacker asked them to expose areas on their bodies where they were carrying holstered pistols. Soon thereafter, two FBI agents who were qualified to fly the B-737 arrived, and the hijacker was informed that they instead of the present flight deck crew would have to fly the airplane if it was to leave the Atlanta area. The FAA pilots were dressed in Frontier Airlines' captain and first officer uniforms, briefed by me on use of the special earphones, and told by the FAA negotiator to stand by to board the airplane. As time passed, the hijacker spoke with his partner and parents, who unsuccessfully encouraged him to surrender, released the 11 remaining male passengers, and was visited on the airplane by the attorney who would be representing him and his partner in their trial. After the attorney and hijacker met for about one-half hour, the hijacker walked to the back of the airplane, sat in a passenger seat, and shot himself in the heart. I followed the FBI Special Agent-in-Charge and Atlanta's coroner onto the airplane immediately after hearing that the hijacker had taken his life, and witnessed the grim scene that ended the hijacking. Several weeks later, I heard that the special earphones had been destroyed.

In early 1979, Dr. Reighard and I were appointed to the Senior Executive Service of the U.S. Government, with the advantage of receiving priority consideration for Senior Executive positions that might open in the government, hopefully with higher salaries. About that time, Dr. Reighard suggested that I join a group of Civil Service physicians who were "lobbying" for a $10,000 annual bonus that physicians in several other civilian branches of the Government were already receiving. The salary of Civil Service physicians in the U.S. Government had been capped at $37,500, the maximum salary for members of Congress. I joined the group, and over several weeks we met with many members of Congress and their staff, all of whom agreed with us that the bonus should be applied equally to all non-military physicians working in the U.S. Government, but took no action on this.

DOUGLAS E. BUSBY

In the late spring of 1979, my wife Barbara completed her doctorate in immunology and was planning to conduct post-doctoral research for at least a year, and our daughters, Suzanne, Sharon, and Stephanie, were expecting to enter college within four years. Consequently, I started to give thought to leaving the FAA for higher-salaried, non-governmental employment. In June of 1979, I unexpectedly received a telephone call from Dr. Joseph "Joe" Tomashefski, Chair of the Department of Pulmonary Medicine at the Cleveland Clinic in Cleveland, Ohio, who had been one of my professors in the aerospace medicine residency program at Ohio State. He said that he had recommended me to be the Chair of the new Department of Environmental Health at the Clinic and that I would soon be contacted by Abraham "Abe" Brickner, the Clinic's Director of Development, regarding this position.

9. As Chair of the Department of Environmental Health at the Cleveland Clinic (Cleveland, OH)

In our lengthy conversation by telephone, Mr. Brickner informed me that the Cleveland Clinic had recently studied the feasibility of developing an occupational medicine program to support industry in and beyond the Cleveland area. He said that the report of the study led the Clinic's Board of Governors to approve the program and place it in a newly-formed Department of Environmental Health in its Division of Medicine. He stated that the Board had recommended that the program be headed by an occupational medicine specialist who would primarily be a consultant on occupationally-related medical problems in patients referred to or within the Clinic. Moreover, the program would employ an RN with clinical and administrative experience in occupational medicine to help the local industry get occupational medicine support, and an industrial hygienist to conduct hazard evaluations required by the Federal Government's Occupational Safety and Health Administration (OSHA). Finally, he added that the board had suggested that the Clinic's executive health evaluation program be placed in the Department of Environmental

MY EXPERIENCES

Health, as a conduit for introducing its occupational medicine services to executives whose companies might need them.

I gave much thought to the possibility of leaving my position as the FAA's Deputy Federal Air Surgeon to become the Chair of the Department of Environmental Health at the Cleveland Clinic, and a few days later telephoned Mr. Brickner to express interest in visiting the Clinic to discuss the position and to meet physicians with whom I would be working. My first meeting at the Clinic was scheduled with Dr. Richard "Dick" Farmer, Chair of the Clinic's Division of Medicine and Department of Gastroenterology, who would be my direct superior. After I waited for him in his reception area for over an hour, he arrived, asked his secretary who I was, and standing with his back to me loudly berated her for scheduling my visit with him at an inconvenient time for him. I immediately decided that I would be unable to tolerate Dr. Farmer as my superior, and as I started to leave the reception area, he turned around, warmly welcomed me to the Clinic, and ushered me into his office to discuss how the Department of Environmental Health might function. Thereafter, I visited with Dr. Tomashefski, and with each of the chairs of several other Clinic departments, including Neurosurgery, Ophthalmology, Orthopedics, Audiology, Cardiology, and combined Psychiatry and Psychology. Finally, I met together with Dr. William "Bill" Kiser, Chair of the Clinic's Board of Governors, Dr. Shattuck "Shad" Hartwell, Jr., Director of Professional Staff Affairs (Chief of Staff), and Mr. Brickner, to review the anticipated responsibilities of the chair of the Clinic's Department of Environmental Health. Dr. Kiser stated that if I wished, I could also perform executive health evaluations and FAA airman medical certification examinations, and be a consultant in aerospace medicine beyond the Clinic. As our meeting ended, Dr. Kiser made me a verbal offer of employment, with substantial increases in salary and fringe benefits over what I had been receiving from the FAA. He noted that the Board of Governors would have to approve his offer, "as a formality." During my visit to the Clinic, my family found a possible home for us on Lyman Circle, a quiet, tree-lined street in Shaker Heights.

Three days after my visit to the Cleveland Clinic, Dr. Kiser informed me by telephone that its Board of Governors had approved me to be the Chair of its Department of Environmental Health. After I received the formal offer of this position and accepted it, I resigned from the FAA and we purchased the Shaker Heights home. Then, 10 days after my visit to the Clinic, Dr. Kiser called me by telephone and said that the Board had just decided not to have an occupational medicine program in the Clinic for the reason that some of the Clinic's orthopedists and neurosurgeons had become concerned that the program would burden their departments with chronic workers' compensation cases, especially fabricated and exaggerated chronic lower back problems. My reply initially focused on the marked impact that the Board's change of mind would have on me professionally and financially, in that I had resigned from a senior position in the FAA, and my wife and I would probably lose the large deposit that we had made to purchase the Shaker Heights home. Then I expressed my bewilderment to him over the fact that none of the Clinic's physicians who had interviewed me had voiced concern for the Department of Environmental Health burdening their departments with workers' compensation cases. Consequently, he invited me to return to the Clinic for the second round of interviews, during which I downplayed the potential for the department to become a referral center within the Clinic for persons receiving workers' compensation, and stressed the much wider range of clinical activities in occupational medicine. A day after my second visit to the Clinic, I was hired by its Board.

In late August of 1979, we moved to Shaker Heights, one of several small cities that closely surround Cleveland. Shaker Heights is widely known for its educational excellence, and stringent building codes and zoning laws. Suzanne entered the John Carroll University in nearby University Heights. Sharon was to stay in Potomac for her last year of high school, but transferred at mid-year to the Case Western Reserve University and then to the Cleveland Institute of Music.

MY EXPERIENCES

Stephanie went to the Shaker Heights High School for a year, immediately after which she was invited to participate in an early-entry program at the Wilfred Laurier University in Waterloo, Ontario, Canada. Barbara began post-doctoral research in immunology at the Case Western Reserve University Hospital in Cleveland.

Until the day that I started to work at the Cleveland Clinic, I was unaware that the Board had formed an oversight committee to monitor and guide all of the occupational medicine activities of the Department. The committee consisted of Dr. Tomashefski, Joseph "Joe" Hahn, Chair of the Department of Neurosurgery, Dr. Froncie Gutman, Chair of the Department of Ophthalmology, Dr. Kenneth Marks, representing Dr. Alan Wilde, Chair of the Department of Orthopedics, Dr. Richard "Dick" Steinhilber, Chair of the Department of Psychiatry and Psychology, and Mr. Brickner. This committee met with me monthly for over a year, primarily to review my progress in developing the department. However, our meetings were usually rendered unconstructive by Dr. Gutman making negative remarks on allowing the practice of occupational medicine in the Clinic, Dr. Marks reiterating Dr. Wilde's concern for the Department of Orthopedics being burdened by chronic workers' compensation cases referred to it by the Department of Environmental Health, with Dr. Tomashefski and Dr. Steinhilber refuting their views and Mr. Brickner being silent.

My initial activity in the Department of Environmental Health was to standardize and optimize its executive health evaluation program since the content of the health evaluations varied remarkably among the companies which were participating in the program. The department's three internal medicine specialists who were conducting the evaluations and I decided that every executive should have a detailed medical, social, and work history, a thorough physical examination, a comprehensive battery of laboratory tests, an audiogram, and a resting EKG. And if indicated, an executive should also have a chest x-ray, and under current medical guidelines, all executives a proctosigmoidoscopy and female executives a mammogram and Pap test. We decided that other studies (e.g., cardiac exercise stress testing, colonoscopy) should be considered diagnostic, and therefore beyond the scope of an executive health evaluation. Finally, we believed that every executive should, if necessary, be offered the opportunity to have a consultation with the department's nutritionist. This standardized evaluation protocol was well received by the participants in the program, and soon led to a substantial increase of participants in it.

The occupational medicine activities of the Department of Environmental Health began with visits by Mr. Brickner's associate and me, and then by an independent consultant in occupational medicine management and me, to several companies in northern Ohio, to assess their needs for occupational medicine support. Some companies had medical departments to conduct pre-employment medical examinations, drug screening, and the employee health monitoring required by OSHA, as well as to treat occupational injuries. Other companies were using clinics that provided limited occupational medicine services. Our visits identified the need for occupational medicine support by free-standing and hospital-based clinics staffed by physicians with broad expertise in occupational medicine in several areas of northern Ohio. They also identified the need for industrial hygiene services, even within the Cleveland Clinic. Consequently, I proposed to add to the department an RN with clinical and administrative experience in occupational medicine to help companies identify and meet the need for occupational medicine support, and an industrial hygienist to conduct on-site, OSHA-required occupational hazard evaluations. Meanwhile, I began to serve as a consultant on possible occupational medical problems in patients referred to me within the Clinic and by various companies.

Unforgettable Memories: Serving as an Expert Witness in Friends for All Children v. Lockheed Aircraft

In the late fall of 1979, Dr. Reighard gave my name to an Alexandria, Virginia law firm to be a possible expert witness in suits that Friends for All Children (FFAC) had brought against the Lockheed Aircraft

MY EXPERIENCES

Corporation. This suit was for the cost of treating minimal brain dysfunction (MBD) among the 150 orphaned Vietnamese infants who had survived the crash of a USAF Lockheed C-5 Galaxy transport airplane that was transporting them from South Viet Nam to the United States on April 4, 1975. My anticipated role in this suit would be to testify on the possible contributions of environmental factors to the MBD.

With permission from Dr. Kaiser and Dr. Farmer, I joined a team of other selected expert witnesses in Washington, DC, to learn in detail about the accident and MBD and to testify in the first suit to be presented in the Court of Appeals for the Third Circuit. We were told that with the war in Viet Nam rapidly coming to an end, on April 3, 1975, President Ford had authorized "Operation Babylift," to evacuate as many orphaned infants and children as possible from South Vietnamese orphanages on 30 USAF flights using C-5 and Lockheed C-141 Starlifter transport airplanes. The FFAC was one of several adoption organizations in the United States and abroad that had petitioned the U.S. Government for the evacuation, and had subsequently found homes for 2,600 infants who were evacuated. The disastrous first C-5 flight originated at Saigon's Tan Son Nhut Air Base. It carried about 313 people, including 243 orphaned infants and children, 44 escorts, 16 flight crew, and 10 medical crew. Over 150 orphaned infants were placed in this airplane's upper compartment, with 150 of them surviving and most of their escorts perishing in the crash. Almost all of the 175 adults and orphaned infants and children who were placed in its lower compartment perished in the crash.

The loading of the ill-fated C-5 took several hours in South Viet Nam's hot (average 94°F) and humid (average 65%) April daytime weather. The infants in its upper compartment were passed brigade-style up a stairway and strapped in pairs into hard bucket seats. The C-5 took off at 4:00 PM local time for Clark Air Base in the Philippines. When the C-5 reached 23,000 feet in altitude, its large, rear pressure door suddenly opened and detached, causing an "explosive decompression" of its cabin atmosphere, and severing all control cables to its rudder and elevator. The C-5 went into an uncontrolled descent that could be partially reduced by increasing the thrust of its four jet engines, but not enough to get the airplane back to Tan Son Nhut Air Base. We were told that the C-5 struck a dike along the Saigon River, and was broken into five sections – cockpit, fuselage, wings, and tail – all skidding in various directions and distances across the rice paddies beyond the dike, with the impact weight of the upper compartment of the fuselage crushing its lower compartment. We were also told that armed conflict was occurring around the crash site as survivors were being evacuated from it, so only a few pictures were taken of the site; moreover, an accident investigation team could not reach it. The pictures showed infants being passed to rescuers through a post-crash, ground-level door of the upper compartment, which had a half-cylinder shape like a Quonset hut.

The briefing continued with our being told why we had been asked to serve as expert witnesses for the FFAC. Several adoptive parents of infants who had been in the C-5 crash had informed the FFAC that as their infants grew into childhood, they developed signs of minimal brain dysfunction (MBD), such as hyperactivity, learning disability, and short attention span. The FFAC had funded a study to verify this, by having several children examined by pediatric neurologists, psychiatrists, and psychologists in university medical centers. Included in the study were several pairs of twins, with every twin who had been in the crash having MBD, and every twin who had not been in the crash not having MBD. The FFAC and its pediatric medical consultants raised the question of whether the cause of the MBD was whiplash due to an abrupt, rather than a gradual deceleration of the C-5's upper compartment as it skidded across the rice paddies, since recent human factors research had found that an infant who sustains whiplash in an automobile accident is prone to develop MBD, probably for the reason that the bones of the skull are not yet fused to fully protect the brain. However, descriptions of the C-5 crash indicated that deceleration of the upper compartment containing the infants was gradual, and whiplash was dismissed as a likely cause of the MBD. Then I was asked

MY EXPERIENCES

what other environmental factors might have been causative. Initially, I suggested that hypoxia from exposure to atmospheric altitudes from 23,000 down to 8,000 feet should be considered a possibility. However, I then proposed that prolonged exposure of the infants to the high environmental heat and humidity during the long process of loading the C-5 could have rendered them hyperthermic and dehydrated, and their brains much less able to tolerate hypoxia, and therefore prone to injury from a combination of hyperthermia and hypoxia. I felt that the nature of the C-5 crash precluded exposure to spilled jet fuel or fumes as a risk factor for brain injury. Finally, I stated that low-intensity whiplash should not be ruled out as contributing to brain injury, especially when combined with hyperthermia and hypoxia.

Over a several-month period, I testified in three individual trials on these possible environmental causes of MBD children who had been involved as infants in the C-5 airplane crash. While the law firm for FFAC was preparing for the fourth trial, a package with numerous pictures of the C-5 accident scene was placed in the firm's doorway one morning. Later that day, the firm's lead attorney for the FFAC trials informed me that the pictures clearly showed that scene was visited by Lockheed and U.S. Department of Defense accident investigators after the accident, and most important to the MBD issue, that the upper compartment had been abruptly stopped by a large mound of dirt as it skidded across the rice paddies. Later, the attorney told me that because of this revelation, the Court of Appeals had issued a "guilty" judgment against Lockheed and the United States on all of the FFAC cases, without retrial or trial.

Back at the Cleveland Clinic, I now participated in the executive health evaluation program, performed FAA airman medical certification examinations and consultations, received consultant requests for patients with possible occupational health problems, and began to assess percentages of permanent partial impairment from occupational injuries and illnesses for workers' compensation service companies. And beyond the Clinic, I gave lectures on protection from lead exposure to the employees of two brass foundries, was asked to

DOUGLAS E. BUSBY

design a free-standing occupational health clinic to serve a cluster of companies in the Akron-Canton area of Ohio. I and joined the Tri-State Occupational Medical Association and Western Reserve Medical Directors Association, eventually serving each as president. After several months as the Chair of the Clinic's Department of Occupational Health, I felt that the growing scope and amount of my work in occupational medicine justified the addition of an RN with occupational health experience and an industrial hygienist to the department, and the Clinic's Board of Governors approved searches to fill these positions.

In the fall of 1980, I was appointed, again on the recommendation of Dr. Reighard, to a committee of medical specialists formed by NASA to advise NASA on medical standards for the selection of mission specialists, and the in-flight and post-flight medical tests to be performed on them in NASA's Space Shuttle Program. We had three, two-day meetings at NASA's Lyndon B. Johnson Space Center in Houston, Texas, during which the aerospace medical specialists and physiologists who worked at the center briefed us on what was presently known about the effects of space flight on human beings, gave us a tour of the Center, and participated in our deliberations. In the tour, we were shown the shuttle's crew compartment and fuselage modules used in training the shuttle crews, and how special tiles were attached to the outer surface of a shuttle to absorb the intense heat generated by its friction with the atmosphere during a shuttle's return from space. Later, a colleague at NASA whom I knew expressed her concern to me over the possibility that a tile could become detached from a shuttle during atmospheric re-entry, and the shuttle be destroyed.

The committee's third meeting was on April 14, 1981, the day that the first space shuttle, Columbia, was launched for a 55-hour, 36-earth-orbit test spaceflight. The committee was invited to sit in an observation room above and behind the Space Center's new mission control facility, to observe information on spacecraft functioning, location, and direction, as it appeared on projection screens in front

MY EXPERIENCES

of the five rows of flight controllers, and to watch the two astronauts "bed down" for the night. A gentleman seated next to me remarked how much spaceflight monitoring had advanced over the years. I introduced myself to him and smiling, he introduced himself to me as "Commander Shepard." I will never forget this moment in my career in having the privilege of meeting Alan Shepard, the first American in space (Project Mercury), the fifth astronaut to walk on the moon (Project Apollo) - and the first astronaut to hit a golf ball on the moon. We continued to talk for several more minutes about the future of spaceflight and our past experiences at the Lovelace Foundation.

In the summer of 1981, I served as an expert witness in a court case in Toronto. Several airline flight inspectors who had been retired early by Transport Canada were suing Air Canada as a group for denying them employment as pilots because their ages exceeded its Air Canada's age limit for the hiring of pilots. The retired flight inspector pilots were being supported in their suit by Canada's Equal Employment Opportunity Commission, which enforces the Age Discrimination in Employment Act (ADEA) of 1967. At the time, Air Canada was an independent Crown corporation, wholly-owned and regulated by the Canadian government so, in essence, this case involved the Canadian government suing itself. To further complicate matters, CALPA, the professional union for Air Canada's pilots, was supporting Air Canada in defending the age limit.

The hearing of this case took about a week. On the first day, I took an early-morning flight on Air Canada from Cleveland (Ohio) to Toronto via London (Ontario). In London, I was temporarily retained, along with the airplane, by an Immigration Canada official as he tried to determine whether my being an expert witness on Canadian soil in a case of Canada v. Canada should be considered the unapproved, gainful employment of a citizen of the United States (I did not know that I was a dual citizen of Canada and the United States at that time). After a half-hour delay, the official shook his head in confusion and dramatically waved me onto the airplane.

DOUGLAS E. BUSBY

Air Canada placed me in a suite in the Sheraton (now Westin) Harbour Castle Hotel overlooking Lake Ontario and Toronto Island with its small but very busy airport. I mention my rather elaborate accommodations for the week because my daughter, Stephanie, was able to leave Wilfred Laurier University in Waterloo to spend two memorable days in Toronto, watching me testify in court and visiting with several Air Canada pilots while dining in Toronto's finer restaurants.

In the late summer and early fall of 1981, the *status quo* of the Department of Environmental Health was shaken by three events directly involving it. First, the planning team for a new Cleveland Clinic central building decided to relocate the department in this building, with substantially less floor space and consequently no room for its expansion. Second, a highly-qualified occupational health RN and an industrial hygienist, according to their resumés and references, were employed by the department and did not fulfill what was expected of them, so their employment had to be terminated. Third, the Clinic's Board of Governors rejected a proposal that the department conduct the comprehensive health evaluations portion of a large, long-term epidemiologic study, called the Air Force Health Study.

The purpose of the Air Force Health Study was to determine whether USAF personnel who had served in Viet Nam had experienced adverse health effects from Operation Ranch Hand, which involved spraying the herbicide, Agent Orange, to defoliate trees and brush along rivers and roads to expose enemy troops. During a visit to the Clinic, the study's coordinator, Colonel Roy DeHart, Commander of the USAF School of Aerospace Medicine, informed Dr. Kiser, Mr. Brickner, and me that the Clinic would be ideal for the study because it had a department of environmental health headed by a physician who is familiar with research planning and budgeting, a national reference laboratory for accurate biochemical and blood cell analyses, and an onsite hotel for two-night stays by the study participants. Immediately after Dr. DeHart's visit, I sent a proposal for the study, outlining it many benefits to the Clinic, to Dr.

MY EXPERIENCES

Kiser, Dr. Farmer, and Mr. Brickner. A few days later, Dr. Farmer personally informed me that Dr. Kiser had presented the memo to the Clinic's Board of Governors, which had decided not to become involved in the study because the Clinic had a policy of not conducting government-funded research. I asked him to clarify this policy for me in light of a substantial number of clinical research projects at the Clinic being supported by the National Institutes of Health as an agency of the Federal Government. He replied that the policy probably related to the Clinic's decision not to engage in medical research for the U.S. Department of Defense, and then advised me to give no further thought to the study. I notified Dr. DeHart of the board's decision. At a subsequent annual meeting of the Aerospace Medical Association, he told me that the 1,242 health evaluations in the first of six cycles of the study were being performed over one year at the Kelsey-Seybold Clinic in Houston and that the other five evaluation cycles would be conducted at the Scripps Clinic and Research Foundation in La Jolla, California.

After these three events, I requested a meeting with Dr. Farmer and the oversight committee. I reviewed successes and failures in my attempt to establish an occupational medicine program in the department over the prior two years, noting that space for it, including an expanded executive health evaluation program, would now be quite limited in the new clinic building. I suggested that for the time being, the department's activities be limited to its successful executive health evaluation program, FAA airman medical certification examinations and consultations, and my consultant activities in occupational and aerospace medicine. Dr. Farmer and the committee agreed.

10. In the Practice of Occupational and Aviation Medicine (Cleveland, OH)

In November of 1981, the administrator of Cleveland Lutheran Hospital in Cleveland, Terrence "Terry" White, asked me by telephone to consider being employed by the hospital as the medical director of a freestanding medical clinic that had recently been created by the Federal Government in downtown Cleveland for the U.S. Public Health Service and then given to Lutheran. Mr. White said that he had heard of my difficulties in establishing an occupational medicine program in the Cleveland Clinic, and was wondering whether the Lutheran facility, having been named "Lutheran Downtown Healthcare Services," might be better than the Clinic for this program. I toured it and was quite impressed by its large parking lot, spacious reception area and administrative offices, several well-equipped examination rooms and treatment room, an audiometric booth, an x-ray facility, an automated clinical laboratory, and a large meeting room. I agreed with Mr. White that the facility could support an occupational medicine program, and resigned from the Cleveland Clinic. I became the Medical Director of Lutheran Downtown Healthcare Services and formed a medical corporation to provide its physicians, including me. Soon the program was performing pre-employment and executive health evaluations for banks (e.g., Society National, First National) and home-office companies (e.g., PPG, Sherwin-Williams) in downtown Cleveland, pre-employment medical examinations, comprehensive annual health evaluations on FBI, U.S. Secret Service, and CIA special agents, medical examinations on physician and pilot applicants for the USAF, FAA airman medical certification examinations and consultations, and occupational and aerospace medicine consultations. The program treated very few acute occupational injuries and illnesses, no doubt because of its distance from most of the industry in the Cleveland area. However, several people who were working in downtown Cleveland visited Lutheran Downtown Healthcare Services for the treatment of minor health problems.

My work in Lutheran Downtown Healthcare Services included a return to the assessment of percentages of permanent partial impairment from occupational injuries and illnesses for workers' compensation service companies. I also visited the medical clinic in the human resources department of the Eaton Corporation's headquarters nearby one morning a week to perform pre-

MY EXPERIENCES

employment medical examinations and treat minor medical problems. In late 1982, I was an expert witness in two court cases. One case was a suit brought against Western Airlines in Los Angeles, California, by two pilots and a second officer (flight engineer) who wished to work as flight engineers beyond Western's mandatory retirement age of 60 for its pilots and flight engineers. The other case was a suit against Piper Aircraft in Birmingham, Alabama by the estate of one of the three men who died in the crash of a Piper PA 28-151 airplane after carbon monoxide leaked through failed-metal cracks in its muffler, incapacitating them.

In early 1983, Barbara and I were divorced after she decided to move to Florida to obtain an M.D. degree and then use both her training in medicine and her Ph.D. in immunology to engage in medical research and practice somewhere in the United States. And in late 1983, Bobbe Moran and I were married and purchased a home on Stonewood Court in Westlake, Ohio, after she unexpectedly refused to move with me if I accepted an offer to become the Medical Director of the International Telephone and Telegraph Corporation in Manhattan, New York. (On my recommendation, Dr. DeHart, who had recently retired from the USAF, took the position.)

In May of 1984, Mr. Whiter in Cleveland, informed me that within two weeks, Lutheran Parkside Occupational Health Services in Chicago would be taking Lutheran Downtown Healthcare Services and the medical clinic in the human resources department of the Eaton Corporation's headquarters. I soon learned from Lutheran's assistant administrator that I would be replaced by a manager from the automobile-manufacturing industry who had no management training or experience in medicine. Next, Mr. White said to me that Parkside hoped that my medical corporation would continue to provide physicians to work in the facility. However, the head of Lutheran's radiology department and the nation's first local television doctor, Dr. Theodore "Ted" Castele, who strongly supported Parkside's management of the facility, suggested to Parkside that his medical corporation provide the physicians to staff it. Finally, Dr.

DOUGLAS E. BUSBY

Castele asked Mr. White to have me removed from Lutheran Downtown Healthcare Services for the mistaken reason that I had allowed its x-ray technician to take a few x-rays for a medical unit in the nearby U.S. Navy Regional Recruiting Office without having them interpreted by his department at Lutheran. The x-ray technician told me that this arrangement had been made by Lutheran's assistant administrator, who, along with Mr. White, vehemently refused to clarify this with Dr. Castele. When I attempted to resolve this misunderstanding with Dr. Castele, he angrily assaulted my integrity and in essence forced me to resign from Lutheran Hospital

In the following month, so many organizations telephoned me to ask whether I would continue to serve them as a consultant that I decided to set up an office for this in downtown Cleveland.. Fortunately, my daughter, Stephanie, who had just graduated from university, helped me immensely in getting the practice started, especially with organizing it and learning the medical terminology that I use when I dictate medical reports. The practice was located in downtown Cleveland, initially in an unused medical office that was part of a medical insurance company, and then in a medical office suite that I designed in the nearby Statler Office Tower. After Stephanie left the practice to pursue her career, I employed an RN with occupational health experience, a medical receptionist-transcriptionist, and a medical transcriptionist.

The practice was in full operation within four months after I Left Lutheran Downtown Healthcare Services. During this "slow time," I became formally recognized as a specialist in occupational medicine by the American Board of Preventive Medicine. In the practice, I continued to perform pre-employment medical examinations, comprehensive annual health evaluations on FBI, U.S. Secret Service, and CIA special agents, medical examinations on physician and pilot applicants for the USAF, FAA airman medical certification examinations and consultations, and occupational and aerospace medicine consultations. I also continued to assess permanent partial impairment from occupational injuries and illnesses for workers'

MY EXPERIENCES

compensation service companies. The FBI became a special part of my practice, with it having 190 special agents in the Cleveland area. The assistant agent in charge of the local FBI office, Philip "Phil" Urick, showed me the highly-diverse work of the FBI and interestingly, I saw a remarkable similarity between conducting FBI investigations and diagnosing an illness.

Early in 1985, I became the medical advisor to the Oglebay Norton and Interlake Steamship companies, which operate large ships that transport iron ore, grain, and coal on the Great Lakes, as Oglebay Norton's SS Edmund Fitzgerald had been doing when it sank in Lake Superior on a stormy November day in 1975. Before the Great Lakes' shipping season began each spring, I conducted comprehensive health evaluations in my office on the ships' officers, including the captains, first mates, and chief engineers, and shipboard health screening examinations of its seamen (non-officers). For the onboard examinations, my nurse, Bobbie Moyer, and I had to travel to where the ships were docked for the winter in Conneaut, Ashtabula, and Toledo, Ohio, in Detroit, Michigan, and in Duluth, Minnesota. We usually had to climb steep ladders to reach the decks of the ships, and then work quickly in a small crew lounge. On two occasions, we had to work while a ship was underway, and then disembark from ship by walking down a narrow ramp that was lowered to a lifeboat tender, and with the tender pitching about in the waves, had to board it for the trip to shore.

Even though Parkside took over my involvement with the medical clinic in the Eaton Corporation's headquarters, I continued the health maintenance and FAA airman medical certification program for the pilots in Eaton's Flight Operations department. And on several occasions, Bobbie accompanied ill and injured Eaton employees being transported by its executive jet airplanes.

Occasionally, workers' compensation service companies asked me for an "informal" opinion on whether persons who had been receiving workers' compensation for many months, reportedly due to an occupationally-related injury, appeared to be physically impaired by the injury in surveillance videos of them. In several videos, persons who had purportedly sustained severe lower back injuries at work were engaged in strenuous physical activities, such as building a garage onto the side of a home and moving lumber and bags of cement to the back of a home. In one video, a person on workers' compensation for a leg injury was handing out small paper bags for cash through the front door of his home and periodically walking down the steps of his home and driving away in his pickup truck, without a limp or use of a cane for support. (I suggested that a copy of the video be shown to the police). In another video, a person who claimed to have injured his lower back and a leg at work slowly walked from his car to his orthopedist's office, bent over and limping, and using a cane for support. When he came out of the office, his walk was brisk, erect, and without a limp; although he still used the cane which he held in his other hand.

My continuing association in aerospace medicine with the Eaton Corporation led to it asking me to serve as an expert witness in a court case. The wife of a former Eaton employee was suing for workers' compensation because her husband had died from a ruptured brain aneurysm that occurred while he was traveling on a commercial airplane flight from Cleveland, Ohio to Albany, New York, where he had been enrolled to take an educational course for his work at Eaton. Reportedly, her husband suddenly developed a severe headache in flight. The headache persisted that evening, so he went to an outpatient clinic, where he was given analgesic and decongestant medications for a "sinus block." The following day, his headache was worse and he was vomiting, so he decided to return to Cleveland. When he arrived at the Cleveland air terminal, he was immediately taken by automobile to the Euclid Clinic several miles away, where ruptured aneurysm was diagnosed and he died during emergency surgery to stop it from bleeding.

A few days before I was to appear in court as an expert witness, the lead attorney representing Eaton on the case scheduled me for a

MY EXPERIENCES

deposition by the attorney representing the deceased employee's wife. He strongly warned me that the wife's attorney had a reputation for being unscrupulous and confrontational. He also warned me that the wife's attorney planned to use a local "specialist in aerospace medicine" as an expert witness, who would attribute the rupture of the aneurysm to an "explosive decompression," in spite of Eaton having determined that the airplanes on which the employee flew to and from Albany did not sustain any unusual change in cabin pressure or aircraft altitude. Eaton's lead attorney assured me that he would attend my deposition especially to prevent it from becoming argumentative, but an Eaton attorney who was not familiar with the case had to take his place at the last minute. The first question of me from the wife's attorney was, "Why did you leave Lutheran Downtown Healthcare Services," and before I could answer him, he stated, "I have proof that you were fired for stealing money from it." I was unable to counter his unmerited remark due to his continuously interrupting me with additional horrific accusations. Eaton's substitute attorney just sat and listened to the mounting uproar until I asked for a recess in the deposition, and briefed him on what the opposing attorney was trying to do: prevent me from using my expertise in aerospace medicine.

When the deposition resumed, the wife's attorney immediately asked me if an explosive decompression could cause a brain aneurysm to rupture, and I replied that I did not have to answer this question because it was irrelevant: an explosive decompression did not occur. He then stated that the airplane flying the employee from Cleveland to Albany actually had a sudden drop in altitude which caused the brain aneurysm to rupture, and asked me if the drop in altitude could cause a brain aneurysm to rupture, and I again replied that I did not have to answer this question because it was irrelevant: a sudden drop in airplane altitude did not occur. The wife's attorney returned to his personal attacks on my integrity and the Eaton's substitute attorney remained silent, so I terminated the deposition.

DOUGLAS E. BUSBY

The wife's attorney subsequently told the lead Eaton attorney that he had lost the videotape of the deposition, but during the court case produced a highly-edited version of the videotape which cast me as not being responsive to his questions. The lead Eaton attorney felt that the judge could see that the rupture of the brain aneurysm had nothing to do with the employee's travel by commercial airplane, and decided not to have me testify. The judge suggested an out-of-court settlement of the case, to which Eaton's lead and the wife's attorneys agreed.

For over a year, I flew around the Eastern United States on FBI and commercial airplanes with two-person "exchange" teams of FBI agents, to provide medical care to Angelo Lonardo, the former boss of the Cleveland mafia. He had been released from having begun to serve life in prison, by agreeing to testify in court against his counterparts and in a hearing before a U.S. Senate committee. During this period, he was hidden in various places by the FBI, and after his testifying was over was placed in the Federal Protected Witness Program operated by the U.S. Marshall's Service. I remember quite well the imperiling experience that I had when I was flown with two FBI agents to La Guardia Airport in New York, to examine Mr. Lonardo and take a portable EKG on him on the day before he was to testify in the famous Federal case against Mafia boss John Gotti and his associates. Immediately after the airplane landed, I was taken to a heavily-guarded motel in New Jersey by car. Mr. Lonardo sat between two New York FBI agents in the front seat of the car, and I sat between two Cleveland FBI agents in the back seat with a case containing an Uzi submachine gun on my lap. When I asked why all of this protection was necessary, an FBI agent sitting next to me said that the night before, a witness in the Gotti case had been murdered. My examination of Mr. Lonardo went well, after which he and I were separately driven away from the motel. This was the last time I saw Mr. Lonardo, for he soon went into the Protected Witness Program.

Another daunting time in my practice occurred after the LTV Steel Company in Cleveland sent me one of its truck drivers after he had

MY EXPERIENCES

failed his U.S. Department of Transportation medical examination to drive a commercial motor vehicle because he had diabetes requiring insulin for its control. When the driver arrived at my office, he handed me a letter from his family physician, which stated he had diabetes and did not have to take insulin for it. I asked the driver for a urine sample, which tested "four-plus" for glucose, and told him that his diabetes was out of control and that he should not drive a commercial motor vehicle unless he could control his diabetes with diet and exercise. A few days later, he stormed into my office, in an intoxicated condition, and demanded a repeat urine test. I told him that I would his urine to a clinical laboratory to be tested for glucose and insulin, and ask it to send copies of the test results to LTV Steel and me, to which he agreed. His urine was negative for glucose and positive for insulin. A few days later, I received an anonymous telephone call which I recognized as likely coming from the LTV Steel driver. He angrily told me that I had been the cause of his being fired from his job and that he intended to "shoot and kill" me when I left work at the end of that day. I notified LTV Steel of the incident and was told that the driver's employment by it had just been terminated because he lied about his diabetes status. I also notified the police, which said that they could do nothing to protect me because I had not been shot at and advised me to take different routes for a few days when leaving and entering my office at the Statler Office Building.

In the spring of 1991, I was engaged to be married to Christina Dougherty, who lived and worked in the Chicago area. We decided that opportunities for leading fulfilling careers and social lives together would be much greater in Chicago than in Cleveland. I had heard that the Euclid Clinic had decided to have a satellite office in downtown Cleveland, to offer much the same services as I was providing in my practice, and sold my practice to it. Soon thereafter, I received a telephone call from a physician recruiter who was searching for a medical director for the LTV Steel Company in East Chicago, Indiana, a salaried position to be filled at least for one year during which the company was likely to be closed or sold.

11. As the Medical Director of the LTV Steel Company (East Chicago, IN)

I was employed as the Medical Director of the LTV Steel Company in East Chicago, Indiana in August of 1991. I initially lived on my boat, which was docked in New Buffalo, Michigan, and when Christina and I were married, we moved into a condominium on North Lakeshore Drive in Chicago. Our condo was across "the drive" from the walking and bicycling paths along the shore of Lake Michigan, and 15 minutes by bus from the Chicago Loop. My drive from New Buffalo to work passed by the farmland of Northwest Indiana and through the brown smog from the steel mills in Gary, Indiana, and my drive from Evanston to work went along the Lake Michigan shoreline and through the south suburbs of Chicago – with these routes having remarkable contrasts in scenery.

The Indiana Harbor Works of the LTV Steel Company included two blast furnaces and several hot-rolling mills, and LTV's nearby Chicago Coke Plant. The process of steel-making involved pellets of iron ore, called taconite, being combined with coke, made by thermally removing the volatile chemicals from coal. This combination in a blast furnace produced liquid steel, which was then poured from the furnace into square and rectangular molds. Later, individual blocks of steel were milled, or reheated and rolled into the thicknesses specified for bodies of automobiles. Even though much of this process was automated, it was also hot, noisy, and dirty for the majority of employees, including the blast furnace and milling-machine operators, oilers, shovel operators, fork-lift, and crane operators, and cleaners. Everyone had to wear a hard hat, shoes with steel toes and heat-resistant soles, and, if indicated, shatter-proof eyeglasses, safety goggles, safety ear muffs, or earplugs, an appropriate respirator, and flame-resistant jacket, pants, and gloves. Fortunately, water hoses were available to wash the brown dust from the blast furnaces off employee cars, but not so for the boats docked in a nearby marina.

MY EXPERIENCES

An onsite, free-standing, medical facility was among the many buildings in the Indiana Harbor Works of the LTV Steel Company. It contained a reception room and adjoining medical records office, a nurses' office, treatment, examination, and recovery rooms, an x-ray unit, and the medical director's office. Because a blast furnace used in steel-making had to function continuously to prevent loss of its costly fire-brick lining, LTV Steel operated around the clock, seven days a week. Consequently, the medical facility had to be continuously staffed by nurses who were trained and experienced in caring for employee injuries and illnesses that occurred during work hours, and in assessing employees for return to work after recovering from minor injuries or illnesses. Employees who sustained major injuries or became seriously ill while at work were transported by ambulance to the emergency department in the nearby St. Catherine's Hospital in East Chicago.

I assessed and treated work-related injuries, performed all pre-employment medical examinations, and evaluated employees for return to work after being off work due to major injuries or illnesses. A special aspect of my work was fulfilling and documenting OSHA's requirements for the pre-employment and annual medical surveillance examinations of employees in the Chicago Coke Plant, all of whom had potential exposure to the chemical carcinogens that I had learned about in the applied toxicology course that I took many years before at The Ohio State University. I worked closely with the two industrial hygienists at LTV's Indiana Harbor Works and Chicago Coke Plant in preventing and investigating causes of occupational injuries and educating everyone on injury prevention. Some of our work together involved visiting dangerous areas where serious accidents warranted periodic safety reviews with supervisors and employees. I recall that one collaborative effort involved deciding whether the operator of an overhead sliding crane for moving steel-making materials could effectively perform his work while being treated for rheumatoid arthritis. This required the crane operator, accompanied by an industrial hygienist, his supervisor, and a union representative, to walk unprotected along the 3-foot-wide top of a high wall between enormous materials bins, then up a 20-foot ladder to the operator's cage. My fear of heights immediately kicked in, so from a distance I watched the group go to the cage. The crane operator demonstrated that he could safely get to his workstation and effectively perform his work there.

On my first day at the Indiana Harbor Works of LTV Steel, its human resources director showed me a remarkably-long list of Indiana Harbor Works and Chicago Coke Plant employees who were currently and repeatedly off work and receiving workers' compensation, the majority of them complaining of work-related lower back injuries. I mentioned to him that workers' compensation service companies in Ohio were successfully using surveillance videos to identify exaggeration and deception in worker's compensation cases, and he decided to shorten his off-work list by getting surveillance videos of employees suspected of abusing the workers' compensation system. I recommended to him that any involvement that I might have in surveilling company employees be confidential between us, to which he agreed. However, someone informed the employees' union that employees on long-term workers' compensation were subject to video surveillance. The union accused us of conducting unauthorized investigations of its members and began to threaten us with all sorts of legal action. This ended our effort to control workers' compensation abuse among Indiana Harbor Works and Chicago Coke Plant employees.

About two months before my one-year anniversary with the Indiana Harbor Works, it shut down one of its two operating blast furnaces. Consequently, the medical department had a reduction in the number of employees it served which led to it only being open at reduced staff during the morning and afternoon work shifts on weekdays, with any injured employees in the Indiana Harbor Works and Chicago Coke Plant at other times receiving care in the emergency department of St. Catherine's Hospital.

MY EXPERIENCES

12. As the Medical Director for Medicare in Illinois (Chicago, IL)

With my employment by LTV Steel soon to end, I was introduced to a wonderful employment opportunity by Jonathan "Jon" Shattuck, who was a longstanding friend of my wife, Christina. At the time, Jon was a senior vice president of Blue Cross Blue Shield of Illinois (BCBSIL), a division of the Healthcare Service Corporation (HCSC). He said that the HCSC had the contract to manage Medicare in Illinois for the Health Care Financing Administration (HCFA) in the U.S. Department of Health and Human Services (HHS), and that HCSC had just started to respond to HCFA's request for a written proposal to manage the coverage of durable medical equipment (DME) for Medicare nationally. He noted that the proposal would have to identify the medical director and other key individuals who would be involved with the contract, so HCSC management had decided to hire a physician who would be the future DME medical director, and meanwhile help to write the proposal. It had also decided that if HCSC did not receive the DME contract, the physician hired for it would replace the current full-time Medical Director for Medicare in Illinois, Dr. Charles "Charlie" Henderson, a general surgeon who had come up from Texas to temporarily fill this position.

I joined HCSC in early July of 1992, and immediately began to work on the DME proposal on the Medicare side of HCSC with William "Bill" Kotowski, whom I assumed would be the manager of the DME contract if HCSC received it. After spending most of my medical career in aerospace, occupational, and emergency medicine, and most recently had been the medical director of a steel mill, I certainly felt out of place when Bill told me what the DME contract, especially my responsibilities in it, would entail. He showed me that in Medicare, "DME" encompasses an immense number of devices and accessories, purchased or leased by Medicare for use in the home and community by ill and injured persons as aids to achieving a better quality of life. He described many types of DME, including motorized and non-motorized wheelchairs, walkers and crutches, continuous positive airway pressure (CPAP) and respiratory assist devices, patient lifts, commode chairs, oxygen equipment, and blood glucose monitors. He said that in the proposal, I would be writing about the principal responsibilities of the DME medical director, including the development of Medicare coverage criteria and payments allowed for DME, and reviewing DME claims whenever necessary. Within a few days of my being at HCSC, I felt quite enthusiastic over this new and fascinating challenge in my medical career. We completed the DME proposal in less than a month.

While I waited for HCFA to decide on which Medicare contractor would receive the DME contract, I spent much of my time with Dr. Henderson and his nurse assistant in learning about his four basic day-to-day Medicare Part B activities. He had come to HCSC in 1989 after HCFA directed its 32 Medicare Part B contractors to hire medical directors. At the time, HCSC was managing separate contracts for Medicare. The Medicare Part A contract served parts of Illinois in paying for inpatient care in a hospital, skilled nursing facility, and hospice, and for home health care. The Medicare Part B contract served all of Illinois in paying for physician services and procedures, medical tests, outpatient care, home health services, DME, and some preventive medicine services. HCSC had hired Dr. Henderson to be the medical director for both Part A and Part B.

Dr. Henderson showed me that one day-to-day activity was to create local coverage policies (LCPs) which provide the medical necessity requirements for the coverage of various medical services, procedures and items, including DME, by Medicare Part B in Illinois. Although HCFA had already published several national coverage policies (NCPs) for Medicare Part B, it expected Medicare Part B medical directors to develop LCPs encompassing a much greater number of medical services, procedures, and items than its NCPs. Dr. Henderson said that HCFA had confused this process in two ways. First, it had told the medical directors to create LCPs independently of each other, when in fact it advised them to form specialty committees among themselves to develop "model" LCPs. Second, it had told the medical directors not to develop LCPs to prevent abusive and

MY EXPERIENCES

fraudulent billing of Medicare Part B for medical services, procedures, and items, when in fact the basic purpose for the majority of LCPs created by the Medicare Part B medical directors to date was to do just that or, as Dr. Henderson said in his broad Texas accent, "to prevent gaming the system." Dr. Henderson and I agreed that for political reasons, HCFA was trying to avoid the appearance of assigning its contractors the primary responsibility for bringing substantial "Medicare abuse and fraud" under control with LCPs rather than its NCPs, because the development of NCPs is limited by the fact that they have to go through a lengthy notice-and-comment period before they can be put into effect. Interestingly, concern for the coverage-deciding power of Medicare contractors as compared to HCFA was expressed in Congress, which in 1993 led HCFA to change "local coverage policy (LCP)" to "local medical review policy (LMRP)," apparently to point out that LMRPs focus on informing the medical community when medical services, procedures, and items are medically necessary, and therefore covered, rather than on controlling abuse and fraud in billing Medicare for them. With some lingering concern about LMRPs being a tool to control abuse and fraud in billing Medicare Part B, and subsequently Part A, HCFA invited me to its headquarters in Baltimore, Maryland, to give a presentation on the history, purpose, and development of LMRPs to its administrator and senior staff, and representatives of several health care organizations. Although I was asked not to mention the use of the LMRP in controlling abuse and fraud in billing Medicare. I declined to do so and cited several outstanding examples where LMRPs markedly controlled abuse and fraud. HCFA did not comment on this part of my presentation.

In another activity, Dr. Henderson worked on the correct coding of medical services, procedures, and items covered by Medicare Part B. He had helped to set up an alphanumeric coding system in California for use in submitting medical insurance claims and had been an advisor on Current Procedural Terminology (CPT®), a system similar to that developed and maintained by the American Medical

DOUGLAS E. BUSBY

Association in collaboration with HCFA for claims submitted to Medicare Part B and most medical insurance companies. He also showed me how the CPT® is linked to Medicare's resource-based relative value scale (RBRVS), which assigns a relative value unit (RVU) to each service and procedure as the sum of the three costs of providing a service or procedure: the total physician work involved, the practice expenses, and the malpractice expenses. I soon learned from Dr. Henderson that effective use of the CPT® takes considerable training and practice, especially in the selection of appropriate codes and code modifiers for various types and durations of patient visits and procedures. Medicare Part B claims were constantly being submitted to Dr. Henderson by claims-processing clerks and claims-review nurses to be checked for coding accuracy, a task that we soon began to share.

Yet another of Dr. Henderson's activities was to render medical coverage opinions to the Medicare Part B hearing officers. These employees of HCSC had been given the authority by Medicare to render final coverage decisions on claims for services, procedures and items that were initially denied, then reviewed, and still denied, usually on the basis of medical necessity. For this, Dr. Henderson would often ask local medical consultants to Medicare Part B for their views on the coverage of claims.

Finally, Dr. Henderson showed me how he was engaged in controlling abuse and fraud in billing Illinois Medicare Part B for services, procedures, and items. As directed by HCFA, all of the Medicare Part B medical directors had to review random samples of claims submitted by a specified percentage of physicians practicing in the geographic areas served by their Medicare Part B contracts. At the time, audits of physicians submitting high-frequency claims with certain CPT® codes had been initiated by several Medicare Part B medical directors, but, for some reason were yet to occur in Medicare Part B of Illinois.

Dr. Henderson was also the Medical Director of Medicare Part A. He pointed out that even though Medicare coverage under Part A is

MY EXPERIENCES

also determined by medical necessity, Part A does not use the CPT®, but a diagnosis-related group (DRG) classification system based on the World Health Organization's International Classification of Diseases, Ninth Revision, Clinical Modification (ICD-9-CM). He said that the Medicare Part A medical directors help the Medicare Part A auditors to determine whether claims for hospitalizations or other services under Medicare Part A had been assigned appropriate DRGs, and for assisting the Medicare Part A in audits where the excessive assignment of services to DRGs was suspected. He predicted that Medicare Part A medical directors would soon be busy writing LCDs for Medicare Part A.

In September of 1992, HCSC was informed that it had not received the DME contract. I succeeded Dr. Henderson as Medical Director for the Medicare Part A and Part B contracts in Illinois, and Bill Kotowski became the Director of Program Integrity for the Medicare Part B contract. Bill soon developed a computer program to identify possible abuse and fraud in billing Medicare, based on the identification of a statistically-significant increase in claims for a specific service, procedure, or item by a Medicare provider or number of providers. The supervisor over us, as well as the hearing officers and a unit for training staff in physician offices in the CPT® coding of claims, was Ann Shannon, Vice President of Administration for HCSC's Medicare Part B contract. Ann's counterpart was William "Bill" Gowan, Vice President of Operations for the Medicare Part B contract, which included all Medicare Part B telephone assistance personnel, and claims processors and reviewers. At the time, the Medicare contracts under HCSC employed over 1,000 persons in Chicago, Mattoon, and Marion, Illinois, with Mr. Gowan, an expert in claims-processing software, spending most of his time in the claims-processing operations in Mattoon and Marion.

For the following 6 years, I continued all of the activities of Dr. Henderson, and attended twice-yearly, two-day meetings of the Medicare medical directors at HCFA headquarters, where the medical directors were updated on changes in Medicare's medical coverage system and developed "model LCDs," which were later called "model LMRPs." After two years as a Medicare contractor medical director, I was invited by HCFA to serve on a panel consisting of physicians from its medical coverage staff and Medicare Part B medical directors, which met annually in Baltimore to review proposed additions to the CPT® and the RBRVS work values assigned to new CPT® codes and many existing codes. And about the same time, HCFA formed another physician panel consisting of physicians from its medical coverage staff, Medicare contractor medical directors, and physicians from the Veterans' Administration and the National Institutes of Health. This panel reviewed the results of research on new medical technologies and medications, and advised HCFA whether Medicare should cover them. It was disbanded after two years of meeting every few months, reportedly because it was viewed by Congress as bypassing the long notice-and-comment period for creating NCPs. HCFA subsequently formed a new panel of physicians from various national medical specialty organizations, to review and accept proposed NCPs after the notice-and-comment periods on them. Moreover, HCFA directed the individual Medicare Part B contractors to do the same for all LMRPs.

During my time at HCSC, I made several presentations on Medicare Part B at local meetings of physicians and annual state-wide physician events, including the annual meetings of the Chicago Medical Society, the Illinois Society of Internal Medicine, the Illinois Chapter of the American College of Cardiology, and the Illinois Optometric Association. After the expert panel was disbanded, each Medicare Part B medical director had to form a Medicare Part B advisory committee of representatives from all of the medical specialty organizations in their states, to meet at least twice a year to be updated on Medicare and review and comment new LMRPs. Dr. Joseph "Joe" Messer, a past president of the American College of Cardiology, and I co-chaired the meetings at HCSC. For my last two years at HCSC, I supervised the Medicare Part B unit that trained staff in physician offices in the CPT® coding of Part B claims.

MY EXPERIENCES

In 1994, my workload had increased to such a degree that Ann decided to hire an associate Medicare medical director for Illinois, Dr. Richard Baer. As the only specialist in psychiatry and trained writer among the Medicare medical directors, he soon created various model LMRPs for Medicare Part A, including policies on hospice, skilled nursing, and home health coverages. In 1996, Richard became the Medical Director of HCSC's Medicare Part A contract.

I guess that I was somewhat unique among the medical directors of the Medicare Part A and Part B contracts, in developing a strong interest in combatting Medicare abuse and fraud. In retrospect, this interest may have stemmed from my earlier exposure to the work of the FBI. The biggest abuse-and-fraud case of many with which I was involved followed a technically-failed investigation of a group of Chicago ophthalmologists who were billing Medicare Part B for a remarkably large number of cataract operations followed by droopy-eyelid repairs called blepharoplasties, many of which appeared to be medically unnecessary. An interesting turn of events occurred after a claims examiner in Bill Kotowski's area asked me why a patient would need to have an extensive and expensive battery of blood tests for allergies before cataract or droopy-eyelid surgery, especially when the tests were ordered by a physician who is not an allergy specialist, and the results of these tests would not be reported until a day or so after either surgery was performed. I asked the examiner to "pull up" a sample of claims for this service. It was subsequently determined that this physician had ordered hundreds of batteries of these tests, and that he had illegally obtained his license to practice medicine in Illinois. But this was not the end of the story, for I subsequently trained OIG and FBI investigators to mimic various medical conditions for their "sting" to show that a South Chicago hospital owned by an ophthalmologist in the group was paying kickbacks to doctors and other individuals to encourage patient referrals to the hospital, and was submitting claims to Medicare Part A for medically-unnecessary services and procedures.

Another large case of Medicare Part B abuse began when I was asked by one of Bill's claims examiners why a psychologist had to conduct a comprehensive and expensive battery of psychological tests on all Medicare-age patients admitted to several nursing homes. We discovered that psychology students at a local college were doing this testing to meet their degree requirements, with the income from this enterprise going to a Chicago area psychologist and politician who, when she learned that her scheme had been discovered, tried unsuccessfully to meet alone with me, which I declined to do.

A remarkable instance of a highly-profitable case of Medicare Part B fraud which was discovered by another of Bill's claims examiners involved the submission of claims for daily EKGs on all of the residents of several nursing homes over short periods of time. I immediately reported this to all of my Medicare Part A and Part B colleagues, and soon learned that claims for this daily service totaling several million dollars had also been submitted to other Medicare Part B contractors. Interestingly, only one individual was doing this, using addresses of United States Post Office boxes and even a cemetery address to bill collect the checks for this service from Medicare!

In late 1997, I heard that investigators from the Office of the Inspector General (OIG) in HHS were visiting the Medicare Part B facility in Marion to investigate a matter regarding claims processing there. In late December, the vice presidents and directors (including Richard and me) of HCSC's Part A and Part B Medicare contracts for Illinois were invited to a confidential meeting with top HCSC management. We were told that several medical claims which had not been processed by the former Medicare Part B contractor for Illinois had been destroyed by certain Medicare Part B employees at the Marion Medicare facility. Moreover, HCFA's system for monitoring the quality of Medicare Part B claims processing had been altered at this facility to show that HCSC was more efficient in Medicare Part B claims processing than it was. This meeting ended with a description of an integrity program to begin in January of 1998 for all of HCSC's Medicare Part A and Part B employees, with this program to be administered by a retired FBI official. In the last week of December 1997, HCSC's president and its chief legal officer went to Baltimore to brief HCFA officials, including its chief contracting officer, on HCSC's integrity program for its Medicare Part A and Part B contracts. January of 1998 began with the vice presidents and directors of HCSC's Part A and Part B Medicare contracts for Illinois again being invited to a

MY EXPERIENCES

confidential meeting with top HCSC management. This time, we were told that HCFA and HCSC had agreed to terminate the Medicare Part A and Part B contracts in about 6 months, with HCSC assuring HCFA that the process of transitioning the contracts to new contractors would be seamless. Then all Medicare employees were informed of the decision, along with the assurance that HCSC would do everything possible to encourage the new Medicare contractors to hire them.

Over the following several weeks, several facts about the demise of HCSC's relationship with HCFA came to light. The abrupt decision to terminate the Medicare Part A and Part B contracts was made by HCSC's president after HCFA's chief contracting officer made a "no-confidence" remark directed at him during the Baltimore briefing. The federal government fined HCSC $144 million for these offenses, the person in the Marion Medicare facility who reported them received $29 million under the Federal Whistleblower Protection Act, two managers in this facility received several-month jail sentences and five other managers and supervisors were indicted but apparently not tried for engaging in them. In late 1997 and again in early 1998, the OIG investigators and even the FBI tried unsuccessfully to interview Bill Gowan, who had been in charge of all Illinois Part B claims processing when the misdeeds occurred. He was suffering from terminal cancer and refused to communicate with these agencies

My work with HCSC ended on July 31, 1998. In the interim, I worked with the medical director of the new Illinois Medicare Part B contractor, Wisconsin Physicians Service (WPS), in "coordinating" our LMRPs, as well as continuing my regular day-to-day activities as the medical director for Medicare Part B in Illinois. During this period, I spent a day at WPS in Madison, Wisconsin, being interviewed to be its associate medical director for Medicare Part B in Illinois, where I would work in WPS's new satellite office in Chicago four days a week at 80 percent of my HCSC salary. After my visit to Madison, Ann Shannon told me that she and others in Illinois Medicare Part B management had received similar offers, which were suspected as being precursory to being offered full-time employment at WPS, but at a lower salary. By the end of July, I was looking for another position in medicine, receiving six months of severance pay from HCSC.

DOUGLAS E. BUSBY

13. As an Information Analyst for Medtronic and other Medical Technology Companies (Home Office, IN)

In August of 1998, I received a telephone call from the senior information analyst at Kathpal Technologies in Baltimore, who invited me to serve for two years on a panel d me whether I might be available to help him complete a project which HCFA had given to TRW Inc., to conduct a comparative analysis of LMRPs developed by the Medicare Part B medical directors. He said that Kathpal had gathered LMRPs for several services and procedures which had been selected by HCFA to determine how much they differed among Medicare Part B contractors. For over two months, I traveled to Baltimore weekly by airplane to work on the project for three days, with the analyst and I periodically visiting HCFA to present our findings. Then, without warning or explanation, HCFA terminated the project.

For several months in 1999, I worked three days a week as a consultant to AdminaStar Federal in Indianapolis, Indiana, which had the Medicare Part B contract for Indiana. I reported to Dr. Arnold "Arnie" Krubsack, a nuclear medicine specialist from Madison, Wisconsin, who was the contract's temporary medical director. My major responsibilities were to assist the claims review nurses and hearing officers in making Medicare coverage decisions and to create LMRPs. In the fall of 1999, a sales manager of Medtronic in Minneapolis, Minnesota whom I had met socially, informed me that Medtronic was looking for a physician with experience in information analysis and technical writing, to conduct state-of-the-art reviews, or so-called "white papers," on new medical technologies. He said that Medtronic used white papers for the development and marketing of its medical devices, and in requesting Medicare coverage of the devices. I expressed my strong interest in this position to him, and the following day had a successful telephone interview with Alexandra "Alex" Clyde, Medtronic's Corporate Vice President of Global Health Policy, Reimbursement, and Health Economics, to whom I would be reporting. Ms. Clyde stated that she would be relaying review requests to me from any one of the company's 31 product groups, and that I would responsible for identifying and Medtronic would be responsible for providing published scientific reports that I might need for my reviews. She said that I would work at home, would receive a generous hourly consultant fee, and be as free as possible from time pressure in my work. When I informed the manager of Medicare Part B at AdminaStar Federal that I would be conducting information analyses for Medtronic, she immediately terminated my employment by AdminaStar, as Arnie later told me, due to a misperceived conflict of interest between my two consultant functions. Now I was back to where I had started in my medical career at the Lovelace Foundation in 1964 – doing information analyses!

Over the subsequent 14 years, I wrote 37 major white papers: 26 for Medtronic and 11 for six other U.S. new technology companies. During this time, Christina and I lived in our new log home on North Pine Country Drive in Rolling Prairie, Indiana, then in our conventional home on West Timber Ridge Road in La Porte, Indiana, and finally in our ranch-style condominium on Allison Circle in Valparaiso, Indiana.

My initial work for Medtronic was for its cardiac rhythm products group, which had me write on the need for a tilt table test before implanting an insertable loop recorder when cardiac arrhythmia is a suspected cause of syncope, use of an insertable loop recorder in the management of atrial fibrillation, use of the T-wave alternans test to identify patients at risk for life-threatening ventricular arrhythmias, termination of atrial fibrillation with an implantable cardioverter-defibrillator (ICD), catheter ablation of atrial fibrillation, prevention of sudden cardiac death with an ICD, treatment of chronic heart failure with an implantable cardiac resynchronization system, remote electronic analysis of the ICD, and insurer coverage of automatic external defibrillators for use in the home. The neurological products area had me write on neurostimulation for complex regional pain syndrome, neurostimulation for failed back surgery syndrome, intrathecal drug therapy for chronic intractable cancer pain, and intrathecal drug therapy for chronic intractable non-cancer pain, with Medtronic publishing each paper as an article for physician education. The ear, nose and throat products area had me on the treatment of Ménière's disease with a low-pressure pulse generator, pharyngeal surgery for obstructive sleep apnea, and hyoid suspension for obstructive sleep apnea using a bone screw system. And the spinal and orthopedic products area had me on the instrumentation of the cervical and lumbar spine, percutaneous vertebroplasty, anterior lumbar interbody fusion using recombinant human bone morphogenetic protein-2, computer-assisted guidance of pedicle screw placement in spinal surgery, and accuracy of sacroiliac joint fusion.

During this period, several other companies asked me to write white papers on new medical technologies. Some of them were referred to me by Katherine "Kathy" Francisco, President of the Pinnacle Health Group in Yardley, Pennsylvania, which had been remarkably successful in giving many of these companies marketing and pricing advice on their products, and in obtaining Medicare and private insurance coverage for them. I wrote on percutaneous closure of the left atrial appendage to prevent stroke from atrial fibrillation, endoscopic gastroplication in the treatment of gastrointestinal reflux disease, scintimammography in the diagnosis of breast cancer, percutaneous cryoablation of breast fibroadenomas, intraoperative radiation therapy for early-stage breast cancer, and deep regional hyperthermia in the treatment of cancer. I also wrote on unattended portable home monitoring of breathing during sleep for diagnosing sleep apnea, palatal implants for the treatment of snoring and mild-to-moderate sleep apnea, biofeedback in the treatment of urinary incontinence, detection and measurement of microalbumin in the urine, and peripheral arterial tonometry in the management of coronary artery disease.

My years of writing white papers were fulfilling in many ways, especially in allowing me to participate in many remarkable technological advances being made in medicine. I was invited to several research-planning meetings at Medtronic, where I met with persons who had requested my work. On one occasion, two other physicians and I participated in a "brainstorming" session with several Medtronic bioengineers to identify the need for new technologies: I suggested that Medtronic's infusion pump to control severe chronic pain be modified for the continuous administration of insulin in diabetes mellitus, which soon happened. And I spoke on LMRPs at a meeting of the local chapter of the life Sciences Alley Association.

E. MY EDUCATION IN THEOLOGY

1. Background

As I described above, I became interested in theology from attending Sunday school, confirmation classes, and worship services during my growing-up years at St. John's Anglican Church in Kitchener. All of the theology that I learned during this period of my life came from the Holy Bible, which I was led to believe was the "Word of God," and therefore infallible, factual, or true. For example, I accepted the biblical teachings that: God rules over Heaven and Earth; God created the Earth in six days; sin originated when Adam and Eve disobeyed God and ate the forbidden fruit from the Tree of the Knowledge; the Jews are God's chosen people; God rewards us for being good and punishes us for being bad; Mary was a virgin when she gave birth to Jesus; Baptism washes away original sin; Jesus was the "son of God;" Jesus performed many "miracles;" Jesus died on the Cross to save all humans from their sins; Jesus arose from being dead and ascended into Heaven; and, Jesus will return to judge the living and the dead to determine whether or not they be sent to a beatific place called "Heaven" or a horrific place called "Hell". And the key facts on which Christianity was founded were incorporated into two ancient, doctrinal statements of belief, the Apostles' and the Nicene creeds, either of which I would cite in every worship service.

As I grew into my teens, my theology was challenged by many thought-provoking questions which simply came into my mind, especially while I was serving as an acolyte, or server, and then as a crucifer, or cross-bearer. Such questions included: who is God and by whom was God created; did Creation take only six days; why did God allow the Holocaust to occur to God's chosen people; did Jesus really arise from being dead and then pass through solid structures; is Christian belief and practice necessary for entry into Heaven; and, did my out-of-body experience in childhood confirm the existence of the

DOUGLAS E. BUSBY

soul? As I entered my adult life, I decided that if the Bible is literally the "Word of God," then it will answer questions that God wants me to know the answers to in this life, and leave any other answers for my next life when, hopefully, I will be better able to comprehend them. However, I would eventually realize that this fundamentalistic approach to theology was quite naïve.

Until 1983, my first wife, Barbara, our three daughters, Suzanne, Sharon, and Stephanie, and I were members of Anglican churches in Canada and their virtually-identical Episcopal churches in the United States. We sang in church choirs, our daughters went through Confirmation, I served on music and stewardship committees, and Sharon played the clarinet and I the trumpet in church services. And in these churches, I had learning experiences that broadened my perspectives on theology.

When we lived for a year in Grandview Heights, Ohio in the mid-1960s, we attended St. Mark's Episcopal Church nearby. In an adult religious book study group, I volunteered to be trained on how to lead theological discussions with the instructor using Harvey Cox's classic new book, *The Secular City.* In this thought-provoking book, Dr. Cox considered the relationship between the rise of urban civilization, the decline of hierarchical institutional religion, and the place of non-religious people in society. Over a several-week period, intense debates over its content opened our minds to how religious beliefs are shaped inside and outside of the church, hopefully with divine guidance always being available.

When we lived in Norman, Oklahoma in the mid-1970s, we joined St. John's Episcopal Church in Norman, adjacent to the campus of the University of Oklahoma. We soon became involved in a theologically-driven split of its congregation and the formation of a new Episcopal church in Norman. The turmoil that led to the split started about two years before we arrived, under its new pastor, Rev. David Penticuff, who had left the business world to attend a Roman Catholic Seminary and then be ordained as an Episcopal priest. He was strongly hierarchical and authoritarian. Soon after he began to serve at St. John's, he became part-owner of a local golf course that had just failed financially and required a substantial amount of his time for its recovery. About a year later, he was delivering a sermon on

MY EXPERIENCES

Stewardship Sunday when he "went off script," and expressed his hope that the congregation would give as much money to St. John's as to "Ole John's," the only liquor store in Norman's otherwise "dry" community. And within two weeks in our second year at St. John's, he gave sexually-explicit advice to a husband and wife in the congregation who were having marital difficulties, announced that he instead of the congregation would be selecting the senior warden (president of the vestry, or church board) of St. John's, and asked the head acolyte of St. John's, who was African-American, not to participate in the marriage service of a couple from two prominent local, white families. The racial issue in particular raised quite a furor, which culminated in a visit of several members of St. John's, including me, to the Episcopal Bishop of Oklahoma, who listened indifferently to our expressed concerns over Rev. Penticuff's behavior. This led about 40 percent of the members of St. John's to leave St. John's and form St. Michael's Episcopal Church in Norman, aptly named after the archangel who champions justice and heals the sick. It also led to the bishop being forced to send "those rabble-rousers" a just-ordained priest, Rev. Donald "Don" Owens, who was so well-loved by the St. Michael's congregation that he served it for many years.

When we moved to Potomac, Maryland in the late 1970s, we became members of St. James' Episcopal Church in Potomac, while occasionally attending Sunday morning worship services at the Episcopal Cathedral of St. Peter and St. Paul, more commonly known as the Washington National Cathedral. Most memorable for me at St. James was an adult class on the Bible, conducted by its minister, Rev. Almus Thorp, Jr., who was a biblical scholar. He presented a lecture series on the origins of the Bible, casting doubt on its infallibility. To do this, he showed how the Bible's historical and literary accuracy were blurred by its numerous authors relying on word of mouth, and its hand-copiers and translators inadvertently and deliberately altering it. As examples of significant theological differences among various Bibles, Rev. Thorp drew upon identically-numbered passages in the original Greek, King James, and Revised Standard versions of the Bible. Although he still believed that the Bible as a whole can be considered the "inspired" Word of God, he reawakened my thinking about the reality of what I had been taught are the theological

DOUGLAS E. BUSBY

"truths" in the Bible, especially those contained in the doctrines and liturgy of the Episcopal Church.

From late 1979 to early 1983, we were members of St. Paul's Episcopal Church in Cleveland Heights, Ohio. Its charismatic minister, Rev. Dr. William Chave McCracken, often related the theology of the Bible to the existence and management of current world problems. In addition to his parish ministry, he strongly supported civil rights and social justice in the community and led St Paul's to become more consciously inclusive. In 1963, he invited Dr. Martin Luther King, Jr. to visit St. Paul's, and Dr. King gave an early version of his *I Have a Dream* speech. Dr. McCracken showed that renaissance thinking can go hand-in-hand with theological thinking in a local television show entitled *The Meaning of Greatness*, in which he described the work of great writers and painters. As an aside, he was always willing to quote, dramatically from memory, especially-interesting parts of Mark Twain's *Adventures of Tom Sawyer* and *Adventures of Huckleberry Finn*. He believed that the worship of the church should be supported by a strong music program, in which we participated under its renowned organist and choir director, Karel Paukert.

After Barbara and I were divorced in early 1983, I lived for several months in an apartment in downtown Cleveland and on my boat in Vermilion, Ohio. I began to attend Sunday morning worship services at the Trinity Episcopal Cathedral, and other Episcopal churches around Cleveland and Vermilion. Three unusual church experiences occurred during this time. One Sunday, the cathedral's organist and choir director stepped out of the organ loft and into the pulpit to give a sermon that was so inspiringly "theological" that I again began to wonder whether it was time for me to seriously study theology. On another Sunday, boating friends invited me to worship with them at their church, the Hungarian Reformed Church of Lorain, Ohio, which is a part of the United Church of Christ (UCC), but gives stronger attention to the Bible being the Word of God and the ultimate rule of the Christian faith and practice than the UCC. And on yet another Sunday, my fiancé, Bobbe Moran, and I attended Grace Episcopal Church in Sandusky, Ohio, where she introduced me to its interim minister and her longstanding friend, the Rev. Robert "Bob" New, who described how his ministry functions in the period between ministers,

MY EXPERIENCES

and the how the Episcopal Church was adapting to the charismatic, or spiritually-inspiring, movement within it.

This brings me to describe a spiritually-painful chapter of my life. Bobbe and I were married by Rev. New in late 1983 and purchased a home on Stonewood Court in Westlake, Ohio. In preparation for our wedding, we met on two occasions with Rev. New, during which we discussed my interest in theology and desire to continue worshiping in the Episcopal Church. Bobbe said that she had been raised in the United Methodist Church, and even though she had not been involved with any church since she left home for college, she told Rev. New and me that she now wished to live a more "religious" life. However, in the first month of our marriage, she emphatically informed me that she did have any interest in theology or wish to participate in the worship of any church or say any prayers except grace when guests dined with us in our home. If I subsequently mentioned something of theological interest, she would immediately interrupt me and say that the sole driving force of her faith was the "Golden Rule," or the principle of treating others as she wished to be treated. So I had inadvertently entered a marriage void of any spiritual relationship with my wife – a "spiritual desert" as a friend once said. This lack of a spiritual life with Bobbe was a cause of our divorce in early 1990.

In 1990, I spent Christmas in Chicago with Sharon and Stephanie who had moved there, and Suzanne who went along with me from her home in Cleveland. Sharon arranged for me to attend a concert of the Music of the Baroque with Christina Dougherty, a professional businesswoman and singer with whom Sharon had lived for a period of time in her apartment in Evanston, a suburb of Chicago. This concert of classical choral and instrumental music was held in a very large Roman Catholic Church. We had to sit in the uppermost row of the balcony where, as we later agreed, the sound was both etheric and bonding! Soon we began to share our joys of music, family, friends and boating on alternate weekends in Cleveland and Evanston while attending St. Paul's Episcopal Church in Cleveland Heights and the First Congregational Church of Wilmette (FCCW), a member church of the UCC next to Evanston. Our courtship led to my leaving Cleveland for a new life in the Chicago area, and our entering a wonderfully-spiritual marriage in December of 1991.

DOUGLAS E. BUSBY

We regularly attended FCCW, where Christina was a long-standing member, sang in the choir, and was a vocal soloist. I soon learned that in contrast to the Episcopal Church being hierarchical, or having ministerial levels of control up to the bishop in a cathedral office, the UCC is covenantal, where its members, including ministers, agree to work together in their churches, churches agree to work together in local associations, and associations agree to work together in regional conferences - with all of these levels of relationship receiving support from a central UCC office in Cleveland, Ohio. I also learned that in contrast to the Episcopal Church always using its *Book of Common Prayer* for worship services, most UCC churches use various worship resources, including the *Book of Worship, United Church of Christ*. I discovered that most churches of the UCC do not use the Apostles' Creed or the Nicene Creed in their worship services as does the Episcopal Church, but may use the less-doctrinal and more-encompassing United Church of Christ Statement of Faith in them.

The FCCW was a remarkably-active church, in that everyone seemed to be busy doing something in support of its religious life and the welfare of the surrounding community. Its minister, Rev. Dr. Robert "Bob" Lee continued the work of its charismatic former minister, Rev. James "Jim" Kidd, who energized the Asylum Hill Congregational Church in Hartford, Connecticut to rapidly become one of the UCC's largest urban churches. Under Dr. Lee, the Wilmette church continued to be an open and affirming (ONA) church, which by definition welcomes lesbian, gay, bisexual, transgender, and queer (LGBTQ) members. It was also a strong voice in the community on justice issues and provided support to a mission in Latin America. Periodically on Sunday afternoons, FCCW's choir gave a concert or FCCW presented a well-known guest speaker. And an annual joyous event for the entire congregation was family camp every week surrounding July 4 at the UCC's Tower Hill facility near Sawyer, Michigan, close to a Lake Michigan beach. In the fall of 1993, I became a member of FCCW and, in turn, the UCC.

I was on the family camp committee for 1992, and was sort of "pushed" into being committee chair for 1993 by members of the committee who learned of my interest in theology and felt that this would be a good way to "introduce me to congregationalism." I

MY EXPERIENCES

opened the first meeting of the committee by requesting suggestions for a camp theme and related program activities, such as morning worship, crafts and education, contests, group meals, a parade, and a talent show. Everyone immediately provided input that led to indecisiveness which someone commented was typical of congregationalism. I realized that the only way for me to get a consensus on the theme and related program activities without my leadership seeming to be hierarchical was to have a vote to select the theme, and then ask the committee for volunteers for subcommittees to conduct related program activities. The theme was "Get on Board," as on passenger trains, with over 160 campers of all ages being handed classical railroad engineer hats and red bandanas to begin a fun-filled, railroad-oriented week of Christian fellowship.

While I was at the FCCW family camp in 1993, I had the opportunity to talk about my interest in theology with several fellow campers who were current and past students at the Chicago Theological Seminary (CTS). I learned that CTS is affiliated with the UCC and is a member of the Association of Chicago Theological Schools (ACTS), which enables any student in its group of 12 seminaries in the Chicago area to cross-register for theological courses in the other 11 seminaries. I also learned that while studying at CTS, the eight members of FCCW continued to work almost full-time in their various careers because many courses were given in the evenings. At last, I saw an opportunity to study theology, but I wondered whether I might have the time to do so since I had just become the Medical Director for Medicare in Illinois. However, in the fall of 1993, I had a religious experience that set me on a path to my career in theology.

This experience occurred while I was in San Francisco, California, participating in a seminar on Medicare. Before dinner one evening, I decided to visit Grace Episcopal Cathedral to "walk" its indoor labyrinth, a replica of the labyrinth embedded in the floor of the ancient Chartres Cathedral in France. During my first exposure to this ancient spiritual practice, I was quite impressed by the "divinely-peaceful" effect that it had on me. As I stepped out of the labyrinth, I heard a loudspeaker voice announce that the cathedral's evening worship service would soon begin in its Chapel of Grace. I decided to attend the service to ponder over the meaning of the labyrinth experience to me, and to thank God for it. The minister who led the service gave a brief sermon in the service that contained a message surprisingly applicable to my deliberations on whether or not to begin to formally study theology at this point in my life. The message was that through God's grace, we can never stop learning. As background to it, the minister told a story about one of the early monarchs of England, King Alfred the Great. King Alfred believed so strongly that one should never stop learning, that he promoted learning and literacy amongst his subjects and built one of the largest libraries in the world for them to use throughout their lives. The message in this sermon and the story of Alfred, the first name of my father, caught my attention, and I sadly recalled how Dad had been denied an education in theology by Grandpa Busby. I asked myself, "Given the same opportunity, should I now turn away from it?"

2. In Seminary

My experience at Grace Episcopal Cathedral led me to enroll in CTS for the Master of Divinity (M.Div.), and begin to take courses in January of 1994. At the time, I wanted to study for a career in academic theology, but I soon became interested in pastoral ministry as an alternative. Since the M.Div. degree could be the first step toward education in theology and was mandatory for ordination as a minister, I felt that was on the right track for either option.

My M.Div. adviser at CTS was Rev. Dr. W. Dow Edgerton, the Academic Dean and an expert on pastoral ministry. Even though I assured my superior at HCSC, Ann Shannon, that I planned to take all of my courses in theology during evening hours, she kindly said that if necessary, I could take off work for a half-day a week for courses and activities in CTS, such as guest lectures, staff-student worship services, and practice preaching. And Christina said that she would be pleased to give her full support to my back-to-school experience by having to miss some social events because of it, having to sit with me in our library watching television with its volume turned down, and looking for hours at a time at the "top of my head" as I read and wrote at my desk. Fortunately, Christina had recently received a Master of

MY EXPERIENCES

Business Administration (MBA) degree from the Kellogg School of Management at Northwestern University, and repeatedly reassured me by saying, "I know what it takes to follow a dream."

My M.Div. required 27 course credits, six of which were awarded for my previous academic work for my M.D. and M.Sc. degrees, and 800 hours of field education. Although the 21 courses that I took at CTS and other ACTS seminaries provided me with a solid foundation for a career in theology, some were especially informative and memorable to me.

The first of the two courses that I took in the winter quarter of 1994 was entitled "The Epic of Creation," given at the Lutheran School of Theology Chicago (LSTC) by Rev. Dr. Philip Hefner, a theologian. It compared Biblical accounts and modern scientific knowledge of Creation in lectures on the Creation Story by biblical scholars at LSTC, on man being God's co-creator by Dr. Hefner, on the development of the cosmos by scientists from Fermilab, and on evolutionary biology by professors from the University of Chicago. The other course, "Engaging the Powers," was taught at CTS by Rev. Dr. George Cairns, a psychologist and professor of theology, who described how evil can occur and be managed in various organizations, such as churches.

Next, I learned how theology can be involved in family life in a course at CTS entitled "Jungian Perspectives on Family Dynamics," given by Dr. Robert Moore, a psychologist, who for the entire course used analytic psychology founded by the eminent Austrian psychiatrist, Carl Jung, to show how the four different male and four different female archetypes, or models of behavior, affect family relationships. Later, another course, given by a CTS professor whose name I do not remember, described how theology can be applied in pastoral counseling a form of psychotherapy that uses spiritual resources as well as psychological knowledge for healing and growth. I recall that both of these courses were quite interesting to me in light of my past training and experience in psychiatry not having given any attention to the relationship between our emotional and spiritual selves.

My first Old Testament course was on the Book of Job. It was taught at McCormick Theological Seminary (MTS) by Rev. Dr. Robert

DOUGLAS E. BUSBY

Boling, a theologian and biblical archeologist. The course was an analysis of the rather-complicated Old Testament story of Job, culminating in each student writing a term paper on a possible theological message that was embedded in this story. A message that I saw pertained to my growing interest in spiritual healing, especially in prayer for healing. It becomes evident when Job is described as a rich and righteous man who, for no reason that he knew of, lost everything except his wife, and ended up in the local garbage dump, scratching a serious disease on his skin with a piece of broken pottery. His wife and some friends desperately tried to convince him that his misfortunes were God's punishment for his sins, so he should repent for his sins in the hope that God will be merciful and relieve him of his suffering. Since Job believed that he had never sinned, he disagreed with them and boldly demanded a face-to-face debate with God on God's justification for punishing him. God responded by pointing out to Job that since all of Creation is the work of God, Job has no right to demand anything of God. Job meekly apologized to God for challenging God's authority and power, and God restored Job's wealth and health. So in my paper, I said that this part of the story of Job advises us not to demand anything of God, but to ask God for it humbly, acknowledging that God acts according to God's will and for the greater good. Dr. Boling agreed with the theological message that I saw in the Book of Job. However, he strongly disagreed with my mentioning in the paper said that Jews adopted the story of Job from ancient Mesopotamian folklore, even though I referenced a credible source of it. Consequently, I received my only "B" while I was at CTS!

Whenever I think of this seemingly-fundamentalistic view of the Book of Job by Dr. Boling, I recall an "extremely-short" introductory course in the Old Testament that I took at the Northern Baptist Theological Seminary (NBTS). The professor, whose name I have forgotten, stepped up to the lectern about 5 minutes before the first lecture was scheduled to start, and then turned to gaze intently at the classroom wall clock. When the clock reached the starting hour for the lecture, the professor asked a student to close the door to the

MY EXPERIENCES

classroom and announced that anyone late for a class that he teaches is not allowed to attend it. He took attendance, gave an incredibly-difficult quiz on the Old Testament, and before starting his lecture, held a Bible up high and stated, "If any person in this class believes that any word in the Bible is not the infallible word of God, that person should not come back after the class break." I was so surprised by this declaration of biblical infallibility and the consequence of not agreeing with it, that I decided not to wait for the break to leave the course. I calmly put my pen in my shirt pocket and my writing pad in my briefcase, and slowly stood up and walked out of the classroom, gently opening and closing the door to the hallway.

I soon had the opportunity to take an alternative introductory Old Testament course at the Catholic Theological Union (CTU). It was given by a Roman Catholic priest and Franciscan biblical scholar, the name of whom I do not recall, who had lived for many years in Jerusalem and was teaching at CTU that year. A new textbook on reading the Old Testament and his interests in Jewish history and Judaism made the course quite fascinating and informative.

I took three courses on the New Testament, all at CTS. They were respectively entitled "The Synoptic Gospels," "Healing in the New Testament" and "The New Testament Letters" These courses had several interesting aspects that I should mention here. Rev. Dr. Theodore "Ted" Jennings, a biblical theologian, showed how the Synoptic Gospels of Matthew, Mark, and Luke were derived in large part from a "lost" gospel, and how the Gospel of John markedly differs from them in its stories, theology, and spirituality. For homework during the course, Dr. Jennings suggested that every student read the gospel that he would be covering over and over as quickly as possible to best understand its purpose and content. Known for his wise applications of theology to the contemporary world, Dr. Jennings finished the course with: "I hope the world will someday get the message [in the Gospels]." Rev. Dr. Graydon "Grady" Snyder, a New Testament scholar, stated that all spiritual healing described in the New Testament was of various psychosomatic conditions generated

DOUGLAS E. BUSBY

by the social and religious stresses of the day. In support of this, he translated every healing "miracle" from the Greek New Testament into English, focusing on words for conditions that he believed had psychological causes. Early in the course, I agreed with him that some of the conditions could have been psychologically caused, or psychosomatic, and offered some alternative, non-psychosomatic diagnoses, but was ignored, so I just sat back and enjoyed the course. Finally, Dr. Snyder gave me a one-to-one tutorial on the letters of the New Testament, focusing on the letters attributed to the Apostle Paul. He showed me how Paul's theology was influenced by Jesus' teaching and Greek philosophy, and how biblical scholars have identified which of these letters were unlikely to have been written or dictated by Paul, specifically Ephesians, Colossians, 2 Thessalonians, 1 and 2 Timothy, Titus, and Hebrews.

I remember taking several other courses at CTS, especially for their practicality in ministry. The highlight of a course entitled "Theology of Mysticism," given at CTS by Dr. Cairns, was the class practicing a form of meditation called "centering prayer," developed and publicized by Rev. Thomas Keating, a Trappist monk. A course entitled "Theological Ethics" was presented at the Garrett Theological Seminary (GTS) by Rev. Dr. Kenneth Vaux, a biological and theological ethicist. He showed the class how The Ten Commandments and The Golden Rule can be used to construct a broad system of ethics for humanity. A course entitled "Good and Evil," given at CTS by Rev. Dr. Susan Thistlethwaite, President of CTS and a theologian, dealt with theodicy, or defense of God's goodness and omnipotence given the existence of evil. I remember her scolding me in front of several prospective seminary students who were sitting in on the class, for my colloquial use of the racially-inappropriate term, "black and white" while I was trying to answer a difficult question that she had asked me; later that day, one of the visiting students told me Dr. Thistlethwaite had used this term in a speech to the prospective students.

To continue, separate courses entitled "Practice of Ministry" were given at CTS by Dr. Edgerton and by Rev. Dr. Christopher Miller, a pastoral counselor at the First Presbyterian Church in

MY EXPERIENCES

Evanston, Illinois. Both of their courses dealt with issues that might be encountered by those in parish ministry, such as how to manage debates on churches being ONA, and conducting same-sex marriage (or union). In an introductory course entitled "Preaching," Dr. Edgerton covered different styles of preaching, including its distinctive form in African-American churches. And at CTS, Rev. Elizabeth "Betsy" Bueschel, a minister at FCCW, presented a course entitled "UCC History and Polity (organization)," which I subsequently taught many times in an abbreviated form to potential UCC members.

The principal courses for the M.Div., which all M.Div. students were obliged to take near the end of the CTS M.Div. Program, were entitled "Constructive Theology I and II" (in many seminaries called "systematic theology"). Given by Dr. Jennings, these courses had each student construct and communicate his or her own positions on key elements of Christianity, including theological method, God, Jesus, good and evil, baptism, communion, ministry, and the church.

Finally, the CTS M.Div. Program required each student to have two field education experiences, each of at least 400 hours in total duration. The designated experiences were clinical pastoral education (CPE), which usually involves learning to provide spiritual care in a hospital setting, and field placement, which usually involves being a minister-in-training in a church setting. As a physician and a medical director in Medicare, clinical pastoral education was thought to be a potential conflict of interest for me. Consequently, I had both of my field education experiences in 1995-96 at the First Congregational United Church of Christ in Elmhurst, Illinois, under its minister, Rev. Dr. Ernest "Ernie" Huntzinger.

From his past work with several field education experience students from CTS, Dr. Huntzinger believed that while at First Congregational, I should receive as much hands-on experience in ministry as possible, and arranged for me to become a licensed minister in the UCC so that I could perform the rites of the Church. Dr. Huntzinger was an excellent preacher and teacher, having a comprehensive knowledge of the Bible, a photographic memory, a dramatic personality, and countless stories from his childhood and youth in rural Pennsylvania. He was always ready to give me

DOUGLAS E. BUSBY

constructive advice. After I completed my second field education experience with Dr. Huntzinger, I continued as his part-time Associate Minister through 1997.

In my field education   With Rev. Dr. Huntzinger

Unforgettable Memories: From My Field Education

Dr. Huntzinger believed that an important step to preaching a sermon from the pulpit was learning how to give children's message that captures the children's (and adults') interest and uses words that children understand. One Sunday morning, I had several children sitting around me on the steps up to the altar, while I attempted to draw the children's attention to the just-restored, beautiful, stained glass windows of the four Evangelists above the altar. I asked the children, "What do you see in the church that makes you think of God?" The children pointed to the baptismal font, the church flag, the altar, and the cross on the altar, but not the windows, when Luke, with his remarkable biblical knowledge for being just five years of age, started to hyperventilate as he generated what I anticipated would certainly be the correct answer to my question. So that everyone would hear the answer, I held my lavalier lapel microphone in front of him. He said, "I know what reminds my dad of God." I replied, "So, Luke, what reminds your dad of God?" Luke answered, "When my dad hits his thumb with a hammer." What a roar of sustained laughter occurred, while Luke smiled and pointed to the windows!

The organ and choir in First Congregational were located at the opposite end of the church from the altar, lectern and pulpit. I still do not know whether Christina, who led the alto section of the choir, was the instigator of thumbs-up and thumbs-down responses of the choir to my sermons, and when the ends of my stole were uneven. Believe it

MY EXPERIENCES

or not, I found this type of critique both constructive and humorous. Dr. Huntzinger never said anything about it.

My first baptism ever was of a baby at First Congregational. t the request of the baby's parents, it was conducted privately between Sunday morning worship services rather than conventionally at one of them. During the Service of Baptism, I intended to add to the water already in the baptismal font, some water that I had obtained from the Jordan River while visiting the Holy Land, and had stored in small, plastic bottles which had contained liquid soap for blowing bubbles at weddings. As I began the service, I poured the water, supposedly from the Jordan River, into the font water, and immediately realized that the content of the bottle was liquid soap. Acting as though I was engaged in a routine procedure, I removed the font's basin and took it to the nearby men's washroom, where a member of the congregation who watched me wash it out remarked on how clean it will be with all of the soapsuds I was generating. After the brief pause that this incident created in the baptism service, it went on without a glitch – but without water from the Jordan River.

The first wedding that I ever performed was at First Congregational. The bride was the granddaughter of a prominent Illinois judge, who participated with me in it. The planning of the wedding service went well except for my having to resolve a disagreement in the bride's family on whether the bagpiper, whom the bride's mother had hired to play at the wedding, should lead the newly-married couple down the aisle and out of the church, or play on the church's parking lot after the service. Contrary to the decision finally being reached for the bagpiper to play outside of the church, someone reversed it without telling the organist, the bagpiper, or me, so that the departure of the newlyweds from the church was somewhat delayed until the bagpiper came into the church, and took over from the organist and led the newlyweds down the aisle. The service went well after I prevented an incident that could have disturbed it. When I visited the bride just before the service, I found her quite pale and standing alone in the middle of the "bride's room" of the church, saying she was going to "throw up. After the judge had someone place an empty pail behind the altar and both of us told the bride that we would care for her at the altar, I decided to *go ahead with the service. When the bride and groom initially stood facing the judge and me at the altar, I saw that the bride was now extremely pale and starting to faint. I grasped her hands and loudly said: "Marriage can be a stressful moment in our lives, so I am asking everyone here, including the bride and groom, to slowly take three deep breaths along with the judge and me." Many smiled and some even laughed or clapped as they participated in this little exercise. The bride quickly recovered.*

I graduated from CTS with my M.Div. on June 7, 1997, after receiving 16 A, 1 B, and 4 "passing" grades in 21 courses, and completing two field education experiences. I was ordained by the United Church of Christ on March 8, 1998. This process involved my being approved by: a guidance-and-support committee at FCCW, which periodically met with me while I was at CTS; by a career development service, which gave me a battery of psychological tests over a two-day period; by the ministerial qualifications committee of the Chicago Metropolitan Association of the UCC, which evaluated my understandings of ministry; and by a local group of clergy and laity, which examined me on a position paper that I had to write on my religious beliefs.

3. In Interim Ministry

During the fall of 1997 and winter of 1998, I received basic education in interim (transitional) ministry from the Interim Ministry Network (IMN), which trains ministers from several denominations to meet the ministerial needs of churches during the often-stressful periods between a church's ministers. My class included ministers from the Church of God, Christian Reformed, Church of the Brethren, Congregational Christian, Disciples (DOC), Episcopal, Lutheran (Evangelical and Missouri), Mennonite USA, Presbyterian USA, United Methodist, and UCC churches.

The IMN training took place at the Cedar Valley Center in West Bend, Wisconsin. In the first session of five days, three highly-experienced educators from the IMN described congregational systems and experiences of congregations during the interim period. Then they and other IMN ministers supervised inter-church

MY EXPERIENCES

group discussions on resolving issues that might occur in the interim period. At the end of this session, each of us was assigned a congregational system project, with directions on how to write a paper on it for review and discussion of the project by the IMN staff and students.

My congregational system project involved the failing ministry of a congregation of the Evangelical Lutheran Church of America (ELCA) in Elmhurst. From the initial meeting that I had with the minister and several members of this church, the failure of this church's ministry appeared to be due to a pervasive lethargy of the minister and congregation. The minister's lethargy seemed to stem from the church's board allowing the former minister's widow to live indefinitely in the manse, or clergy home, which was indirectly lowering his income, and from his having to perform most of the administrative and janitorial duties within the church, which was interfering with his time for ministry. The congregation's lethargy seemed to stem from many years of ineffective council leadership and minimal council turnover. I subsequently met on several occasions with the minister to design a system that would empower the church to operate more effectively, and then present it to the church's board. We decided that because I was not a member of his church, I should not attend his presentation. He met with the board to give his presentation, but at the last moment decided not to give it out of concern that it would result in his immediately being fired by the board. About a year later, Dr. Huntzinger told me that the minister had left this church, which was then sold and its congregation scattered to other ELCA churches in the area.

In the second session of three days at the Cedar Valley Center, the original three IMN educators reviewed the material on the interim ministry that they had presented to us in the first session, and then had the students present their project reports to mixed groups of educators and students for review and discussion. At the end of this session, we had worship and social time together. I was deeply grateful for the comprehensive knowledge of interim ministry that I had obtained in a highly-friendly, inter-church environment

4. In Graduate Theological Programs

In the fall of 2002, I decided to study for a Doctor of Ministry (D.Min.) degree, from which I could see potential benefits for me as an educator, interim minister, and, at the time, a new teacher and author on spiritual healing ministry. As an aside, a D.Min. is a professional degree, and a doctor of philosophy (Ph.D.) is an academic degree, so my D.Min. would be much more aligned to ministry than theology.

I returned to CTS to take courses and conduct a doctoral project. I was assigned a new D.Min. advisor whose name I do not recall. In our first meeting, she said that I would have to take all of my D.Min. courses at CTS and that she would have to approve each course in order to be assured that it was of the "academic quality" necessary for a D.Min student. She then pointed out that the "Theology and Medicine" course that I was teaching at CTS did not meet this requirement, even though several D.Min. students at CTS had already taken the course and she had just approved two D.Min. students to take it from me that fall. After this first-time meeting with her, I began to wonder whether she was attempting to dissuade me from being in the CTS D.Min. Program

I took two very informative courses at CTS, both from Rev. Dr. Bo Myung Seo, a theologian and culturist. One course, entitled "Interpretation and Contextual Theology," considered experiences of the past in scripture and the Christian tradition, in the context of present-day Christianity. The other course, entitled "Theology and Cultural Analysis," showed how the relationship between culture and religion is revealed in the motivation and manifestation of cultural expression. I received an "A" in both courses.

After the second course, I returned to my D.Min. advisor to discuss my next two courses and a possible topic for my doctoral project. Because I had not found another course at CTS that pertained to my interests in ministry, I handed her a list of such courses offered at other ACTS institutions. She simply glanced at the list, pushed it across her desk towards me, said "take any course you wish," and dismissed me with a hand motion. Now I was so convinced that she wanted me out of the CTS D.Min. program that

MY EXPERIENCES

I decided to transfer from it to another ACTS D.Min. program. Shortly thereafter, a minister, religious author, teacher, and friend, Rev. Dr. David Moffett-Moore, introduced me to the Graduate Theological Foundation (GTF) and its D.Min. program.

The GTF is a prestigious ecumenical and interreligious community of scholars that provides educational opportunities to credentialed professional theologians and ministers. Since GTF was formed in 1962, it has evolved from institution-directed to mostly self-directed online educational programs in partnership with leading academic institutions around the world, including the Oxford University Department for Continuing Education and the *Centro Pro Unione* in Rome, Italy. Its headquarters are in Sarasota, Florida.

In the spring of 2003, I successfully transferred my two course credits from the CTS D.Min. Program to the GTF D.Min. Program. That summer, I took a group of three courses at the Retreats International Institute at Notre Dame University in South Bend, Indiana. They were entitled "Dreams and Spirituality," "The Plunge into God: Women and the Mystic Tradition," and "Nature, Cosmos and God: An Exploration of Ecology, Spirituality and Ethics." All of my fellow students in these courses were Roman Catholic priests and nuns, which led to my participation as the lone Protestant in some very interesting discussions. And in the summer of 2004, I took a course on Reiki, a Japanese form of energy healing, at the Holistic Alliance Training Center in St. Joseph, Michigan. I also received "A's" in the Notre Dame and Holistic alliance courses.

After the coursework for my D.Min. at GTF, I worked on my doctoral project and wrote a dissertation on it entitled "The Healing Service: Expressing God's Unconditional Love." Dr. Moffet-Moore, who had received a D.Min. and a Ph.D. from GTF, was my project director. As I said in the dissertation, the purpose of this project was to develop a unique spiritual healing service that enables us to connect with God and each other, with uplifted spirits and untroubled minds, for spiritual healing. The dissertation began with a brief history of spiritual healing in the Judeo-Christian tradition, giving particular attention to spiritual healing by Jesus of Nazareth and how he demonstrated the various ways that we can connect

DOUGLAS E. BUSBY

with God and each other in a healing service. Then it described how each of these ways of connecting can shape the design and conduct of a healing service. Finally, it provided a framework and some resources for a healing service, and a summary of my experience as a minister in conducting a service. The dissertation was approved by Rev. Dr. John Morgan, Founder and President of GTF, and I received a D.Min. from GTF on May 6, 2005. My dissertation was subsequently published as a book, entitled *We Can Help God Heal Us*.

In the fall of 2013, I decided to return to GTF to broaden my knowledge of theology in 10 courses and a doctoral thesis leading to a Ph.D. in Theological Studies. My interest in the "biblically-based" practice of spiritual healing had turned to understanding the nature of spiritual healing and the role of the spirit world in it, which I now planned to do in the GTF Ph.D. Program. I was interviewed for this program by Dr. Morgan, who approved my stepping "out of the box" of conventional theology, as usually studied for a Ph.D.

My first course, entitled "Search for the Human Soul," was given by Rev. Dr. Paul Kirbas, the President of and a theologian at the Kirbas Institute in Wheaton, Illinois. It was an excellent starting point for my Ph.D. studies, in considering whether humans have a soul, or spirit, which leaves the body when it dies and returns to the reconstituted body at the end of time (dualism), or whether humans do not have a soul but the body dies and is reconstituted at the end of time (physicalism). Next on the course list was the first of three independent-study papers, on subjects selected by me, which required a course-equivalent number of hours to research. They were entitled "Can Disincarnate Spirits Help Us Heal?", "How Do 'Gifted Healers' Function?", and "Christianity and Spiritism." I should note here, that Spiritism is defined as **the moral philosophy and observational science that is concerned principally with the nature and destiny of spirits and their relationship to the mortal world.**

The next course, given by Rev. Dr. Jennifer Little, a theologian at the Anabaptist Mennonite Biblical Seminary, in Elkhart, Indiana, was entitled "Process Theology; Perspectives for Ministry." The rather complicated description of process theology begins with the

MY EXPERIENCES

premise that our reality is comprised of a series of momentary events of experience initiated by God's creative will and subjected to our selective decision-making. Interesting, but I wondered whether process theology could fit into the practice of ministry.

I took two more courses from Dr. Kirbas, entitled "God, Nature and Us," which considered our responsibilities and difficulties in protecting nature, and "A Biblical Theology for Biotechnology," which considered how the Bible might be applied to ethical decision-making in various biotechnologies. Then I took a course entitled "Mystical Theology" from Rev. Dr. Dennis Billy, C.Ss.R., a theologian at St. Mary's Seminary and University in Baltimore, Maryland, which raised my awareness of how mysticism has contributed to Christianity from ancient times to the present. Certainly mystical was a fascinating course that I took from Dr. Ann Graber, a practicing psychologist in logotherapy in St. Charles, Missouri, with a self-explanatory title of "Near Death Experiences and Their Life-Transforming Impact." Finally, Dr. Morgan gave a course entitled "The Modern Search for Personal Meaning," based on the writings of the Viktor Frankl, a philosopher, psychiatrist, neurologist, and Holocaust survivor, who founded a school of psychotherapy called logotherapy, based on searching for a life's meaning as the central human motivational force.

The coursework for my Ph.D. was quite challenging for me academically, especially with my having to write both weekly and final papers on each course topic, and discuss them with the professor covering that topic. I received an "A" in all 10 Ph.D. courses.

My doctoral thesis was entitled "Can the Spirit World Provide Us Help in Healing? Seeking an Answer from What is Known About the Nature of Disincarnate Spirit Existence, and from the Spiritual Ministries of Harry Edwards and John of God." The thesis began with a review of belief in the soul and spirit in the Bible and Christianity and a description of how nonbelievers in the soul and spirit are being challenged by the near-death experience (NDE). It continues with a summary of what we know about spirit existence, drawing upon information provided by the spirit world, including a prominent, departed LSTC theologian. Then it considers how spirits might help God heal us from the perspective of energy healing, and gives many examples of spirits providing help in spiritual healing by working through spiritual healers such as Harry Edwards and John of God. Finally, it suggests how help in spiritual healing from spirits might be requested and used in the ministry of spiritual healing and in the practice of energy healing.

I received a Ph.D. degree from GTF on December 1, 2015. My thesis was subsequently published as a book entitled *Spirits Can Help God Heal Us.*

F. MY CAREER IN THEOLOGY
1. Introduction

Since 1999, I have served four UCC churches as their interim, or transitional, minister. One church was in Michigan, two churches were in Indiana, and one church was in Illinois. An interim, or transitional, minister fully replaces a "called," or "permanent" minister who has left his or her church. During the interim period, the church will form a search and call committee and develop a church profile that gives prospective candidates for the empty ministerial position key information to consider in applying to be the church's new minister. UCC Headquarters usually manages the search process after it approves the church profile for distribution. An interim minister can assist the church with the development of its profile, but is not involved in any way with the search and call process when it begins. She or he can serve from a few to several months and, as I experienced, can encounter unforeseen situations that lead to an early departure.

Between the interim ministries, I continued to work as an information analyst in medicine and served many times as "pulpit supply," or substitute minister, from one to several Sundays. I did pulpit supply in Goshen, South Bend, Plymouth, Elkhart, Bremen, La Porte, Woodland, Wanatah, Chesterton, Merrillville, Hammond, Highland, and Crown Point in Indiana, in Frankfort in Illinois, and in Niles, Portage, and New Buffalo in Michigan. I also taught courses entitled "Medicine and Theology" at CTS, "Introduction to Ethics," "Ethical Philosophy," and "Western Religions" at Purdue Northwest in Indiana, and "Spiritual Healing" at Sancta Sophia Seminary in Tahlequah, Oklahoma.

And since 1999, I have studied, practiced, lectured, and written on spiritual healing. I have learned that each of us has a subtle energy body that appears to be our immortal spirit, that each of us is capable of performing spiritual healing, and that the spiritual world can help God in spiritual healing. My involvement with interim ministry and spiritual healing is described below. My major writing on spiritual healing has been published in books entitled *We Can Help God Heal Us* and *Spirits Can Help God Heal Us*.

2. As Interim Minister of the First Congregational Church, United Church of Christ (Benton Harbor, MI)

My first interim ministry was from December 1999 to August 2000, at the First Congregational Church, United Church of Christ, in Benton Harbor, Michigan. This large church was built in the early 1900s to accommodate its several hundred members in a predominantly-caucasian community. Some of the church's features were an impressive bell tower, many beautiful stained-glass windows that depicted well-known stories in the Bible, a magnificent E.M. Skinner pipe organ, numerous classrooms, and a gymnasium-size, multi-purpose room. First Congregational had not become ONA.

In the 1950s, Benton Harbor's demographics began to shift as it attracted African-American laborers from the South for its automotive parts and appliance industries. The new families who populated Benton Harbor preferred to worship mainly in Baptist and Pentecostal churches, and the membership of First Congregational significantly declined over a several-year period. Then most of the industry moved out of Benton Harbor in the 1990s, causing such an economic downturn that this city became widely known for its unemployment, poverty, empty homes, crime, and illicit drug sales.

The previous minister of this church, Rev. Dr. Richard Taylor, had served it for 12 years. He had accepted a call to be the minister of a UCC church on Rhode Island soon after a consultant on church membership concluded that First Congregational was unlikely to remain viable for more than a few years in Benton Harbor's deteriorating community. Nevertheless, the congregation voted to maintain itself "as is." Since an interim minister should not initiate

MY EXPERIENCES

a new-member drive or alter the times and formats of worship services of a church between its ministers, I suggested that the congregation suggest these possible activities to its future, called minister. I quickly settled into the routine of First Congregational, which was not had about 135 members, a small choir and Sunday school, and an average attendance of 75 at its Sunday morning worship services. I baptized my teenage grandson-by-marriage, Frank Garvey, as an extension of the children's message at a Sunday worship service. And at the request of several church members, I conducted several spiritual healing services on Wednesday evenings.

At my suggestion, the entire congregation had a Saturday "retreat" in its gym to envision its future and, in turn, to decide on the qualifications of its next minister. Thereafter, the church's board formed a search-and-call committee and asked me to help it prepare the church profile to be used in its search for a minister

The over nine months that I was at First Congregational Church had some challenging moments. Women living in a known "crack house" across the street from the parking lot entrance to the church were soliciting passers-by for sex, and others were making illicit drug sales to truckers driving through the church's parking lot. I tried repeatedly and unsuccessfully to meet with the mayor and then the chief of police on this problem, with the chief of police insisting that I meet him at noon in his usual bar, but not showing up. Finally, the Michigan State Police assessed the seriousness of the drug-selling problem with surveillance using unmarked police cars parked nearby the church and a camera mounted on the church's bell tower. The police quickly resolved the problem, and even, became the police force for Benton Harbor for several months.

A challenging situation for me occurred when some boxes of used needles and syringes were discovered in the trash bin behind the church. After this incident, the church secretary informed me that Dr. Taylor had permitted a syringe exchange program based in Kalamazoo, Michigan, to serve cocaine addicts in the Benton Harbor area from the basement of the church. I contacted the medical consultant in the Benton Harbor Department of Health about this,

DOUGLAS E. BUSBY

and he explained that legally, churches should not be involved with syringe-exchange programs. I then asked the representative of the program in Benton Harbor to relocate its syringe-exchange site, and immediately received a telephone call from the director of the program. He introduced himself as a UCC minister, and accused me of deliberately trying to destroy the program in Benton Harbor. Surprisingly, he would not let me to explain why I had asked that the syringe distribution be moved out of the church. Subsequently, he openly demanded an apology for this from me at a meeting of Southwest Michigan UCC clergy in Kalamazoo, and would not allow me to explain why.

Soon thereafter, a woman in the congregation who was the leader of a Girl Scout troop at a local Seventh Day Adventist Church. As a step toward several scouts in the troop receiving their "My Promise, My Faith" pins, she wished to bring the scouts to First Congregational to have me show them the stained-glass windows depicting biblical stories. After I agreed to do this, she strongly advised me not to tell the stories from memory or make any remark about their authenticity beyond what the Bible specifically states, because, in contrast to the UCC, the Seventh Day Adventist Church teaches that every word in the Bible is the infallible Word of God. In reply, I told her that for me to comment to her scouts on the authenticity of a biblical story or even describe its theological purpose would be inappropriate, but I should at least draw her scouts' attention to the artistry in each window, and ask them what biblical story that the window depicts and why its artist might have selected that story. At first, she neither agreed nor disagreed with me, and said that she needed to consult with the other leaders of her troop on whether or not to go ahead with the visit. Soon thereafter, the visit occurred and I had a delightful time letting the scouts teach me!

Midway in my interim ministry at First Congregational, a wealthy, elderly member of it asked me to tell its search and call committee not to call a female minister. He said that he was talking about this to me rather than to the committee because I would know that females should not be ordained ministers from reading the letters of the Apostle Paul, and cited two passages from Paul's letters to Timothy to support this. I told him that Timothy's letters were not written by Paul and over 25 percent of UCC ministers are women. After I gave him this information, he said that he would not worship, let alone take communion, in a church led by a female minister. Then, he inferred that he would withdraw his substantial financial support of First Congregational if a male was not selected to be its new minister. I did not say anything more to him about his views on and potential responses to a female being called, for I knew that the search and call committee had just offered a male candidate the position.

I greatly enjoyed my interim ministry at the First Congregational Church in Benton Harbor. Unfortunately, I did not have the opportunity that an interim minister usually has about a month after a called minister arrives, to have a constructive visit with the incoming minister, in this case, Rev. F. Russell Baker. I would have described for him my interim ministry experiences at First Congregational, and this church's current and future challenges that I saw in serving it. Rev. Baker arrived an hour late for my appointment with him. After he introduced himself, he immediately showed me a picture of his wife, who was an African-American, and stated that he would learn from her how First Congregational should function in its African-American community. Surprised by the way that our visit began, I said that my reason for visiting him was not to tell him how to manage his church, and he replied that he already knew everything about operating a UCC church, and abruptly ended our meeting. Thus began his six years at the church, ending in its failure to thrive, being given to Trinity United Church of Christ in Chicago for a failed attempt to restart, and finally sold to the Legacy Group of Benton Harbor, which restored it for use as a community center with an emphasis on youth.

3. As Interim Minister of the First Congregational Church, United Church of Christ (Elkhart, IN)

My second interim ministry was from December 2002 to May 2003, at the First Congregational Church, United Church of Christ, in Elkhart, Indiana. The history of this church goes back to the 1840s. Although its 1940's architecture looks more like an office building than a church, inside it has a spacious main worship space with a large pipe organ and abundant choir space, a chapel, and several large offices and

DOUGLAS E. BUSBY

classrooms on two floors. This church was located in downtown Elkhart on the edge of an area of deteriorating homes and businesses, and increasing criminal activity, in selling illicit drugs. It was an all-white, middle-income church disinterested in promoting diversity and growth of its congregation, or in becoming ONA.

When I arrived at the First Congregational Church, it had about 220 members, fairly large choir and Sunday school, and an average attendance of about 100 at its Sunday morning worship services. This church's previous minister, whose name I do not recall, was an ordained Missionary Baptist minister, farmer, and clinical psychologist who was invited to conduct a Sunday morning worship service at First Congregational after its previous minister left. He stayed on as its minister for eight years, "as the permanent interim minister." He used the 1986 UCC Book of Worship as his resource for Sunday worship and other church services. Meanwhile, the congregation remained in the UCC in name only.

The council of First Congregational began to form a search and call committee for a new minister in the spring of 2003. At that time, it decided to re-engage with the UCC and asked me to give a series of lectures on UCC history and polity after Sunday morning worship services. I gave four lectures along with handouts of the slides that I used during them. At the end of the last lecture, I mentioned the national UCC website as a source of additional information about the UCC. On the following Sunday, I was informed by the president of the church's council that three families had abruptly decided to leave First Congregational after looking at the UCC website and taking issue with the ONA and gay marriage policies described on the website. He noted that these families had followed the former interim minister from the local Missionary Baptist Church to First Congregational, and that they had become very active members of First Congregational. At this point in our conversation, a prominent member of First Congregational, who had just returned to Elkhart after a long vacation, interrupted us and angrily accused me of forcing ONA and gay marriage policies on the congregation. He would not listen to me when I tried to inform him that in my lectures, which he had missed, I had stated that individual congregations in the UCC can decide whether or not to adopt ONA

MY EXPERIENCES

and gay marriage policies. Our very tense discussion concluded with the president of the council ordering me not to attempt to resolve the three families' issues with policies. Later, I learned that the families had followed the former interim minister of First Congregational to the Goshen Church of the Nazarene, where he had become its co-minister

Monday morning two weeks later began with the director of the Sunday school coming into my office in tears and shaking, to report that when she had returned to the church to pick up a personal article on the previous Sunday afternoon, she found the church's choir director sitting on the couch in the foyer, with a young girl, whom she did not know, lying across his lap. He said that he was giving grief counseling to the girl, who had come to him on her way to see her deceased grandmother in a nearby funeral home. I telephoned the president of the church council to report this incident, and a meeting of the council was held that evening to discuss it. In the interim, the president of the church council asked me to consult with the attorneys for UCC Headquarters and the Indiana-Kentucky Conference of the UCC on how the UCC would recommend that First Congregational handle the incident. The headquarters attorney said that the choir director should be fired immediately. The conference attorney recommended that the girl's age be determined, and if she was over 16 and her mother had given her permission to meet with the church's choir director for grief counseling, to drop the issue; he did not suggest what should be done if the girl was under age 16. I reported what the UCC attorneys had recommended to the council that evening, and it decided to have the church's attorney contact the girl's mother regarding the girl's age and her mother's permission. I understand that a few days later, the church's attorney informed the council that the incident had been resolved after the choir director and the church's attorney, who were close friends, and the choir director's sister, who was a UCC minister, "put their heads together." Interestingly, I subsequently learned that the former interim minister of First Congregational had not instituted the UCC's safe church policies, which could have prevented this apparent boundary break. I also learned that the church's choir director, who conducted the choirs at one of Elkhart's high schools, had been placed on probation for inappropriately touching a young girl, and that as a School Board member, the president of the church council would have known about this.

Despite the incidents described above, I did not receive a negative comment my interim ministry until May of 2003. I had gradually introduced a more conventional format for UCC Sunday morning worship services than the former interim minister had been using. I was making regular "communion" visits to the homebound members of this church, which had not been done for years, and is usually not done by interim ministers. At the request of the church's board of deacons, I was providing copies of my sermons to the congregation. During Lent, I conducted evening worship services on Wednesdays, including Ash Wednesday. I had begun to assist the church council in developing a church profile. But in my sixth month in interim ministry at Elkhart's First Congregational UCC Church collapsed. I believe that the story of what happened to cause it can now be told..

Unforgettable Memories: Mention of the Invasion of Iraq in a Sermon

On Sunday, May 11, 2003, I briefly commented in my sermon that I was saddened by a picture and article on the front page of the Chicago Tribune that morning regarding a fully-occupied civilian bus in Baghdad, Iraq, that had been accidentally destroyed by a USAF air-to-ground missile. I went on to say that I hoped that the United States would find weapons of mass destruction in Iraq, to justify its invasion of Iraq to search for them.

When I returned to the church on May 13 after speaking on spiritual healing at the noon meeting of the Elkhart Downtown Kiwanis Club, I found the president of the church council and the chair of the church's board of deacons sitting in my office. After I greeted them, the chair of the board of deacons said that "many" members of the congregation were upset with me for having made a "treasonous" statement during my sermon that Sunday. When I said that I could not recall what I had said that was upsetting, the chair of the board of deacons stated that I had "insulted the

MY EXPERIENCES

President of the United States" by criticizing him for ordering the invasion of Iraq.

Since neither the president of the church council nor the chair of the board of deacons had attended the worship service, I reiterated to them what I had said. Moreover, to further defend myself, I drew their attention to a letter on my desk that I had just received from the President of the UCC, Rev. Dr. John Thomas. This letter asked all UCC ministers to join their colleagues in other mainline Christian churches, in preaching against the invasion of Iraq.

Frustrated by my response to his accusation, the chair of the board of deacons said that if I had committed such an act in an early congregational church, I would have been "hanged for treason." Then he added that the same upset members of the congregation had complained to him about my inappropriately "praying for innocent victims of war" during Wednesday evening Lenten services. I responded to him by saying that I had also done so – as Jesus taught us – in every worship service that I had conducted in First Congregational since the invasion of Iraq began that March 19.

At this point in my confrontation with these two leaders of the congregation, I asked the president of the church council if I could propose a resolution to this misunderstanding of what I said about the justification for our country's invasion of Iraq in my sermon, and why I was praying for the innocent victims of war. My first suggestion was for me to meet with the upset members of the congregation, and the second was for me to address these issues from the pulpit, which they rejected without discussion. My third suggestion was for me not to renew my six-month contract as First Congregational's interim minister, which they accepted under the condition that I not discuss the circumstances of my upcoming departure with anyone else in the congregation. During my remaining two Sundays at First Congregational, I noticed the unusual absence of only two families from worship. On my last Sunday, the president of the church council came to the front of the church's sanctuary, thanked me for my service to the church and wished me well, adding that I was leaving became First Congregational to complete a writing project in medicine that I had been conducting before its interim minister.

DOUGLAS E. BUSBY

About two weeks after I left First Congregational, I was invited back to it for an exit interview, chaired by a local UCC minister who had been appointed by the Association Minister. It was attended by 10 members of the church's congregation, with some coming from its council and board of deacons. The chair introduced himself and, giggling nervously, stated that he did not know why he was there. The president of the church council said that he was to preside over my exit interview and asked me to describe my ministerial experiences at First Congregational. I concluded my presentation with a summary of the meeting in my office with the president of the church council and the chair of the church's board of deacons. When I referred to the issue over my praying for the innocent victims of war, a member of the church council, stormed out of the room, loudly slamming the door behind him, consequently causing the interview to end. Surprisingly, no questions or comments were made about the circumstances of my leaving First Congregational. Moreover, the UCC minister who chaired the interview contributed nothing to it, and I received no follow-up report on it.

4. As Interim Minister of the First Congregational United Church of Christ (Bremen, IN)

As repeatedly requested of me by the Association Minister, I agreed to serve as the interim minister of the First Congregational United Church of Christ in the town of Bremen, Indiana, starting in October of 2007. I was somewhat familiar with this church from being its pulpit supply minister for two Sundays about four years before, just after the congregation split when its minister insisted on replacing its traditional Sunday morning worship service with a contemporary worship service, including praise music. I had been reluctant to be its interim minister when the Association Minister told me that its previous minister, Rev. Susan Sickelka, had two "bad" experiences in this church, that caused her such emotional distress that she had to resign. Later, I learned that certain recently-elected members of the church council with fundamentalistic leanings had announced their dissatisfaction with the UCC ordaining females. Then a member of the church council had accused Rev. Sickelka of stealing

MY EXPERIENCES

money from the church's bank account, when the money was authorized by the church council and made to her by the church's treasurer for the tuition necessary for her to begin courses at the Christian Theological Seminary in Indianapolis, Indiana, in its D.Min. program.

When the chair of the church council contacted me by telephone and asked me to meet with the council for an interview to be First Congregational's interim minister, I agreed to do so. However, only two members of the council were present for the interview, and did not wish to speak for the council when I began to ask questions about my responsibilities as this church's interim minister. Consequently, I asked that the interview be rescheduled, if possible with the entire council. The two council members agreed and the interview was held, albeit with no answer being given when I asked why Rev. Sickelka had resigned from being the church's minister. I accepted First Congregational's invitation to be its interim minister after it approved my request for a renewable six-month contract for this.

The First Congregational United Church of Christ in Bremen does not appear to have published its history, but as compared to the architecture of other Bremen churches, the church building probably dates to the early 1900s. When I arrived, it had about 130 members, an average Sunday morning worship attendance of about 65, no choir, and a few children in its Sunday school.

First Congregational had a large women's Bible study group which was being taught by a church member with its minister functioning as back-up. In my first week at the church, I was asked to lead the group through one of the Psalms, at the end of which one of the women pointedly asked me, "Do you believe in the devil?" Startled by a question that had nothing to do with the psalm being studied that day, I said, "You mean the fellow with the horns coming out of his forehead, a red jumpsuit, and a pitchfork?" Silence, then laughter by everyone but the woman who had asked the question. By her reaction, I guessed correctly that the woman and her husband were farmers, so I immediately apologized for my remark. I then gave the group a short lesson on the theology of the devil, for which she thanked me. I never did answer her question.

DOUGLAS E. BUSBY

My day-to-day ministry at this First Congregational went well. I conducted weekly worship services at the UCC retirement home in Bremen, made regular communion visits to the church's homebound, and continued to have copies of my sermons available, as I had done at the First Congregational Church in Elkhart.

The First Congregational United Church of Christ in Bremen was not ONA, as I soon learned when a prominent member of it told me that she and her family would leave the church if I ever allowed a "gay or lesbian" to worship in it. Subsequently, other members of the church told me that Bremen's population of over 4,000 people had just one African-American adult, that the Ku Klux Klan was still active in Bremen, and that a church member may be a Klan officer. Also disturbing to me was an attitude that members of the congregation had towards the Amish, in addressing their Amish domestics disparagingly as "girls."

Two issues touching on my responsibilities as interim minister at First Congregational warrant being mentioned here. The first issue revolved around who would conduct the 2007 Christmas Eve worship service. This church had traditionally held a minister-led worship service on Christmas Eve. For a reason that I was unable to determine, Rev. Sickelka had allowed a new family in the church to conduct the Christmas Eve worship service the previous year, during which she sat in the back of the church. I was told by the chairs of the church council and the worship committee that this family would again conduct the service and that I did not have to attend it.

The other issue was the unnecessary cancellation of a Sunday morning worship service by the chair of the church council. After an overnight snowfall, my wife and I arrived for the service to find the church's walks and parking lot cleared of snow, but its doors locked; I had not been given a key to the church. We then drove home to La Porte, observing that all of the other churches that we passed in Bremen were open and active.

To compound this issue, Christina and I had anticipated the overnight snowfall in the Bremen area, and after attending an evening concert of the South Bend Symphony Orchestra, planned to drive to Bremen and stay in its only lodging, a downtown motel. Our motel room was unbelievably filthy and odorous, and consequently,

MY EXPERIENCES

we spent a sleepless night. Later that Sunday, I learned that the chair of the church council had canceled the worship service without any attempt to reach me before doing this. And on Monday, I reported our horrible experience at the motel to Bremen's public health department and was told that the department was well aware of the uncleanliness of the motel, but was reluctant to take action on it since the motel was owned by Bremen's Chief of Police.

In April of 2008, my initial six months at the First Congregational were coming to an end, so I repeatedly tried unsuccessfully to schedule a meeting with the church council to discuss whether the church wished to have me continue as its interim minister for another six months. I mentioned this problem in communication to the church secretary, and she had no explanation for it. Then, a day before my contract was to end, the chair of the church council telephoned me and said that my ministry had been successful and that I did not need to have an interview to continue it. The following morning, the church secretary came into my office, crying. She said that for six months, had been carrying a secret: the reason for my first interview by the church council was to see the color of my skin. After I consoled her, I decided not to sign a new contract.

5. As Transitional Senior Minister of the Glenview Community Church, United Church of Christ (Glenview, IL)

From August 2011 to February 2013, I served as the transitional senior minister at the Glenview Community Church, United Church of Christ, in Glenview, Illinois. This church was founded in 1897 as the Community Church of Glenview and became the Glenview Community Church (GCC) in 1941 as it began to provide an ecumenical ministry in a rapidly-growing suburb of Chicago that was yet to have churches of other denominations. By the late 1940s, the membership of GCC had swelled to over 5,000 members, and a large church building was built to accommodate them. Featured in a 1955 *Life Magazine* article, GCC has been regarded as one of the first "megachurches." To expand its outreach, GCC joined the UCC in

DOUGLAS E. BUSBY

1961 and became one of the largest UCC congregations in the United States. It has been ONA since 2010.

My daughter Sharon and her family were active members of GCC, and consequently, I learned about GCC's search for a transitional senior minister after attending her daughter Melissa's confirmation at a GCC Sunday morning worship service in May of 2011. GCC's Associate Minister, Rev. Dr. Pamela "Pam" Keckler, encouraged me to apply for this position. I was interviewed for it by a search-and-call committee, which appointed me to replace its Senior Minister, Rev. Dr. Harold Roberts on August 1. This gave me time to have a brief vacation from my information analysis work and to find an apartment in the Glenview area for the 18 months of my anticipated ministry at GCC.

When I arrived at GCC, I learned that it had just over 1,500 members and an average Sunday morning worship service attendance of 425 children and adults. The average Sunday school attendance was 125, and there were 61 teenagers in the confirmation class and about 40 teenagers in the youth group. GCC had an impressive music program, led by its music director and highly-accomplished organist, Gary Wendt, with an adult choir of about 45 members. Two children's choirs had a total of about 60 members. At the time, the church's music board was engaged in a search for new directors for its adult choir and children's choirs.

Dr. Keckler served as GCC's Minister for Spiritual Formation and Operations. Spiritual formation encompassed all of the Christian education activities in GCC, including the children's and youth programs and the confirmation classes. She was assisted in the youth program by Elizabeth Hartung-Ciccolini, who was also a seminarian at CTS. Church operations were conducted by GCC's administrative coordinator, a communications and media administrator, a part-time business administrator, and a facility manager.

GCC had a full-time "Faith Community Nurse," Marilyn Belleau, who had been involved in developing the remarkable specialty of parish nurse as an international professional specialty. She worked with me to assure that the medical, residential, nutritional, social and transportation needs of homebound members of the church

MY EXPERIENCES

were being met. We also made regular visits to the homebound and led a twice-yearly Sunday afternoon service called "Remembering Our Loved Ones."

During my interview to be GCC's transitional senior minister, I was asked if I would conduct an early Sunday morning worship service of a more "spiritual nature" than the later, traditional worship service, and I replied that I would be pleased to do so. Called "A Time for Spiritual Reflection," this service was held in the main church at 8:30 a.m. on Sunday mornings, with Gary Wendt kindly arriving early to prepare its attendees for worship with background music on the organ or piano. I designed the service for a broad spiritual experience, using traditional modalities of worship plus meditation, as follows: a shortened hymn, an invocation, the reading of a biblical passage with a brief sermon on it, a shortened hymn, a guided or silent meditation of at least 20 minutes in duration, a pastoral prayer ending with The Lord's Prayer, a shortened hymn, and a benediction; communion was added on the first Sunday of the month. As I noted above, an interim minister should not alter the times and formats of worship services of a church between its ministers. Consequently, I advised the group of about 20 who regularly attended this service, that the new permanent minister would decide whether or not to have it.

Dr. Keckler and I always started the Sunday morning regular worship service together, and she would often have to leave it to conduct the worship service in Sunday school. She preached and gave the pastoral prayer once a month, and officiated at communion on alternate months.

From the beginning of my ministry at GCC, I was impressed by the structure of its volunteer, lay administrative organization, and the competence and dedication of the leadership of this organization's numerous boards and committees. The authority of the congregation was vested in a 28-member executive council, which met monthly. It consisted of the senior and associate ministers, present moderator, vice moderator, and past moderator, the treasurer, the church clerk, eight at-large members, 12 board chairs, and the Women's Association chair. The boards, which also met monthly, were for adult education, confirmation and youth,

DOUGLAS E. BUSBY

finance, membership, missions outreach, music and pastoral care, services and sacraments, and stewardship. The committees, which usually met periodically, were for planning, operating, leadership, and technology and communications. I was expected to attend all executive council and board meetings, and when needed, various committee meetings.

GCC was a remarkably-active church, in large part reflective of its commitment to ecumenical outreach in the community. Its facilities were wide open to the community, being used by such organizations as the Glenview Community Church Nursery School, the Resale Shop (operated by the Women's Association of GCC), Boy Scouts, Girl Scouts, Hands of Peace, Common Ground, Alcoholics Anonymous, Al Anon, Senior Housing and Wellness Fairs, LifeSource Blood Drives, the local Breast Cancer Survivor Volunteer Choir, and Simple Gifts Music Concerts. And GCC had a large gym that was used by local sports programs in volleyball, basketball, and pickleball.

GCC was also extensively engaged in mission outreach. Some of the numerous organizations that it was supporting were Habitat for Humanity, Leap Learning Systems, Northfield Food Pantry, A Just Harvest, Hands of Peace, Interfaith Refugee Immigration Ministries, Back Bay Mission, PADS (for providing advocacy, dignity, and shelter), and The Night Ministry.

I was fully occupied at GCC, spending weekdays, Sunday mornings, and at least two evenings a week at the church. I worked on my sermons in evenings and on most Saturdays at the apartment. Some leisure time enabled me to play my trumpet in the Glenview Concert Band, which rehearsed one evening a week and had a busy summer concert schedule, attend "make-up" meetings of various Rotary International clubs in the area, and join the American Legion in Glenview. I also went home to Valparaiso for a day every other week, and fortunately, my wife Christina could take time from her year as a District Governor of Rotary International to visit me every other weekend. And often alone or with Christina, I would spend a joyful Friday evening with Sharon and her husband at the nearby Hackney's Restaurant.

When I started at GCC, I was age 76, and except for arthritic pain in my right hip which was controlled by cortisone injections into it.

MY EXPERIENCES

Preaching at GCC   A Christina visit

In the fall of 2011, my prostate-specific antigen (PSA) blood test was significantly elevated, and biopsies of my prostate identified low-grade cancer in it. The cancer was treated with 45 doses of radiation with the innovative Calypso® 4D Localization System™, which uses global-positioning-system (GPS) technology to deliver radiation to cancer with minimum side effects. At the time, the only Calypso unit in the Chicago area was in Glenview, which enabled me to have every 45-second radiation treatment on the way to GCC in the morning.

Unforgettable Memories: Loss of the Functioning of Muscles that Control Vision in my Right Eye

I had my last radiation treatment for prostate cancer on February 22, 2012. That evening, I developed a dry cough and a right-sided headache, which persisted despite my taking over-the-counter pain medications and a pulmonologist prescribing an inhalant medication for the cough. On a Friday morning in mid-April of 2012, I was working at the computer in my office at GCC, when the muscles that lift my right upper eyelid and enable my right eye to look upwards stopped working. Consequently, the images of everything that I saw with my right eye when I raised the upper eyelid with a finger, would quickly move upwards in my field of vision, making me disoriented and nauseated. I immediately went to the emergency department in the Northshore University Hospital, where diagnostic testing ruled out stroke as a cause of my vision problem, and an appointments were made for me to see a neurologist, a rheumatologist, and a neuro-ophthalmologist the coming Monday.

DOUGLAS E. BUSBY

Over the weekend, my daughter Sharon's husband, who makes eyeglasses, gave me a black eyepatch to wear over my right eye and covered the right lens of my eyeglasses with black electrician's tape. Fortunately, Dr. Keckler was scheduled to preach that Sunday.

My visits to the three specialists led to a biopsy of my right temporal artery on the next day, which showed that the artery was completely blocked by an arteritis (also called Horton's or large cell arteritis), a rare, auto-immune disease of unknown cause that often blocks arterial blood flow to the interior of the eye, producing blindness. This condition had blocked the arterial blood flow to muscles in my right upper eyelid and around my right eyeball. Moreover, it also affected my major pulmonary arteries to produce the cough. Later that day, the rheumatologist started treatment with an intravenously-administered, high-dose steroid to prevent the arteritis from progressing to produce blindness in either or both of my eyes; thereafter, I took an oral steroid, initially at a high dose, but then at gradually-decreasing doses over for two years. The headache and cough disappeared overnight, but the paralysis of the muscles in my right upper eyelid and around my right eyeball persisted. This led the neuro-ophthalmologist to say that at best, I might have only a slight recovery of the eyelid and eye muscle function over several months, after which a prism in the right lens of my eyeglasses might enable me to fuse the images in my visual field. However, he then pointed out that to his knowledge, this rare consequence of temporal arteritis never recovers completely.

As my right eye condition continued, I had to learn to turn my head slightly to the right so that I had a good field of vision with my left eye; this became automatic over a several-day period. And every morning immediately after awakening. I would sit on the end of the bed with my right eye closed and, after pushing my right upper eyelid upwards with a finger, count how many seconds it would take for the image of a small painting on the wall in front of me to ascend to the ceiling. The five seconds that I consistently counted simply did not change – at least until Wednesday, July 4, 2012.

I believe that during the night of July 3, I experienced spiritual healing that restored the functioning of the muscles in my right upper eyelid and around my right eyeball, paralyzed as a

MY EXPERIENCES

consequence of right temporal arteritis. I believe that contributing to this event was my sermon on spiritual healing followed by a hymn for healing and a healing prayer for "family members and friends," during the main Sunday morning worship service at GCC on July 1. And I believe that the Healing Touch therapy that Christina gave my right eye before we went to sleep on July 3 contributed to my healing. And remarkably, two members of the congregation subsequently told me that they had experienced healing of their different orthopedic problems during the healing prayer on July 1.

So what did I experience after I awoke on July 4? As usual, I moved to the end of the bed to check for the possible recovery of function of the muscles in my right upper eyelid and around my right eyeball. When I placed a finger on my right upper eyelid to push it upwards, I realized that the lid was already raised and the small painting on the wall in front of me was not moving upwards. Completely baffled by this, I decided to let Christina sleep while I went to the kitchen to make us coffee and to check the strength of the muscles in my right upper eyelid and around my right eyeball, to be sure that the recovery was not temporary. Christina and I were overwhelmed by this miraculous event, for which we will be eternally grateful to God. We then shared my recovery with Sharon's family and church friends at July 4 festivities, including a dazzling fireworks program. In a follow-up visit to the neuro-ophthalmologist a few days later, he found that the functioning of the muscles in my right upper eyelid and around my right eyeball was normal, and simply stated that this was "awesome." And I no longer had to tell those who asked why I was wearing a black patch over my right eye, that I was training to be a pirate to avoid a long explanation for it!

Unfortunately, my time at GCC was preceded by a conflict that carried over into my entire time there. It began two months before I took over the position of GCC's transitional senior minister, when the Director of Music and Choirs resigned his position to direct a well-known mixed-voice church choir in the area. Until separate directors of the adult and children's choirs could be hired, a retired GCC music and choir director was asked to direct the adult choir. The shifts in responsibilities were accompanied by the position of director of music, along with the salary for the position, being given to GCC's

DOUGLAS E. BUSBY

organist, Gary Wendt. The conflict began when the temporary director of the adult choir realized that her pay as an adult choir director would not include that of being the music director, and be much lower than the salary that she had been receiving when she retired. Dr. Roberts had denied her request for her pre-retirement salary, which angered her and several members of the choir. Then one of the choir members telephoned me two weeks before I was due to become GCC's transitional senior minister, and demanded that I honor this request. I immediately passed the request on to GCC's business administrator, who presented it to GCC's finance board, which rejected it for "budgetary reasons." Now the conflict shifted to several members of the choir and me, with several members leaving the choir and a few not returning to it during my transitional ministry at GCC. This conflict was never resolved, no matter how the reason for it was explained to those engaged in it who, I should note, made the selection of a permanent adult choir director quite difficult.

But numerous significant activities with which I was involved at GCC greatly overshadowed my conflict with certain choir members during the 18 months that I was its transitional senior minister. In addition to conducting the new early Sunday morning service, I led two healing services, co-led three Sunday afternoon services for remembering departed loved ones, and was the host minister and preacher at the Fall Conference of the Chicago Metropolitan and Fox Valley Associations, held at GCC. I gave several presentations in the church's adult education program, updated brochures on the church's programs and activities, initiated a system for identifying pastoral care needs and documenting pastoral care visits, and participated in developing and instituting a program for inactive church member retrieval. I developed a system for managing employee grievances, helped to plan the construction of a modern church chapel, supported a church archival project, a highlight of which was a Sunday dedicated to celebrating GCC's heritage, and participated in preparing the church's profile.

Soon in my ministry at GCC, I learned that GCC was committed to engaging in interreligious activities with Jewish congregations in the Glenview area. Because Christina was in the choir of Musical Arts Indiana in South Bend, I had been introduced to the Holocaust

MY EXPERIENCES

Cantata, consisting of music written and sung by the Jewish prisoners of Holocaust concentration camps. Consequently, I proposed that GCC and the Am Yisrael Conservative Congregation, for which Christina had sung on the Jewish High Holidays, invite Musical Arts Indiana to present the Holocaust Cantata in the Glenview area. This highly-successful venture, occurred in March of 2012, at Temple Jeremiah in nearby Northbrook, Illinois..

During my second summer at GCC, I learned about the work of Hands of Peace (GOP), an interfaith organization founded by a GCC member to develop peace-building and leadership skills among Israeli, Palestinian, and American teens. The organization held a summer program, hosted jointly by GCC and Oakton College. Jewish and Muslim clergy. I conducted the program's closing interfaith service at GGC. I gave its sermon, entitled "Water for Life."

The new, called senior minister (subsequently changed to senior "pastor") was Rev. Dr. Charles "Chuck" Mize, a UCC minister from Madison, Wisconsin with many years of large-church experience. I was not involved in his selection, but briefly talked with him when GCC's Search and Call Committee allowed his request to meet the GCC staff before his "call." During our very brief visit, he seemed intent on knowing about my religious and ministerial background, when I expected him to inquire about my experience as GCC's Transitional Senior Minister. Consequently, I assumed that he had put my briefing him on my experience at GCC on hold until about one month from the start of his ministry at GCC, as recommended by the Interim Ministry Network. When I telephoned Dr. Mize after he had been at GCC for a month, he tersely said that the meeting with me would be unnecessary because "I already know everything about the church." So here ends the story of my time at GCC and possibly in interim ministry, as having been a unique privilege in ministry to serve a large and wonderful congregation.

6. My Spiritual Healing Ministry

My interest in spiritual healing, or healing with divine energy, began at 12 years of age at the Martyrs' Shrine in Midland, Ontario, which honors eight missionaries who were killed near it over 350 years ago by Huron Indians. On the morning that my family and I were to return home from our vacation north of Midland, I awoke with a fever, headache, dizziness, and whenever I raised my head off the pillow, nausea and vomiting. On our way home, Mom and Dad had me lie across the back seat of the car, with a bucket beside me, and put my sister upfront between them. As we were about to pass the shrine, Mom asked me if Dad, my sister, and she could visit its church for just a few minutes, and I assured them that as long as I stayed lying down, I would be alright. A few minutes after they went into the church, I suddenly experienced a complete recovery and, to their surprise, joined them. As we walked by a side altar dedicated to the martyrs, my attention was drawn to a roped-off area next to it, which contained numerous crutches, canes, leg braces, and a few wheelchairs. When I stopped to look at them out of curiosity, Dad whispered to me that they had been left there by people who came to the shrine to be healed of various health conditions, which had actually happened. So, I began to wonder whether being at this sacred place had also healed me that day.

Two spiritually-related questions came into my mind while I studied neuroanatomy and neurophysiology in medical school. One was whether the soul, or human spirit, resides in our brains. As I mentioned above, I heard the renowned Canadian neurosurgeon, Dr. Wilder Penfield, say that he had not found any evidence of a soul, so I began to wonder whether it is an energy field in and around our bodies. The other question came from my hearing lectures on how various physical, mental, emotional, and even spiritual stresses can cause or aggravate various health problems, so I wondered whether the soul can interact with our body and mind to affect our health. As I will describe below, I found plausible answers to these questions 35 years later when I began to study spiritual healing and its related area, energy healing. I learned that about 3,500 years ago, the ancient Indo-European people wrote in ancient Sanscrit about a highly-complex energy field, or subtle energy body, which occupies and surrounds every human being and is sustained by a universal vital life force energy, which we now believe has a divine source and appears to be the "Holy Spirit" of the Christian faith. These people imagined, and modern science has

MY EXPERIENCES

verified, that the subtle energy body supports our physical, mental, emotional, and spiritual health, and that universal vital life force energy has the power to heal. Therefore, spiritual healing and energy healing would be to channel physically or mentally, or both, this universal vital life force energy to the subtle energy body to help it heal physical, mental, emotional, and spiritual conditions.

To continue on about my spiritual healing ministry ...

While I was working on my M.Sc. degree in the mid-1960s, I watched with great interest the televised spiritual healing ministries of evangelists Kathryn Kuhlman and Oral Roberts. Both Kuhlman and Roberts impressed me as being charismatic personalities who used remarkably different, yet seemingly effective ways to channel what they called the Holy Spirit for healing.

Kuhlman was a dramatic preacher who began her healing services with a stream of slowly-enunciated theological reassurances and inspirational songs, as she walked about a large stage, raising her arms high as she repeatedly invited the presence of the Holy Spirit. Still on stage, she used prayer and frequently touch to conduct spiritual healing on each person who came before her. Interestingly, many whom she touched momentarily became weak and some also lost consciousness for a few seconds to several minutes - a phenomenon called "being slain in the Spirit" - due to the power of the healing energy that she was channeling. While people were being healed on stage, spontaneous healing was also occurring in the audience, with Kuhlman appearing to know whom and what had been healed.

Roberts was a forceful speaker who began his healing services with a gospel-based sermon that was usually focused on Jesus' healing miracles. After the sermon, he conducted an altar call, which involved inviting those who wished to come forward to signify their decision to commit their lives to Christ. Finally, he sat on a chair at the forward edge of the stage, placed his right hand on the head of each person who came before him, and prayed for that person's healing while often commenting that he was feeling the power of God passing through the hand. During Kuhlman's and Roberts' services, many people appeared to have been instantly healed of impairing physical health conditions including as paralyses, orthopedic deformities, deafness, and blindness.

As I marveled at what I was observing on the television screen, I began to wonder if the power of suggestion or the power of the Holy Spirit - or both - were responsible for these apparent healings. Although I assumed that the power of suggestion was operating to some degree in some people, I also presumed that the healing that I was witnessing was due principally to the Holy Spirit's powerful presence in response to its "invitation" by Kuhlman and Roberts and their respective spiritually-energized audiences.

While I was at CTS in early 1990, the growing number of books and articles on prayer for healing rekindled my interest in spiritual healing. In Dr. Snyder's course on "Healing in the New Testament," mentioned above, he was convinced that his translation of Jesus' healing "miracles" in the ancient Greek Bible pointed to psychosomatic illnesses being generated by the social and religious stresses of the day and being healed by Jesus in a transformative way. Dr. Snyder believed that a major cause of psychosomatic illnesses was the prevailing belief that all health problems were God's punishment for personal or ancestral sin, leading society to push those with health conditions to the bottom of the socioeconomic ladder. He felt that Jesus' charismatic ministry empowered these people to transcend their impairments and become productive members of society. At first, Dr. Snyder's sweeping understanding of Jesus' healing miracles seemed plausible to me. However, when I considered each of them from a medical perspective in light of the ancient tradition of the Jews documenting their oral history with a substantial degree of accuracy, I concluded that most, if not all, of Jesus' healing miracles, were complete healings, or "cures."

My appreciation of the reality of spiritual healing was subsequently bolstered during my field education experience at the First Congregational United Church of Christ in Elmhurst, Illinois, under Dr. Huntzinger. After a Sunday morning worship service, during which I preached on prayer for healing, several who had attended the

MY EXPERIENCES

service told me that they or persons whom they knew had been healed through prayer. I subsequently mentioned to Dr. Huntzinger that I was pleased to hear firsthand from his congregation that prayer for healing works, which led to his sharing with me a remarkable, personal story of spiritual healing. He said that early in his ministry, he decided to visit the home of a teenage girl who was to have surgery for cancer of the brain the following day. After he parked his car in front of her home, he paused to think about what words of comfort and hope he might give to the family which, he noted, had recently experienced several tragic events and was facing the possibility of yet another with the daughter possibly losing her life from brain cancer. Unexpectedly, he suddenly felt intense compassion for the family, burst into tears, and spontaneously cried out, "God, please help them." After he composed himself, he entered the home and provided much-needed spiritual support to the family. The following morning, he went to the hospital to be with the family during the girl's operation, and at the hospital's surgery reception desk was told that the operation had been canceled after a pre-operative neurological evaluation and magnetic resonance imaging (MRI) of her brain showed that the brain cancer had miraculously disappeared.

Forty-five years after I decided on a career in medicine rather than a career in theology because I had not received a call to theology from God, I had simply forgotten about it. Then call occurred in May of 1997, when I was driving alone to the rehearsal for my graduation from CTS with an M.Div. degree. While I was stopped in traffic for several minutes, I began to wonder how I might best put my ministerial training and experience in ministry into use. An inner voice interrupted my thought with, "You will work in healing ministry." I immediately realized that at last, I had received God's call. Soon after I graduated, CTS invited me to teach a course bridging theology and medicine, to be entitled "Theology and Medicine." Over the subsequent five-year period, this annual, well-attended course included a detailed comparison of theological ethics (centering on The Ten Commandments) with medical ethics, medical and spiritual care of the dying, and consideration of the authenticity of spiritual healing. Because spiritual healing was so prominent in Jesus' ministry and had recently been receiving more attention in various Christian churches, my lectures on it included a review of the history of spiritual healing in Christianity, a description of what we know about spiritual healing, and how to conduct spiritual healing services in various settings. They also considered healing prayers in the books of worship of various Christian denominations in light of the recommendations on the nature and content of prayer by various theologians, including Francis MacNutt and Morton Kelsey, internist Larry Dossey, and cardiologist Herbert Benson. Unfortunately, my presentations of this course ended due to an unexpected, yet remarkable event.

Unforgettable Memories: A Spirit Visits My Class on Theology and Medicine
My study of spiritual healing extended into energy healing, when I realized that both involved the channeling of universal vital life force energy for healing. Many books that I read on energy healing began by describing the subtle energy body with its several layers of surrounding energy, or auras, and its many spinning vortices of energy, or chakras, at right angles to the body. Then they described how our hands can be used to detect the auras and chakras, which are altered by adverse changes in one's health, and how some people can see and cameras can photograph the individual, "rainbow" colors of the auras. Then they described how we can channel universal vital life force energy to others through our hands, as occurs in Healing Touch and Reiki, to correct abnormalities in the auras and chakras, and consequently help with the healing of health conditions.

In my course on theology and medicine, I briefly described how energy healing functions, and commented on the similarity between the laying on of hands in spiritual healing and the use of the hands in energy healing. This led a D.Min. student in the course, Rev. Marilee Brown, who was a Reiki Master and Teacher, to suggest that I devote a class in the course to energy healing, and volunteered to give a brief description and demonstration of Reiki in the class, and my wife, Christina, agreed to come to the class and to do the same with Healing

MY EXPERIENCES

Touch. Since the class would be "out of the box" in a seminary, I obtained prior approval for it, first from its students and then from the Academic Dean, Dr. Edgerton. I also told the students and Dr. Edgerton that working with universal vital life force energy can produce unexpected, but benign spiritual phenomena.

With my permission, several of the 20 students taking the course invited friends from CTS and other ACTS seminaries to this session, so that the class size was nearly doubled. I started it with a lecture on the ancient history and known characteristics of the subtle energy body, and its auras and chakras, followed by the students using their hands to detect each other's auras. To give them an appreciation of the power of universal vital life force energy, I showed them how to concentrate this energy between their hands, but failed to inform them how to release it safely by rubbing their hands together. When I announced from behind the podium that Christina's lecture was about to begin, I held up my hands with palms facing the class, and as though by reflex, many of the students did the same to me. A wave of energy instantly struck the front of my chest and pushed me back against the chalkboard, and I became momentarily dizzy and breathless. At this point, I told the class that any universal vital life force energy which might have been concentrated between the hands should be released by rubbing the hands together, rather than by suddenly releasing it, or even throwing it in the direction of another person. To illustrate this, I described an incident when I created a "ball of energy" between my hands and threw it across the room at Christina, sitting in a rocking chair and reading holding a newspaper held up in front of her. She felt the energy strike her chest and was so startled by it that she tipped the rocking chair backward just short of it coming into contact with a large window behind her.

Christina and Marilee respectively described Healing Touch and Reiki, and then showed the class how they channel universal vital life force energy with them. For their demonstrations, they used a padded, narrow, collapsible therapy table that Christina and I had brought with us, and volunteers from the class. Unexpectedly, one of the volunteer students was having an attack of migraine at the time that she received Healing Touch, and its symptoms disappeared during this therapy. The other students who received

DOUGLAS E. BUSBY

Healing Touch or Reiki described feelings of peace, relaxation and wellbeing after receiving either of them.

The most remarkable event of the evening occurred when most of the students had left the classroom for their mid-session break. A guest student who remained with a few of us in the classroom stated that he saw a human figure lying supine on the therapy table, whom he intuitively knew was Jesus. This momentary apparition was also seen by a CTS student who was taking the course and validated intuitively by Christina. I did not mention the apparition when the session resumed after the break, but it and the other events during this session were apparently made known to members of the CTS staff. Soon thereafter, I was told by the registrar of CTS, Cheryl Miller, that I would no longer be giving the theology and medicine course because of deficient funds to pay me and other adjunct staff to teach at CTS. I reminded her that I was giving the course without remuneration, and had done so for the two previous years, and had had intended to continue to do. She then told me that the president of CTS, Dr. Thistlethwaite, was planning to have her husband, a transplant surgeon, teach the course in the future.

During my years of teaching at CTS, I began to conduct healing services in various settings. In churches, I preferred to give a sermon on spiritual healing during their Sunday morning service or services, and then conduct a spiritual healing service in the afternoon. I anticipated doing this in many churches of the Indiana-Kentucky Conference UCC, especially after it invited me to speak on spiritual healing at its Annual Gathering and later announced my availability to conduct spiritual healing services in its monthly bulletin. However, I only conducted about 10 services in UCC churches, with the number being limited for three reasons given to me by a minister who, along with several other ministers, unexpectedly walked out of my presentation on spiritual healing at the Annual Gathering. First, he stated that the Indiana-Kentucky Conference has many ministers who have continued the more conservative traditions of the Evangelical and Reformed Church since it merged with the Congregational Christian Church in 1957. Consequently, they probably have a "dispensationalist" view of spiritual healing held by many famous theologians, including Luther, Calvin, and

MY EXPERIENCES

Barth. This view is: that God dispensed the ability to perform spiritual healing only to Jesus, his apostles, and certain members of the early church, especially to get it established. Second, he said that UCC ministers may be associating "spiritual healing" with "faith healing," a term which not only reflects an incorrect assumption that a person's strength of faith in God determines whether or not healing will occur, but also pertains to the so-called "faith healers," many of whom have been "con" artists. Third, he pointed out that spiritual healing has not been an everyday occurrence or predictable, leading to it being given low priority in ministry.

Subsequently, I was invited to preach and conduct a spiritual healing service in two United Methodist and two Unity churches, and numerous healing services over a three-year period in the local hospital's chapel. Moreover, I was asked several times to perform a modified spiritual healing service for hospitalized and homebound ill and injured persons.

Spiritual healing in the community

As I described in my book, *We Can Help God Heal Us*, Jesus taught us to involve spiritual faith, compassion, prayer, and touch as the laying on of hands in spiritual healing. Whenever I have engaged in spiritual healing, I have prepared everyone who is to participate in it by describing in some detail what we know about it, and then focusing their minds on it with prayers, a guided meditation, and "spiritual" music. I have also had the person for whom we were praying, or a surrogate for a person who is unable to be there, be seated in an open area for at least five minutes, surrounded by everyone who wishes to participate in the laying on of hands and if they desire, to say a prayer for healing.

Over the years, I did not keep a record of people who told me that they experienced spiritual healing, out of respect for their privacy. In my experience, almost everyone who had requested spiritual healing has experienced an improvement in their health condition. This improvement was most often transformational, such as maintaining strength and balance in body, mind, and spirit, adjusting to physical or mental limitations from the condition, and accepting the love of God, family, and friends when approaching death from the condition. The writings of Dr. MacNutt and others indicate that cure of a health condition is more likely to occur from the intermittent laying on of hands and continuous prayer, which he calls "soaking prayer," in spiritual healing sessions that last up to several hours, but these highly-focused sessions been very difficult for me to arrange. Then too, one never knows what might occur during a short spiritual healing service as I recall occurred during a healing service in one of my interim ministries.

Unforgettable Memories: A Woman's Terminal, Metastatic Breast Cancer Disappears after a Spiritual Healing Service

When I was interim minister of the First Congregational Church, UCC, in Benton Harbor, Michigan, I conducted two spiritual healing services in its chapel. The second service was attended by a woman who was brought to it by a member of this church's congregation. The woman was in a wheelchair, appeared to be very thin and weak, and was barely able to speak. Several persons at the service came forward to perform the laying on of hands on her and pray for her healing. I did not see or talk with her again, until ...

I was standing in the buffet line at a social event in St. Joseph, Michigan several months later, when to my surprise a woman in her 60's walked up to me, hugged me, kissed me on the cheek, and said, "You healed me!" "Whoa, who are you?" I asked her. Then she identified herself as the lady in the wheelchair, and told me that she had been suffering from metastatic, terminal breast cancer and only had a few days to live, when a friend who was a member of First Congregational, brought her to a spiritual healing service that I conducted at this church. She stated that the next day, she began to feel better, and that within a few weeks, her strength had returned and tests showed that her cancer had completely disappeared, without its treatment not being resumed. By this time, both of us

MY EXPERIENCES

had tears in our eyes, and I said to her, "Congratulations, but I must tell you that you were healed by God, not by me." I remember that she momentarily thought about God's role in her healing, and said that she agreed with me. A picture of health, she walked away to join her friends at the event.

7. My Observations of Spirit Involvement in Spiritual Healing

In the spring of 2001, Christina said that she had decided to join several of her energy worker colleagues on a two-week visit to the rural town of Abadiânia in central Brazil. There, they wished to observe the phenomenal spiritual healing "ministry" of João Teixeira de Farias, who was popularly known in Brazil as well as around the world as "João de Deus," "Medium João," and "John of God." In this book, I will refer to him as "Medium João."

I had read about spiritual healing that has occurred in the ministries of several other "gifted healers," including Francis of Assisi, Catherine of Siena, Ignatius of Loyola, Francis Xavier, George Fox, and, more recently, Kuhlman, Roberts, and MacNutt, and believed that their way of healing was very much like that of Jesus. Consequently, I was not prepared to hear about the amazing way that spiritual healing was occurring through Medium João, when Christina invited me to a meeting of the group with the trip's guide for an orientation to prepare the group for its upcoming visit to Medium João's healing center

At the orientation, the guide described Medium João first as a "medium," or a person who can connect with the spirit world, and then as a full-trance spiritual healing medium, or a medium who can "incorporate" a spirit, with the spirit taking over the functions of his mind, body, and soul, and then channeling universal vital life force energy through the medium for spiritual healing. Remarkably, this type of medium is not aware of what an incorporated spirit is thinking, saying, and doing, and therefore the medium has no memory of anything that has occurred during incorporation.

I reacted to what I was hearing with skepticism, but refrained from commenting on it as I gave thought to whether to join

DOUGLAS E. BUSBY

Christina on the trip, if possible to determine exactly what was going on in Medium João's healing center, the Casa de Dom Inácio de Loyola, named after a famous religious saint and usually called "the Casa." As a physician, I wondered if the medical profession had conducted a scientific study on the hundreds of thousands of cases of spiritual healing that had reportedly occurred during Medium João's spiritual healing ministry, specifically to authenticate it. Then a speaker at the orientation meeting said that the majority of medical professionals who had come from around the world to observe the spirits at work through Medium João, had not rejected the reality of the spiritual healing that they had witnessed. As a theologian, I had already wondered whether spirits, including healing spirits, actually exist, contrary to the widespread biblically-based belief that our body does not have a soul that lives on as a spirit after our body dies, but will be resurrected at the end of time. Yet, many books had been published on the phenomena of near-death experience and after-life regression, which provide strong support for the belief in a "soul-spirit."

A few days after the orientation meeting, I consulted Dr. Cairns on whether I would be placing my ministry at risk by personally observing Medium João's spiritual healing ministry. He said that a "dark side," in Medium João's ministry was quite unlikely, such as Medium João being incorporated in body, mind, and spirit by a malevolent spirit that may not heal or even harm a person in an attempt to show me, and others, that Medium João's ministry was false. However, Dr. Cairns suggested that I be prepared for this possibility by wearing my clerical cross while in the Casa, and by quietly saying The Lord's Prayer if I ever felt uneasy or threatened. Finally, my curiosity and Dr. Cairn's assuring words led me to decide to accompany Christina on her visit to the Casa, specifically while observing the spiritual healing ministry of Medium João.

During our first morning in Abadiânia, our group went early to the Casa's main hall, so that it could have a good view of Medium João being incorporated by a spirit, which would then perform visible spiritual surgeries. As we waited for this, I became quite anxious in thinking about the medically- and theologically-anomalous scene that I was about to witness. I walked away from the group and stood alone

MY EXPERIENCES

in the back of the hall, wondering whether to leave the Casa and maybe return to it later, or to return to the United States without observing Medium João's spiritual healing ministry. Suddenly, something bumped my right shoulder from behind so forcefully that I momentarily lost my balance and had to take a few steps to avoid falling to the floor. I immediately looked around, wondering who would bump me so hard without an apology, and saw no one nearby. Then I felt a deep sense of peace for about 10 minutes, during which I realized that a spirit had bumped me as a reminder of why I had come to the Casa. I decided to stay and walked back to our group.

Until Medium João arrived, I stood with our group and looked about the hall. It had seating and standing areas for about 500 people, and, at its far end, a low, small stage with a door to either side of it. On its walls were drawings of Jesus Christ, and photographs of Medium João and several of the healing spirits during their mortal lives. On the back wall of the stage was a wooden triangle made of strips of wood, with its bottom strip set forwards so that photographs of individuals could be placed in the triangle and viewed later by a spirit incorporated by Medium João, during which the spirit would conduct distant spiritual healing of the persons in the photographs.

Just before the spiritual healing session began, the people who had gathered in the hall became very quiet. I noticed that everyone wore white clothing, reportedly to enable the healing spirits to better see the colors of auras as reflections of their health. Many carried rosaries and wore crosses. And many were in wheelchairs and on crutches. The session began with several people going on stage to give words of welcome, describe the Casa's functions and procedures, give testimonials of spiritual healing that they had experienced or witnessed, pray for the work of the healing spirits, and finally lead everyone in saying "The Lord's Prayer" followed by one "Hail Mary."

Medium João came into the hall through a door to the side of the stage, and slowly stepped up onto the stage and walked to the front of it, where he welcomed the crowd and said a few words to it in Brazilian. Then he placed an arm around the shoulders of a Casa attendant standing on each side of him, presumably to draw energy from them to help him incorporate a spirit. He momentarily shuddered, leaned forwards, and gasped. Then his face became expressionless, his eyes drifted into a blank gaze, and his voice changed to that of the incorporated spirit as it announced that it would be performing visible surgeries as proof of spirit involvement in spiritual healing. Strangely, in the many, visible surgeries that I would subsequently observe, the subjects spontaneously entered a state of "spirit anesthesia" as the Casa attendants called it, and then surgery was performed with clean instruments, amazingly without antisepsis. The surgeries that morning, which a Casa attendant told me were "the usual," included: making and suturing a full-thickness skin incision on a man's upper arm; removing tissue with the fingers through a similar incision on a woman's back, and then suturing the incision; scraping tissue off of the surface of a man's eyeball with a scalpel and leaving the eye unpatched; and grasping a cotton swab with a surgical forceps, inserting and twisting it inside a woman's nose, and then withdrawing it from her nose. Needless to say, I was "astounded" by what the incorporated spirits were calling surgeries!

After the visible surgeries, our group joined a line of people who were to go before Medium João during their first visit to the Casa. Each person who did not speak Brazilian carried a piece of paper on which a Casa attendant had described, in Brazilian, up to three personal health conditions that the person wished to have healed by a spirit incorporated by Medium João. Some people also carried one or more pictures of family members and friends to present to Medium João for absent healing by an incorporated spirit. The line slowly passed through two rooms in which about 150 people were sitting in meditation, including about 40 volunteer mediums, to create a "chain" of divine energy, or "current," passing through the meditators in both rooms. Everyone seated in a "current room" had their eyes closed and arms and legs uncrossed to maintain this current chain. Later, I was told that the current in the first room cleansed the subtle energy bodies of the people passing in line through it, in the second room enabled Medium João to incorporate a healing spirit, and in both rooms helped the healing spirits work on the people sitting "in current" or standing in line to go before Medium João.

As I moved towards Medium João in the second current room, I experienced an intense buzzing sensation pass downwards deep inside of my body which was apparently due to a spirit or spirits

MY EXPERIENCES

checking my physical, mental, and spiritual health, to report to the spirit incorporated by Medium João. When I was about 10 feet from him, I began to feel lightheaded and weak in my legs and assumed that these symptoms were due to my entering the high-energy field of his incorporated spirit. A Casa attendant read aloud my medical problems list, which simply said, "Anything you find." Through Medium João, the incorporated spirit wrote something on another sheet of paper and a Casa attendant told me that it was a prescription for me to have invisible surgery at 2:00 p.m. the next day. My symptoms in the energy field disappeared as soon as I stepped out of it. Interestingly, scientists have reported that when Medium João is incorporated by a spirit, his EEG shows that his brain is in a hyperarousal state and his electromagnetic field level is at least 500 times greater than when he is unincorporated.

I kept my professional careers as a physician and theologian confidential during my first visit to the Casa. However, that afternoon I was sitting "in current," when a spirit incorporated by Medium João had a Casa attendant tell me to stop meditating and approach Medium João. The attendant said to me that the spirit had called me "a doctor and a priest," and wanted me to sit and pray on a low, wobbly, flower stand that someone had placed beside Medium João. The attendant then gave me a piece of paper on which was written the names of a physician and several members of his family and their address in South Africa, and asked me to pray silently for their spiritual healing. Surprised that the spirit knew about my professional careers, I unthinkingly said that I was a Protestant minister rather than a Roman Catholic priest, and that I needed to know what to pray for. The incorporated spirit simply pointed at the improvised stool, and told me to sit on it and pray "generically" for the physician and his family for about 30 minutes. Then the Casa attendant ushered me back to my seat to continue my meditation.

The next morning, I returned early to the Casa's main hall, where a spirit incorporated by Medium João invited all physicians there to come up on stage and watch from close-up the scraping of an eyeball. A man who was to have this procedure was standing at the back of the stage. He spontaneously entered a state of spirit anesthesia without making any direct visual, verbal or physical contact

DOUGLAS E. BUSBY

with Medium João or a Casa attendant. He was led to a chair and asked by the Casa attendant to be seated and tilt his head backward. I saw Medium João, incorporated by a spirit, scrape a whitish tissue from the surfaces of this man's right cornea and sclera with a scalpel, notably with no scleral bleeding. And during the scraping, the man seemed oblivious to pain and unaware of his surroundings. Immediately after his surgery, the man was immediately lifted onto a wheeled metal chair and taken to the Casa's infirmary to recover from spirit anesthesia and receive a prescription for herbal capsules and instructions to follow during his post-operative recovery period. An American physician who had been standing next to me during the eyeball scraping said that he had seen it done many times by spirits incorporated by Medium João, with everyone who had had it subsequently describing a gritty feeling in the scraped eye for about 24 hours. He said that the manager of the Casa had told him that each of the visible surgeries performed by the spirits incorporated by Medium João can cure many different medical conditions.

Just as I was leaving the Casa's main hall to return to our inn (pousada in Brazilian) to rest before my invisible spiritual surgery, a Casa attendant asked me to follow him into the second current room. There, Medium João, incorporated by a spirit, was standing beside an indigenous Brazilian woman who was sitting in a wheelchair obviously under spirit anesthesia. Through Medium João, the spirit asked me to suture a slightly-bleeding, full-thickness skin incision of about four inches in length in the woman's left lower abdominal wall. Without looking through Medium Joao's eyes, the spirit threaded a straight needle with a white-cotton thread, grasped the threaded needle with a needle holder, and handed the loaded needle holder to me. I glanced at the surgical instrument tray and did not see a thumb forceps with which to grasp the edges of the incision while closing it. I knelt on the floor in front of the woman and started to suture the incision. When I placed the first stitch, I found that the needle was so dull and the woman's abdominal skin was so thick, that I had to hold the skin at some distance from the edges of the incision with my free hand so that I could push the needle through the skin. I also realized that I would not have an even placement of interrupted sutures along the line of the incision or enough thread, so I switched to using a locking-mattress stitch to close the incision which led the spirit to interrupt my work to ask me what type of stitch I was using. When I completed the suturing, I was amazed to find that the suture placements and skin edges were perfectly aligned and that the incision had already healed! After a Casa attendant wheeled the woman away to the infirmary to recover from spirit anesthesia, the incorporated spirit asked me to describe what I had just seen and done "as an American physician"

Unforgettable Memories: I Receive Invisible Spiritual Surgery

At 2:00 p.m. that afternoon, I joined the invisible spiritual surgery line in the Casa's main hall. After a brief wait, a Casa attendant led the line into a large room lined with treatment tables and filled with rows of benches. The attendant asked everyone to sit on the benches with their eyes closed and pray or meditate. About 15 minutes later, I heard a deep, authoritative voice speak in Brazilian, and subsequently told that it was a spirit incorporated by Medium João, which said, "In the name of God, the surgery is complete." Then everyone who had been in the line was asked to leave the room and wait on the porch outside of it for a prescription for herbal capsules and post-operative instructions. Up to this point, I had not experienced symptoms from any surgery that had been done on my body. As I began to stand up, a buzzing sensation shot through me head-to-toe, I became lightheaded, disoriented, and weak, and I had to sit back down on the bench. As I tried to figure out what had happened to me, initially thinking that I might be having a stroke, a person from our group saw that I was in distress, helped me to my feet, and guided me out of the room to sit on a bench on the porch, where my symptoms slowly dissipated. However, I had great difficulty remembering the post-operative instructions, and realized that I was experiencing short-term memory loss. This first-time problem for me was quite severe for about an hour, during which a person in our group located Christina in a current room. She went with me to purchase the prescribed herbal capsules, get me back to our posada by taxi, and get me into bed. I slept for most of the following 24 hours and recovered my short-term memory without experiencing any new symptoms. I also started to take the spirit-prescribed herbal capsules and followed the instructions that came with them not to drink alcohol, eat pork or its derivatives or anything that contains pepper (sweet bell pepper being acceptable), or engage in any sexual activity for 40 days (eight days if one has had prior spiritual surgery). I was never able to determine what invisible spiritual surgery that I received, even two days later when I unsuccessfully asked a Casa attendant to get this information for me while I was going through the "follow-up line."

On a subsequent visit to the Casa, I learned that every prescribed herbal capsule contains the pharmacologically-inert, ground-up flowers and leaves of the passionfruit (*passiflora*) plant. The healing spirits prescribed these capsules to be taken three a day for 45 days, for everyone who has had spiritual surgery and many who have received direct and absent healing. A Casa attendant said that the capsules prescribed for a person are "spiritually energized" for that person. As I describe below, not only did I see a cure after invisible spiritual surgery, but saw prescribed herbal capsules being specific for the person who had the surgery.

Unforgettable Memories: Invisible Spiritual Surgery Destroys a Man's Cancer of the Liver

On Tuesday of my second week in Abadiânia, I was introduced by the owner of our pousada to a very ill man of about 65 years of age and his wife, both of whom had just arrived from Canada. His wife said that the day before, she had signed her husband out of the University of Alberta Hospital in Edmonton, where he had been receiving palliative care for metastatic cancer in his liver. When I met him, he was sitting in a wheelchair, his skin had a yellow-green color from liver failure, and he was taking sips of water as his only nutrition. The next afternoon, he had invisible spiritual surgery. Immediately after it, he still looked quite ill, so while his wife attended him, I took his herbal prescription to the Casa's pharmacy window on the outside of its main hall to get the prescription filled. The pharmacy attendant at the window stated that he had never seen the man or me before, and that a prescription can be filled only when brought to the pharmacy by the person for

MY EXPERIENCES

whom it was written. So, the man's wife and I took the man to the pharmacy window in his wheelchair to get his capsules. About a week days after the man had invisible spiritual surgery, I met him while he was out for a walk with his wife. Smiling, he said that he had just eaten his first full meal in months and was feeling much better. The color of his skin was almost normal. Mentally and emotionally overwhelmed by this remarkable revelation of spirit help with this healing brought tears of joy to my eyes.

Over the following 15 years, I returned to Abadiânia seven times and Christina returned to Abadiânia five times - each time to observe the spiritual healing ministry of Medium João for two weeks. On two trips, Christina and I served as guides for groups of people, and on one trip, I participated in the making of the Discovery Channel documentary, *Miracle Man: John of God*, produced and directed by Bill Hayes, President of Figure 8 Films in North Carolina. As Bill was making the documentary. I had the privilege of accompanying him to interview three distinguished scientists for their opinions on Medium João's spiritual healing ministry. The first was Gary E. Schwartz, Ph.D., a psychologist, parapsychologist, and author who has conducted both energy healing and afterlife experiments. The second was Norman S. Don, Ph.D., a neuroscientist and parapsychologist who performed EEGs and energy field measurements on Medium João and other full-trance spiritual healing mediums. And the third was Amit Goswami, Ph.D., a theoretical quantum physicist who has studied the relationship between physics and consciousness. These scientists gave us remarkable insight into how Medium João functions.

On our second trip to Abadiânia, Christina and I were in the "second-time line," when a spirit incorporated in Medium João informed us that we were mediums, and directed us to sit in current near to Medium João for the rest of our visits to the Casa during that trip. Almost every time I subsequently went to Abadiânia and entered the second-time line at the Casa, a spirit incorporated by Medium João had a Casa attendant take me out of the line and sit in current with the mediums. On one occasion, an attendant helped me ask the spirit that Medium João had incorporated for any advice on how I should be conducting my spiritual healing ministry back home, and the spirit replied, "Tell the story." which a Casa attendant interpreted as meaning that I should to speak and write about the wonderful work in spiritual healing that the spirits at the Casa are doing.

Question of a spirit incorporated by Medium João

The spirits incorporated into Medium João reflect their personalities through him, sometimes quite dramatically, in what they say and do while interacting with those who come to the Casa for healing and at times for advice. The only prayerful words that I have heard incorporated spirits say to persons seeking healing from them have been "Think God," "Trust God" and "Believe in God." Also, the spirits would occasionally remind those who came before Medium João for spiritual healing, that healing comes at a personal cost, such as switching to a healthier lifestyle or showing greater compassion, otherwise healing may be only temporary.

Casa attendants, most of whom I was told were mediums, often channeled universal vital life force energy to Medium João to help him incorporate a spiritual spirit. One afternoon, this happened to me. I was meditating in the second current room before an afternoon spiritual healing session was to begin. Medium João came into the room, stood behind me, and placed his left hand on my forehead and his right hand on the top of my right shoulder. He said a Hail Mary in Brazilian, and as he continued to speak in Brazilian, his voice lowered in volume and became raspy. With his change of voice, I became so weak that I found breathing difficult. A few seconds later, he placed both of his hands on my forehead and then moved one hand to my upper back, during which my strength and breathing rapidly recovered. I also experienced an intense sense of peace, which lasted that entire spiritual healing session.

MY EXPERIENCES

Between my visits to Abadiânia, I gathered information on Medium João, some of which I included in my book, *Spirits Can Help God Heal Us*. This information introduced me to Spiritism, which I defined above and will describe in the last section of this chapter.

Medium João left home as an under-educated teenager, to become a laborer. Soon thereafter, he was identified as a full-trance spiritual healing medium at a Spiritist center. While he was working as a healing medium and uniform tailor for the Brazilian army in the late 1970s, he decided to have a healing center. When he thought about where this center should be, a spirit told him to situate it in Abadiânia and to buy a small ranch nearby. The ranch was rich in quartz crystals and gemstones, including emeralds. He moved into his first spiritual healing center in 1979, and income from the ranch enabled him to complete the Casa de Dom Inácio de Loyola in 1993. Notably, the Casa is on the top of a large hill rich in natural crystalline quartz, and this hill and the valley next to it have a powerful ley line running through them. Crystalline quartz has electromagnetic properties and a ley line is a geological line of electromagnetic energy, both of which may concentrate and transmit universal vital life force energy.

Spirits incorporated by Medium João have recommended four ways that the healing energy they channel for healing can be made more effective. The first is one or more "crystal baths," which involves lying supine on a bed with alternating lights being shone down on the seven chakras through crystals with individual colors matching those seen by some people in the chakras. The crystal bath is said to provide energy to the subtle energy body while balancing its chakras. The second is briefly standing in the "sacred waterfall" which is in the beautiful, forested valley on the Casa property directly over the ley line passing through the property. Visitors to the waterfall are told that the healing spirits there can channel universal vital life force energy to them to help with their healing, but only if the visitors are reverent and pray for healing. The third is drinking so-called "blessed water," also called "energized water" and "fluidized water." Reportedly, the water is electromagnetically "energized" when bottles of it are exposed to Medium João's energy field during a spiritual healing session. And the fourth is consuming "blessed soup," which is reportedly imbued with universal vital life force energy by the healing spirits. This delicious vegetable soup and a piece of fresh French bread were served to anyone at the Casa in the late morning between spiritual healing sessions, and taken to those who are recovering from spiritual surgery.

Among the 36 known healing spirits which have identified themselves while being incorporated by Medium João at various times in a spiritual healing session, are: King Solomon (10th Century B.C.E.), the wise Israelite king; St. Ignatius of Loyola (1491-1556), a Spanish priest and theologian who founded the Society of Jesus (Jesuits); St. Francis Xavier (1506-1552), a Spanish priest and leading missionary to the Far East; St. Rita of Cascia (1381-1457), an Italian nun who suffered throughout her life as a wife, mother, and widow, and eventually during intense devotional worship as an Augustinian nun; Bezerra de Menezes (1831-1900), a Brazilian physician, businessman, politician, and active Spiritist; Augusto de Almeida (died 1908), reportedly a military officer, physician, and rubber tapper in past lives; Osvaldo Cruz (1872-1917), a Brazilian physician renowned for his contributions to public health; Euripides Barsanulfo (1880-1918), a Brazilian politician and active Spiritist; José Valdovino, reportedly a legal judge in a past life; and Adolf Fritz, a German physician who died in World War I. Two spirits, respectfully called "Dom Inácio" and "Dr. Augusto" by the attendants at the Casa, have purportedly directed much of Medium João's work in spiritual healing in and beyond the Casa, to ensure that all of the spirits who help God with healing can be optimally effective in carrying out their healing functions.

Although not widely publicized outside of Brazil, several other full-trance spiritual healing mediums have appeared in Brazi in the 1900's, leading me to wonder whether the widespread practice of Spiritism in Brazil helps to identify mediums with this unique gift. The most popular of these mediums have been: Zé Arigó, the pseudonym for José Pedro de Freitas (1921-1971), a semi-literate mechanic; Edson Cavalcante Queiroz (1950-1991), a gynecologist; Rubens Farias Jr. (1954-), an engineer and computer programmer; and Medium João (1941-), an illiterate rancher, miner, and businessman. Arigó, Queiroz and Medium João have been incorporated by the spirit named Adolf Fritz.

MY EXPERIENCES

In my visits to the Casa de Dom Inácio de Loyola, I have learned that people from around the world have visited the Casa with all sorts of disabling and life-threatening medical conditions. I have observed spiritual healing of such conditions as a crush injury of the ankle and foot; a spinal cord injury with paraplegia; arthritic conditions in the spine and lower extremities; cancers of the breast, brain, and bowel; multiple sclerosis; Lou Gehrig's disease (ALS); atherosclerotic heart and vascular disease; hepatitis C; HIV/AIDS; psychiatric illnesses; and spirit attachments. Casa attendants have told me that about 85 percent of persons who come to the Casa for spiritual healing appear to receive it. The reasons that the attendants gave me for people not receiving spiritual healing have included: weak or no faith in the healing power of God; failure to follow the spirits' post-operative orders, especially to rest; failure to take a herb as prescribed; failure to follow the specified nutritional restrictions; failure to make moral and other lifestyle changes as directed by the spirits; failure to be benevolent to others; excess karmic debt from one or more past lives; and having a medical condition which the spirits believe is too far advanced for spiritual healing.

Unforgettable Memories: A Few Other Examples of Spiritual Healing Through Spirits Incorporated by Medium João

A few hours after an American surgeon arrived at the Casa, he excitedly sought me out to tell me that he had just helped a spirit incorporated by Medium João with a quadruple coronary by-pass operation on a recently-retired, provincial chief of police. Interestingly, the chief had arrested Medium João in the past for "practicing medicine without a license." The surgeon, a urologist, said that the police chief was hospitalized the day before with incapacitating chest pain due to the severe, arteriosclerotic narrowing of his coronary arteries by arteriosclerosis seen in his coronary angiogram. He stated that the chief was scheduled for quadruple coronary bypass surgery that morning, but in fear of not surviving it, the chief had signed himself out of the hospital, and had a friend drive him to the Casa. The surgeon said that the chief was immediately placed on a treatment table in the invisible spiritual surgery room, and that he and two other physicians, and the chief's friend joined a spirit incorporated by

Medium João in placing one of their hands on the chief's chest for several minutes.

The following afternoon, the chief returned to the Casa for a post-operative evaluation by the spirit who had assumedly performed the invisible coronary bypass surgery and had been incorporated again by Medium João. Thereafter, I interviewed the chief through an interpreter, and he told me he had not experienced any chest pain since the invisible spiritual surgery. He showed me his pre-operative coronary angiogram, which showed the arteriosclerotic narrowing of his major coronary arteries. When I mentioned to him that a repeat angiogram would be immensely helpful in showing the effectiveness of spiritual surgery to the medical community, he said that his restored health was enough. Later, I observed the chief walk briskly across the Casa's parking lot to his automobile, and drive it away.

One morning, a Casa attendant introduced me to a five-year-old girl and her parents from Great Britain. The girl had a rapidly-growing brain cancer which had already blinded her in one eye. A team of British neurosurgeons had been unsuccessful in removing the cancer, and her parents had just presented her to Medium João while he was incorporated by a spirit, and nothing happened that would indicate the destruction of the cancer. As her parents had planned before they and their daughter traveled to the Casa, they took her later that day to the renowned Montreal Neurological Institute in Canada for a second surgical attempt to remove the cancer. When a team of neurosurgeons began this operation the next day, it found only benign fibrous tissue where the cancer had been, leaving them "baffled."

Previously unknown to me, a woman in our energy worker class back home had hepatitis C, which was resistant to medication and beginning to threaten her life. She asked a friend who was traveling to the Casa to present her picture to Medium João while he was incorporated by a spirit. The spirit simply told her friend to sit in current for the rest of the healing session and prescribed herbal capsules for the woman to take. At that moment, the woman developed a warm sensation over her liver and slight nausea, with both symptoms disappearing over a few hours. Several months later, the woman informed me of her hepatitis C and its miraculous recovery, saying she

MY EXPERIENCES

was feeling well and her liver enzymes, which had been markedly elevated due to the hepatitis C, had returned to "normal levels."

A woman from the United States told me that her 16-year-old daughter had a spinal deformity that was corrected at the Casa. She stated that while when her daughter was training to be a professional ballerina, she developed juvenile scoliosis, which rapidly progressed to a 20-degree spinal deformity despite use of an external spine-bracing system. She said that she initially went to the Casa as a surrogate for her daughter, and the spirit which Medium João had incorporated looked at the picture of her daughter, sent her to the invisible surgery room to meditate for the remainder of the healing session, and prescribed herbal capsules for her daughter. The mother said that when she returned home, she found that 10 degrees of her daughter's spinal deformity had disappeared "almost overnight." She stated that a few weeks later, she returned to the Casa with her daughter, and the remaining deformity immediately disappeared when Medium João, incorporated by a spirit, simply touched her daughter's upper back.

A psychoanalyst from the United States and I were walking toward the Casa, while being filmed for the Discovery Channel documentary as I listened to her impressions of Medium João's spiritual healing ministry. When my interview with her began, she had a noticeable right limp, and as we entered the Casa grounds, it suddenly disappeared. She stopped walking and said that chronic arthritis in her right hip from an automobile accident seemed to have spontaneously disappeared. Later that afternoon, she went back on film "to tell the world" how a spirit had unexpectedly healed her injured right hip.

At noon one day during my sixth visit to the Casa, Medium João told a woman who guides people to the Casa, to go immediately to the invisible spiritual surgery room and lie face up on a treatment table there. As soon as she did this, she felt severe pain rapidly develop in her right groin and leg. That evening, she asked me to examine her right leg. While I did this, she described having recently developed painful cramps in her calves while walking, and that this discomfort rapidly ceased when she stopped walking. I told her that this symptom is often due to partial blockage of arterial blood flow in the legs by arteriosclerosis. I found that her right leg was warm to touch, had good arterial pulses, and was markedly tender along its entire major artery to the ankle. Since she said that the painful cramping had been occurring in both of her legs, I also examined her left leg, which was cool to touch and had no arterial pulses, indicating that it also needed attention. Five days later, we went to Medium João while he was incorporated by a spirit, to ask the spirit if her left leg will also have invisible spiritual surgery. The spirit tersely replied in Brazilian, "Trust God the Creator." She subsequently told me that she was no longer experiencing discomfort in her left leg while walking.

A Casa attendant told me that a Brazilian girl in her early teens was brought by her mother to Medium João while he was incorporated by a spirit. The mother said that for several months, her daughter had been going into a trance for several minutes, during which she seemed to be performing a dance and shedding "tears of blood." This phenomenon occurred spontaneously in front of Medium João while he was incorporated by a spirit. The spirit asked the mother and her daughter to return to the Casa, and the mother to bring a large photograph of the daughter's maternal grandmother with he, without her daughter seeing the photograph. When they returned to the Casa, this phenomenon recurred spontaneously when they went before Medium João while incorporated by a spirit. The incorporated spirit told the mother to hold the photo in front of her daughter's face and when the spirit ordered the daughter to look closely at the photo of the deceased grandmother, the phenomenon ceased. Then the incorporated spirit announced to the Casa attendants and everyone sitting in current that the attachment of the grandmother's spirit to her granddaughter had been released. By the way, the photo was of the daughter's deceased grandmother, taken when she was performing as an exotic dancer in her mortal life. (I should add that I had occasionally been sitting in current when a person who was brought before Medium João while he was incorporated by a spirit started to scream quite loudly in a high-pitched voice. Sometimes the screaming spread to others in the current rooms, with the screamers often thrashing about, even after falling to on the floor, creating concern for physical injury to them and persons in current. I learned that this metaphysical show occurs when one or more spirits which are attached to a person develop an intense fear of being released.)

MY EXPERIENCES

8. A Brief Description of Spiritism

In my visits to the Casa de Dom Inâcio, I learned that the spiritual healing there is a practice of Spiritism which, as I said above, is defined as a moral philosophy and observational science that is concerned principally with the nature and destiny of spirits and their relationship to our mortal world. I also learned that of the several hundred Spiritist centers and the few Spiritist hospitals in Brazil that engage in spiritual healing, only a few of the centers have a medium with João's gift of full-trance spiritual healing. All other Spiritist centers and hospitals have one or more mediums who have been trained for several years to channel universal vital life force energy for spiritual healing and counseling. This otherworldly support of spiritual healing led me to study Spiritism to determine why it has not been more widely recognized and practiced, especially by Christians. As will be obvious below, I found that many of the principles of Spiritism are incompatible with the teachings of Christianity. To illustrate this, I will describe how the Spiritist principles evolved and list them.

Various manifestations of spirits have occurred most civilizations. However, interest in actually communicating the spirit world did not develop until 1848, when this "fashionable" phenomenon appeared in the United States, and then in England, France, and other European countries. Initially, it involved people from all socioeconomic levels attending "séances," Initially, it during which they sat quietly around a table and evoked spirits, asked the spirits questions, and received the spirit answers through a medium. Spirit answers would occur as a rapping in the table or a movement of it. Soon the answers came through the mediums in various verbal forms, including uncontrolled writing, thoughts, and speech, or an inwardly-heard voice.

In 1854, Hippolyte Léon Denizard Rivail, a distinguished French educator and author in several sciences, became fascinated by the intelligent responses that spirits were giving to questions. He realized that communication with the spirit world offered humanity the unique opportunity to learn about it, its belief system, and its relationship with the mortal world. Rivail initially compiled and codified superior-spirit answers to 1,019 carefully-written questions, each asked by several experienced mediums in France and other countries. Under the pen name of Allan Kardec, he published the answers in 1858, in a book entitled *The Spirits' Book,* which became the foundational knowledge of Spiritism. Soon Spiritism spread throughout the European continent and to Brazil, where it thrived in upper society despite being banned there in 1898 and for several years thereafter. Most of the world's Spiritists are located in Brazil, where Spiritist centers are used for training mediums, performing spiritual healing and counseling, and conducting benevolent and social activities in their communities.

I have selected the following basic doctrines of Spiritism mainly from *The Spirits' Book* and Kardec's subsequent book entitled *The Book on Mediums.* The doctrines of Spiritism vary somewhat in the way they are presented, but usually include the following:

- God is the Creator of the Universe, the Supreme Intelligence and the First Cause of all things, and is eternal, immutable, immaterial, unique, omnipotent, and supremely just and good.

- All natural laws, physical and moral, are created by God. Moral laws were exemplified in the purest form in the life and teaching of Jesus, who is the guide and model for all of humanity.

- A human being is a non-material spirit incarnated in a material body, with the spirit and body being united by a semi-material envelope called the perispirit. When the body dies, the spirit and perispirit separate from the body to enter the spirit world.

- The human spirit is an immortal, intelligent being in the Universe, created by God in an unknowing condition and then evolving, but never actually regressing, both intellectually and morally in both the spirit and mortal worlds.

- A spirit reincarnates as many times as is necessary for its intellectual and moral advancement, and preserves its individuality before and after each incarnation, as well as its memory from its past lives in the spirit and mortal worlds. In the spirit world, a spirit determines its progress through planes of intellectual and moral development, towards the ultimate plane of perfection.

MY EXPERIENCES

- Human beings have free will to act under the Law of Cause and Effect, so they have to bear the consequences of immoral conduct, which includes illness or other misfortune when a spirit is reincarnated into mortal life. Thus each person creates his or her own "hell."

- Spirits have always had a subconscious or conscious communicative relationship with human beings, in providing them guidance, support, and protection. Many, if not most, human beings are mediums, who have the innate ability to communicate in various ways with the spirit world.

- The Universe has countless other planets inhabited by intelligent beings who are evolving intellectually and morally. At some point in its evolutionary advancement, a spirit may choose to reincarnate on one of these planets,

In my book, *Spirits Can Help God Heal Us*, I drew from many sources to clarify certain aspects of Spiritism, which follow:

- <u>Existence of the Creator:</u> Spiritism views God as a universal form of energy which functions only with creative love, rather than as a divine being with human form and attributes as characterized by the religious doctrines of various civilizations and cultures.

- <u>Existence of the Spirit:</u> Spirit existence has been proven through the study of psychic phenomena, including mediumship and countless reincarnations, near death experiences, and out-of-body experiences. Beginning in the astral plane, which is similar to that of Earth, the perispirit of the spirit takes the perfect form of the human body of its previous incarnation, at an earth-age preferred by the spirit. With the spirit's evolution through planes of its intellectual and moral development, the perispirit becomes increasingly diaphanous, or filmy.

- <u>Spirit Evolution:</u> Spirits undergo a process of intellectual and moral evolution that is progressive, never regressive, but can be temporarily stationary. The rate of this evolutionary process varies among spirits, determined by their willingness to take part in the process and apply the benefits derived from their learning experiences in the mortal and spirit worlds. A spirit's passage through the planes of spirit existence, from the lowest to the highest plane and eventually into its intimate relationship with God, may take eons of time.

- Reincarnation: Christianity repressed the widespread ages-old belief in reincarnation at the Second Council of Constantinople in 553 C.E. However, reincarnation appears to have become a reality from credible reports of children who spontaneously recall past life experiences, spirits who describe their past lives through mediums, and psychiatrists and psychologists who use past life and even inter-life regressions in the treatment of treat various psychological conditions stemming from past life experiences.

    According to Spiritism, a spirit selects a human existence compatible with the spirit's evolutionary progress and the life that the spirit needs for its continued improvement. Like the soul, the spirit still retains some memory of its past life experiences and knowledge. This memory can pass into cerebral consciousness to some degree, and generate emotional and mental problems, produce evil behavior, create prodigies, and even influence sexual preferences. And when the soul leaves the mortal body to become a spirit, it takes the intellectual and moral knowledge from its experiences on Earth with it to the spirit world.

- Heaven and Hell: Heaven as a place of eternal bliss and Hell as a place of eternal torment does not exist. A spirit that has just departed the mortal body enters a state of being in which the spirit has a full-life review. The spirit may remain in this state for a period of time, experiencing the mental and emotional suffering that its immoral behavior caused other human beings while it was on Earth. Atonement for immoral behavior while in the spirit world is possible through moral education and behavior that includes good deeds, or while in the mortal world is possible by favorably bearing the burden of illness or misfortune being suffered because of the Law of Cause and Effect.

- Mediumship: A phenomenon that has occurred in virtually all civilizations, mediumship is a universal natural human faculty that exists to varying degrees to enable communication between the

MY EXPERIENCES

mortal and spirit worlds. Through mediumship, the immortality of the soul and spirit has been scientifically proven; false ideas of Heaven and Hell exposed; the purpose of our mortal and spirit existences disclosed, the nature of spirit-life revealed; and communication with departed loved ones, assistance with healing, and advice on personal matters made possible.

Through mediums, spirits can guide "intelligent" energy to treat medical conditions that are of a physical, mental, or spiritual nature. The healing effects of this energy can be physical, mental and spiritual.

Spiritist teaching about mediumship has some strong cautions about it, particularly in being able to identify when an inferior or frivolous spirit is giving misleading or false information and to deal with spirit attachment. Therefore, this teaching recommends that mediums receive appropriate training, particularly in assessing spirit integrity and knowledge, and in identifying spirit attachment in themselves and others.

Christianity and Spiritism agree on the existence of God and have the same moral values as taught by Jesus Christ But much of Christianity does not accept dualism, or the body having a soul which becomes a spirit when the body dies. Although we are seeing more and more proof of the reality of soul-spirit existence from mediumistic communication, the near-death experience, past life regression, and even inter-life regression, dualism is not well supported by the Holy Bible and, in turn, the large, fundamentalistic component of Protestant Christianity.

Will Spiritism grow and thrive in the future? Was my out-of-body experience 85 years ago a key indication of the reality that Spiritism describes? Only God knows ...

Made in the USA
Middletown, DE
01 June 2024